Building the industrial city

Themes
in Urban
History

General editor: Derek Fraser

Building the industrial city

edited by MARTIN DOUGHTY

Leicester University Press   1986

First published in 1986 by Leicester University Press
Distributed in North America by Humanities Press, Inc.,
Atlanta Highlands, N.J.

Copyright © Leicester University Press 1986

Text set in 10/11 pt Linotron 202 Times,
printed and bound in Great Britain at The Bath Press, Avon

British Library Cataloguing in Publication Data

Building the industrial city. – (Themes in urban
history)
1. Housing – Great Britain – History – 19th
century   2. Cities and towns – Great Britain –
I. Doughty, Martin, *1948—*   II. Series
363.5′0941   HD7333.A3

ISBN 0-7185-1238-3

FOREWORD

Urban history is an expanding field of study, sustained by a considerable volume of research. The purpose of this series, originally conceived by the late Jim Dyos, is to open a new channel for the dissemination of the findings of a careful selection from that research, providing a conspectus of new knowledge on specific themes.

For each volume in the series, each of the contributors is invited to present the core of his work: the essays, originating in these but now specially written for this volume, are combined under the control of the editor, who writes an introduction setting out the significance of the material being presented in the light of developments in that or a cognate field.

It is hoped that in this way the fruits of recent work may be made widely available, both to assist further exploration and to contribute to the teaching of urban history.

In this, the eighth volume in the series, Martin Doughty brings together studies on the physical creation of the Victorian city. The volume illuminates the relationship between land, finance and the building industry itself, which receives close and novel scrutiny. Complementing recent work on housing, landlords, tenants and spatial organization, the book makes an important contribution to the reviving interest in all aspects of property and property relations in Victorian and Edwardian Britain.

Derek Fraser

CONTENTS

LIST OF ILLUSTRATIONS

LIST OF TABLES

LIST OF ABBREVIATIONS

Note Places of publication are given only for works published outside the United Kingdom. In abbreviating less frequently cited periodical titles, commonly accepted abbreviations such as *J.* for *Journal, Proc.* for *Proceedings* have been used; other abbreviations are listed below.

CRA	Central Regional Archives
DGC	Dean of Guild Court
EcHR	*Economic History Review*
EDCRO	Edinburgh District Record Office
GMC	Glasgow Municipal Commission on the Housing of the Poor
H of LRO	House of Lords Record Office
HPL	Huddersfield Public Library
IR	Inland Revenue
MDRO	Moray District Record Office
MOH	Medical Officer of Health
PP	Parliamentary Papers
PRO	Public Record Office
RC	Royal Commission
REP	Ramsden Estate Papers
RIBA	Royal Institute of British Architects
RPS	Register of Plans and Sections
SLEC	Scottish Land Enquiry Committee
TCM	Town Council Minutes
TEP	Thornhill Estate Papers
WRRD	West Riding Registry of Deeds

NOTES ON THE CONTRIBUTORS

MARTIN DOUGHTY attended Worcester College, Oxford, and the London School of Economics. He is currently Senior Lecturer in History and Archaeology at King Alfred's College, Winchester, and was Visiting Professor at the University of Southern Maine in 1983. His publications include *Merchant Shipping and War: A Study in Defence Planning in Twentieth-Century Britain* and articles on industrial history and archaeology.

JANE SPRINGETT is currently Lecturer in Human Geography in the Faculty of Education and Community Studies, Liverpool Polytechnic, having worked for two years in health service administration. After taking her first degree in geography at Leeds University, she continued to study there as a post-graduate, receiving her Ph.D. in 1979. From 1976–83 she was Lecturer in Human Geography at Wolverhampton Polytechnic.

MICHAEL YEADELL graduated·at Hull University in 1968 and, following a year at the Leicester University School of Education, was invited back to Hull in 1969 to carry out research for a higher degree. He obtained a teaching post in a Hull comprehensive secondary school in 1972 and moved to his present post as a Head of Year and Head of Economics and Political Studies in an Essex comprehensive school in 1979. He submitted his thesis in 1981.

TOM ROBERTS is currently the Joseph Rowntree Memorial Trust Research Fellow at the Institute of Advanced Architectural Studies, University of York. He is the author of the Clementhorpe Reports which investigate the physical and social changes resulting from revitalization and gradual urban renewal in our inner city areas. His current research topics are the York housing market in the nineteenth century and the post-1919 English housing experience. His essay stems from a working background in the private sector of the Liverpool housing market and a research paper submitted to the Department of Economics and Related Studies, University of York.

RICHARD RODGER is Lecturer in Economic and Social History at the University of Leicester, and in 1982–3 was Visiting Professor and Fulbright Scholar at the University of Kansas, Lawrence. His Ph.D thesis (1975) was on Scottish urban housebuilding, 1870–1914, and his publications include *Bibliography of European Economic History* (1984), contributions to several books and various articles on social and urban topics in *Business History, Journal of Historical Geography, Victorian Studies*.

Introduction

MARTIN DOUGHTY

Introduction

MARTIN DOUGHTY

1

In 1801 there were 1.6 million dwelling houses in England and Wales. By 1911 net additions to the housing stock had brought the total to 7.6 million. Moreover, the same period had seen massive investment in building and construction works associated with transport developments, along with the creation of new public buildings and resources, the town halls, hospitals and schools required by a quadrupled population and expanded conceptions of communal responsibility. The output of the building industry in the nineteenth century was prodigious, and despite the erosion of the intervening years, the impact of this activity remains indelibly stamped on the fabric of almost all British towns and cities. Towns and cities, for it was in the context of urban expansion that the opportunities for new construction were predominantly concentrated.

This book is concerned with the organization and development of the industry which created the towns and cities of nineteenth-century Britain: the industrial cities, major population centres based on the staple industries of the industrial revolution. As such, it is directed to an aspect of urban history which has not received a great deal of attention in the past. In a reflection of nineteenth-century concern about the quality of the urban environment and its effects, urban historians have tended to concentrate on the impact of the products of the industry rather than on the process of production itself.[1] Consequently much information on the building industry has been generated peripherally, by studies whose major focus lies elsewhere, as in, for example, the bulk of the material relating to the role of aristocratic estates in urban development. One of the objectives of this book is to assist in redressing this imbalance, by making available the results of recent research on the building industry in the nineteenth century.

Given the size of the subject, it has been necessary to impose certain restrictions on the scope of the enquiry. Detailed reference to non-residential construction is thus excluded, and the book concentrates on that part of the industry concerned with the provision of dwellings for the working-class sector of the market, and thus on the activities of the speculative builder. The speculative builder is a much maligned character, frequently held responsible for the problems of quality which affected much nineteenth-century housing.[2] Questions of the standards of the industry's products cannot be wholly excluded from consideration, but they do not form the main focus of this book.

Instead, the intention is to explore the mechanics of the processes by which the houses were constructed. The book concentrates on the people – and they were not always men[3] – who possessed the skills, personnel and equipment physically to build houses. This is the overriding consideration which has been used to distinguish between the functions of builder and developer, roles which, in practice, were frequently indistinctly defined. Thus, attention is particularly focused on the structure of the building industry, and the effect that this exerted on its internal operations and dynamics. The sizes of firms, and their respective contributions to output, are considered, along with questions relating to the supply of materials and labour, and to sources for the finance of house-building. The importance of landowners' attempts to control the nature of dwellings erected on their estates is another major theme, joined, so far as the latter years of the nineteenth century are concerned, by the necessity to assess the impact on the industry of the growing volume of building regulations.

Such themes are common to all the essays in this book, and are, in themselves, testament to the complexities of the subject. The four contributions, with their varied emphases and approaches, provide further evidence of the breadth of the topic, and of the range of disciplines which have been brought to bear on it. Jane Springett assesses the industry in nineteenth-century Huddersfield, working from the perspective of historical geography. In discussing the constraints within which the industry operated in the town, she pays considerable attention to the role of local landowners, especially the dominant Ramsden estate. Against the background of property relations and later legislative controls, the structure of the industry is considered, and its responses in terms of the location and types of development are analysed. Mike Yeadell's study also focuses on Yorkshire, but his concerns are centred on the finance of house-building, and in particular on the contribution of building clubs and societies. Investigating the records of societies in the West Riding, Yeadell has significantly expanded the scope of published material, especially in relation to the details of societies' financial practices and organization. Additionally his study has generated new evidence enabling an important reconsideration of existing analyses of the social composition of society membership, which casts interesting light on the nature of building undertakers and the types of building financed by building societies.

Similar points recur in the remaining two essays, by Tom Roberts on Liverpool and Richard Rodger on Scotland. But these studies take a rather wider focus, providing additional indication of the immense complexity of the building process in the nineteenth century, and of the variety of interests involved in it. Roberts explores the role of Welsh builders, revealing the remarkable extent to which this ethnic group dominated most aspects of the building industry in Liverpool. Welsh influence is traced from the production of building materials in their native land, through their control of a wide range of building firms, to the provision of finance through building clubs and societies. Nonconformity and the chapel are seen as crucial factors in the maintenance of ethnic and social cohesion. While such ethnic

3

domination is obviously not paralleled in other cities, there is no reason to suppose that the structure of the Liverpool industry is atypical, and Roberts thus provides a fascinating insight into the diversity of functions and components which combined to create the nineteenth-century city. The morphology of the working-class house in Liverpool is also explored, and Roberts considers the influence of vernacular traditions, building materials and legislative controls on the city's architecture.

Architectural aspects also form a part of Richard Rodger's explanations of the features of urban housing in Scotland. Among these essays, Rodger's takes the broadest canvas, providing a comprehensive account of Scottish urban conditions during the nineteenth century. He describes the intensive nature of Scottish urban deprivation and its effects, and links these to the building industry through the characteristic form of Scottish urban housing, the tenement. Builders' preference for the tenement is explained by a range of factors deriving from the structure of the industry and the constraints within which it operated in Scotland. The size of firms and the volatility of Scottish house-building are related to the influence of land-tenure systems, the comparative weakness of demand for working-class housing, and the effects of Scottish bye-laws on builders' costs and, thus, on rent levels. Comparison with the English experience provides a number of insights which assist in explaining the development and performance of the building industry in both nations.

While the geographical scope of these essays in itself constitutes a major extension of published information on the industry, greater significance attaches to the analyses they develop, which provide new insights and immensely enrich our appreciation of many of the activities of the industry in the period. Given the variety of economic and legal circumstances in the areas considered, it is not surprising that the essays develop a picture of great regional diversity, and emphasize the variety of structures and methods which characterized the industry in the nineteenth century. The multiplicity of regional variations in practices and structures was immense, and constitutes an essential qualification of any generalization about the industry. However, despite regional differences, certain unifying elements and themes can be discerned. Thus, in broad terms, the analysis of industrial structures and practices developed in these essays accord with the findings of earlier work on other areas. In generalized terms, the industry does seem to have been responding in broadly comparable directions to broadly similar stimuli, and while regional variations undoubtedly reflect factors unique to the locality concerned, they also indicate stages, engendered by local market conditions, in a more general process of development. By linking their descriptions of the structure of the industry to detailed investigation of the changing framework of local circumstances which constrained building operations, the essays provide important new evidence of the industry's interrelations with its environment, and enable comparisons which greatly enlarge our understanding of the mechanics by which the industry developed at both local and national levels during the period.

The value of the present essays is thus not limited to the considerable extent to which they augment the volume of published material on the subject, but also extends to their contribution in developing a coherent national picture which can, moreover, provide a comparative framework for future research. Significant also is the wide range of sources which have been used to construct these studies. Twenty years ago it was regarded as axiomatic that 'hard facts about the structure of the building industry before 1914 are difficult to obtain'.[4] While this assertion still embodies an essential truth, perceptions of the range of sources available have expanded, as these essays demonstrate. Taken together, they constitute a major enhancement of published work on many aspects of the history of an important, but hitherto somewhat neglected, industry.

2

For many years the only direct historical attention given to the building industry was provided by economic historians, seeking to assess the importance of building in national economic terms. Part of this activity was directed at clarifying the statistical inadequacy which afflicted even the macro-economic aspects of the industry's activities. A number of valuable series had been compiled by the mid 1960s.[5]

In general terms, economic historians are agreed that the building industry was a component of great significance in the national economy throughout the nineteenth century. However, attempts to provide firm quantification of that significance have exposed substantial differences of opinion.[6] Estimates of the role of building in capital formation are complicated by the fact that the most refined indices available are calculated on slightly different bases for the two halves of the century.[7] The contribution of residential construction to gross domestic capital formation fluctuated sharply early in the century, from around 30 per cent of the national total in 1821–30 to only 15 per cent in 1841–50. In the latter half of the century, the figures settled more consistently between 17 and 20 per cent. These figures, of course, ignore the non-residential sector entirely. An attempt to take account of non-residential construction complicates the calculation, but naturally increases the overall importance of the industry.[8] While non-residential building is not a direct concern of this volume, it must be noted that the division between residential and non-residential sectors is simply an analytical device, and that in reality the sectors could not be precisely separated. Indeed, it is clear that there were few functional aspects which restricted the ability of builders to switch their activities from residential to non-residential construction during the nineteenth century, and many of them no doubt did so as opportunity offered, whether as builders in their own right, or as subcontractors on projects larger than they could themselves undertake. Evidence explored in more detail below suggests that considerable switching of resources from one to the other may have taken place.

Economic historians were also responsible for the identification of fluctuations in the industry's output – the building cycle – and attempts to explain the origin and importance of these phenomena. Once again, by the mid 1960s the basic structure of historical interpretation of these aspects had been clarified.[9] Repetition of these arguments would serve little purpose, but it must be noted that the debate led to an appreciation of the importance of local or regional fluctuations in building, which might bear little relation to national aggregate figures. Explanations of local fluctuations naturally tended to discount macro-economic arguments and to focus on the specific circumstances confronting individual builders as they sought to assess the demand for houses, and the resources available to supply it, in the various localities. But the debate cast little light on how builders monitored demand: indeed, the industry appeared to be particularly insensitive to market changes. It was suggested that this insensitivity might reflect the structure of the industry,[10] but beyond this, little could be said. Thus one result of the building cycle debate was to indicate the need for research into the industry's structure.

Contemporary opinion was not sanguine about the prospects for such research,[11] as information then available was concentrated on those individual builders prominent enough to have generated a personal historical record, a group known as the master builders. Thomas Cubitt was generally regarded as an archetypal figure.[12] Cooney's discussion of the master builder has been criticized for overstating the importance of the group,[13] but recent research has tended to rehabilitate the concept, albeit with certain modifications. Cooney's definition identified three attributes characteristic of the group: large size, new organizational principles, and an association with 'an intensification of competition within the industry'.[14] Of these, it now appears that the new organizational principles were the most characteristic. Two aspects distinguished these principles: the practice of contracting 'in gross',[15] and, more importantly, the introduction of general contracting, to which contracting in gross contributed. Formerly, the industry had been organized on the basis of small master craftsmen in particular trades who directly employed only men of their own skill. The general contractor, however, employed men in all the principal building crafts more or less permanently.[16] There is little doubt that such changes were pioneered in larger firms, nor that they were to be of great significance for the industry. The reasons which prompted such innovations have been only inadequately explored. There seems to be a connection with the size of project involved, larger undertakings requiring more effective control. But the precise timing of the innovations remains unclear.[17]

Even less clear is the extent to which such innovations had been adopted by the industry before 1914. In this connection, the issue of firm size has tended to confuse debate. Although the initial definition of the master builder did presuppose substantial size, it is clear that general contracting in itself did not inherently require this. Indeed, Cooney has recently observed that firms employing as few as a dozen or a score of men could operate perfectly successfully on general contracting principles.[18] Thus the effort directed at disparaging the role of the master builder by demonstrating the relative insignificance of large firms in the size array of the building industry is rather tangential to the real significance of general contracting.

Another issue concerns the relationship between general contracting and speculative building. Although the innovation undoubtedly emerged in public works, Cubitt's example suggests that the maintenance of a permanent labour force of any size required involvement in speculative building from the very beginning.[19] The most comprehensive modern account suggests that general contracting emerged first in those areas where the demand for housing was highest: London and the north-west; had become common by the mid 1820s in the latter, where it was associated with firms of smaller size than in London, and was integrally associated with the growing importance of speculative activity in the industry throughout the nineteenth century.[20]

Indeed, Price argues that speculative activity was a direct consequence of the introduction of general contracting, and that the extent of speculative building is to some extent a measure of the dominance of this system. This is not to suggest that speculative building was unknown before, but that it was in no sense characteristic of the industry.[21] Since it is accepted that, by the late nineteenth century, speculative activity was characteristic, the implication is that general contracting was similarly dominant. Precise quantification of this dominance is elusive and may remain so, since information available on the detailed activities of individual builders does not generally illuminate their contractual practices.[22] It may be suggested, however, that the concept of the master builder with its accumulated connotations might, so far as the residential sector is concerned, usefully be replaced by that of the general contractor as the focus for future investigations.

So far as the smaller builder is concerned, detailed investigations began with Dyos's studies of Victorian London.[23] More recently, the structure of the building industry has been investigated in a number of cities, although studies centred on the topic have been the exception rather than the rule.[24] Apart from their restricted numbers, the main limitation of these investigations lies in their potential for comparative study. Chronological disparities, different source materials and diverse forms of data presentation preclude precise comparisons between their findings. Nonetheless, in general terms, the results of these studies are not incompatible, and in the cases of London, Sheffield and, to a lesser extent, Cardiff (cities where the data are most directly comparable), the similarities between the findings are substantial. In numerical terms, small firms constituted a majority of the individual units in the industry throughout the century. However, it seems clear that the output of the larger firms exceeded that of the smaller, despite the latters' numerical superiority. Moreover, this imbalance became more pronounced as the century progressed, for the numerical domination of the small builder was gradually eroded, giving further impetus to the domination of output by larger operators. The extent to which such changes in market concentration had progressed by the end of the century is unclear. Data of sufficient discrimination are only available for London, Sheffield and Cardiff, and there are disparities between the cities.[25] It does appear that the provincial cities lagged somewhat behind London, both in terms of the chronology and the extent of this development. Given the disproportionate size of the London market, this is not surprising.[26]

The general picture revealed by the essays in this volume confirms the suggestions of earlier work, despite local variations. Unfortunately the problems of data comparability noted earlier remain unresolved. Nonetheless, the disparity between the numbers of firms of different sizes and their respective contributions to output is confirmed in Huddersfield, Liverpool and Scotland. Information on the extent of market concentration, and its changes over time, remains uneven. In Huddersfield, concentration seems to have been increasing even before 1850, despite the rather unusual course of industrial development in the town. Although direct comparisons cannot be made, large firms clearly dominated the industry in Liverpool, and Roberts also provides glimpses of the emergence of general contracting in the city.

In Scotland, the extent of market concentration in the industry appears to have lagged behind that in England. Some degree of confirmation of Price's argument that speculative building was causally linked to changes in the industry's structure is provided by Rodger's observation that the volume of non-speculative building in Scotland remained substantial. Even in Scotland, though, it appears that the extent of market concentration increased during the late nineteenth century, as Rodger's investigation of bankruptcies among building firms implies. The Scottish example may also provide some indications of the origins of increased market concentration, since the levels of concentration in the industry appear to have been related to the size of population in the various burghs. Rodger has suggested that the critical factor in stimulating concentration may have been the existence of a market larger than a certain absolute size, and not the rate of growth of demand. Unfortunately, the data are insufficiently disaggregated to explore this suggestion in detail by the investigation of specific burghs at various points in their growth. So far as England is concerned, existing work concentrates on cities substantially larger than Rodger's posited critical size. This area may provide opportunities for further research.

The changes in market concentration which took place as small firms were displaced by large in the size array emerge as some of the most significant aspects of the structure of the industry in the period. While the extent and progress of such changes remains obscure, the mechanics by which larger firms attained and consolidated their importance seem reasonably clear. Dyos noted a relationship between the emergence of larger firms and building booms,[27] and Aspinall's cumulative frequency distribution curves demonstrate a similar effect. The logical conclusion would seem to be that the greater opportunities for speculative building offered by boom conditions called into existence larger firms to supply the demand. Once these larger firms had emerged, they demonstrated a greater ability to survive the following slumps than did their smaller companions.

The instability of small building firms has been noted by all commentators on the industry. Lightly capitalized, and able to sustain themselves by repairs or subcontracting to a larger concern, nearly all small firms were only temporary participants in house-building. Conversely, larger firms could develop techniques to sustain themselves through bad times. Economies of scale, the development of a diversity of business interests in other sectors of the economy, perhaps the ownership and rental of property: such are some of the advantages of size. Diversification into non-residential construction was another possibility, rendered more attractive by the tendency of this sector to demonstrate a pattern of fluctuation discrete from that of the house-building cycle. The advantages of counter-cyclical construction to a firm whose residential building was declining are obvious, and it is interesting to note some evidence from Sheffield of the process of diversion of resources between the sectors at work.[28] Rodger has also noted examples of larger firms diversifying.

Changes in market concentration have been linked to the industry's insensitivity to demand, and thus to the origins of the building cycle. Saul drew attention to the potential significance of firm size,[29] and Aspinall noted the possibility of a link between the extent of concentration in the industry and the severity of over-speculation in the upswing of the building cycle in a given area. The thesis has a theoretical basis in the possiblity that a more concentrated industrial structure may be expected to be less sensitive to fluctuations in market conditions.[30] Evidence from Scotland, where the average firm size was smaller than in England, does suggest that the industry responded more directly to market conditions, which helps to explain the greater instability of Scottish building fluctuations.[31] Moreover, there is evidence that this instability moderated towards the end of the century as market concentration increased. However, precise information on such mechanisms is limited, and a wide variety of other factors were operative in the market at the same time. Thus these suggestions must be regarded as tentative.

3

Although consisting in detail of a remarkably heterogeneous group of components, the output side of the building industry can be defined with some clarity. Such precision is not so easily maintained in relation to inputs to the industry. Here a discrete definition of the subject is elusive, and many of the components which constitute factor inputs of major significance are topics of sufficient importance to have attracted scholarly attention in their own right. The provision of land for building is a case in point. The provision of land and any restrictions imposed on its use are of central significance as constraints on the building process, but the implications of the land question extend widely into areas of only peripheral relevance to a discussion focused on the building industry. Thus the question of the influence of landowners on the course of development is, in its general aspects, too broad to be considered here.[32] From the viewpoint of the building industry, the crucial points relate to the extent to which landlords' decisions could constrain the opportunities available to builders, and any implications which might follow for the practices or structure of the industry.

Logic suggests that landowners' power ought to have been most effective where the level of concentration of landownership was highest, creating conditions approaching the 'monopoly of land' which so exercised nineteenth-century critics. A monopoly would have facilitated land hoarding, thus raising land costs and building costs, so affecting the type or quality of housing provided. Recent studies have questioned the relevance of such analyses. In most cases, land in alternative ownership was available, and anything approaching a stranglehold over the supply of building land rarely developed. Huddersfield demonstrates this clearly, despite the high concentration of landownership which approached, in Springett's phrase, an oligopolistic situation. Moreover, most English landowners, far from hoarding land in the hope of inflating its value, were characterized by endemic over-optimism concerning the extent of demand for their land, and developments frequently outran demand.[33] Indeed, the relative absence of speculation in land is the classic explanation for the comparatively low cost of building land in England, and thus the absence of high-rise urban development of the type characteristic of Scotland and Europe. While it has been argued that land speculation did occur in English cities,[34] it does not seem to be linked to the concentration of landownership. Neither is conclusive evidence available to link fragmented landownership, and the consequent small size of plots available for development, to the construction of poor-quality houses. While evidence suggests that certain cases can be explained by such factors,[35] contradictory examples are also numerous.[36]

The relationship between land costs and total building costs is a topic of more direct significance. Unfortunately, firm quantification is not currently possible. Present figures for the proportion of land costs to total development costs are insufficiently precise in their contextual definition, especially regarding the type of development to which they refer (the proportion of land to house required for middle-class housing differing substantially from that for working-class developments). More disturbing, however, is the utter lack of consistency in the estimates.[37] In the face of such diversity, no effective comment can be made.

An aspect of landowners' power which has received considerable attention is their ability, in leasehold areas, to influence, and possibly determine, the types of houses erected. This might, on occasion, have unforeseen effects, as Sir John Ramsden's experience with back-to-backs demonstrates.[38] By extension it has been suggested that certain house types can be associated with the tenurial system applying to the land on which they stood. Freehold land, requiring additional capital

9

for development (to purchase the freehold),[39] is said to have encouraged intensive land use, and to be associated with the back-to-back house. This was contrasted with through houses, developed under leasehold tenures.[40]

The proliferation of local studies has exposed the need for caution in generalizing too rapidly from individual circumstances. A detailed study of back-to-backs in Leeds could find no relationship between the cost of land and the design type,[41] and further examples could be multiplied.[42] In aggregate, so far as England and Wales are concerned, such studies have undermined any generalizations identifying tenure as the sole or major determinant of the type of housing created. The extent to which such conclusions can be extended to the Scottish experience is, however, limited, as Rodger's discussion below makes clear. It is argued that the tenurial peculiarities of Scottish law were an important determinant of land costs, which were higher than in England, and thus of the intensity of land use and of the type of dwelling which resulted. The argument, however, does not seek to establish tenure as the sole determinant, but locates it within a range of other influences, including most significantly the strength of the demand for working-class housing.[43]

It has also been suggested that a relationship can be drawn between tenurial system and the structure of the local building industry. If development on leasehold sites required less capital, this may have encouraged speculative building. Conversely, freehold tenure may have placed the speculative builder at a disadvantage. This latter is held to have been the case in Bradford and the West Riding, where freehold tenure combined with the fragmentation of landownership and a high degree of owner-occupation to reduce the scope for speculative building. In Leeds, too, also freehold, the speculative builder was in decline, whereas in neighbouring leasehold towns, such as Sheffield, he flourished.[44] The argument was undermined by the appearance of large-scale speculative building in Leeds at the end of the century,[45] and has received little subsequent support. Nonetheless, the two cities in which the structure of the industry has been most closely studied – London and Sheffield – were both predominantly leasehold towns, and conceivably the need to purchase the freehold hindered, if it did not prevent, the emergence of the speculative builder in other areas. At this stage our knowledge is too limited to allow even a tentative conclusion. It may, however, be instructive to contrast the general perception of the dominance of the speculative builder in the late nineteenth century with the fact that the evidence available suggests that more than 50 per cent of urban land in England and Wales was held under freehold tenures.[46] The general tendency of recent work has been to reduce the significance attached to tenure as a determinant force, and it may be that greater information regarding the financing of building will diminish the significance of the necessity to purchase the freehold as an impediment to the speculative builder.[47]

The significance accorded to landlord power, once virtually total, has thus been partially undermined by recent work. The role of the landlord is diminished, but by no means abolished altogether. Cannadine has persuasively argued that landlords could and did exercise considerable power in relation to the specific features of their estates, but that no landlord, however restrictive his attitude or efficient his administration, could impose a character of development which the market forces effective on the estate did not support. Landowners' decisions might reinforce the operation of the market, but they could not resist its imperatives.[48] The assertion of the domination of the market is, perhaps, appropriate enough in Britain in the 1980s, but our appreciation of the ways in which the market actually functioned in detail at the local level is very limited. Cannadine's conclusion is to assert a type of topographical determinism, coupled with the influence of the strength of local demand for the various types of housing: pertinent observations, but couched in rather general terms.[49] The ways in which such forces manifested themselves and functioned in specific instances have still to be explored.

4

In contrast to aspects relating to the provision of land, other inputs into the building industry have received relatively little attention. This is, perhaps, most surprising regarding the finance of house-building, particularly in view of the significance accorded to the provision of capital in the building cycle debate. Dyos identified four or five major sources of finance for the speculative builder in London.[50] Landowners played some role, and Dyos noted a number of examples of estates funding development, but although this practice seems to have been by no means uncommon, it was equally evidently by no means automatic. Furthermore, the policy of the same estate could differ from development to development, as the example of the Norfolk estates testifies.[51] There were a variety of ways other than by direct lending of capital which landlords could adopt to encourage building on their estate: the provision of investment by the landlord in social overhead capital, the relaxation of building controls, and the terms associated with the early years of the lease, were all common means of reducing the financial burden on builders.[52] The building industry itself operated in a similar manner in certain respects, as in the well-attested practice of builders' merchants in providing materials on credit. No analytical studies of the extent of such practices are presently available.

In London, Dyos found little willingness on the part of banks or insurance companies to lend directly to speculative builders, although, indirectly, such funds must have found their way into the industry, even at the speculative level, through financial intermediaries. Such institutions seem to have wished to avoid direct involvement in the rather unpredictable speculative sector, except in the middle years of the century, when alternative investments may have been comparatively less inviting. The activities of the freehold land societies seem to have peaked in mid century also, by which time they had shed their political connotations and acted essentially as a means of finance for house-building. Little is known in detail about the relationships between such bodies and speculative building, but their significance seems to diminish towards the end of the century[53]

The major direct source of finance for nineteenth-century house-building remains: the building societies. The main outlines of the history of the societies as financial institutions have been clear for some time.[54] Far less is known about the role of these institutions in financing development in specific localities, or about the extent to which speculative builders obtained funds from this source. Dyos noted that society advances to speculative builders had been extensive in mid century, but that the picture was less clear in the 1880s and 1890s, when 'a marked preference for lending instead to owner-occupiers developed'.[55] Some evidence is available from Aspinall's work on Sheffield, which also stresses the importance of the societies in mid century,[56] but it does not extend beyond the 1870s. Building society funds could be channelled into house-building indirectly, through agents such as solicitors. Solicitors constituted the overwhelming majority of the identifiable sources of finance in Sheffield, but it is unlikely they were all advancing money on their own account, and the real role of building societies remains unclear.

Yeadell's essay thus provides a significant extension of our information on the subject. His discussion of the pattern and sizes of advances revealed by the records of the West Riding societies strongly suggests that their importance in funding speculative building did not decline significantly in Yorkshire before 1914. Without precise details concerning the numbers of houses to which each advance related it is not possible to state conclusively that societies were funding speculative building of several units for working-class occupancy rather than single units of high status for middle- or upper-class owner-occupation, but the balance of the evidence is clearly that this was the case. It is certain that societies' role in funding owner-occupation in the working-class sector of the market was extremely limited before 1914.[57]

The view that societies' activities essentially facilitated artisan and middle-class investment in housing is confirmed by records of society membership. The social composition of societies can thus be traced in greater detail than hitherto, and the insignificance of the working class as borrowers is evident. Although the bulk of the information refers to the mid nineteenth century, it is notable that this trend was apparent as early as the 1830s. The tendency may not have been so important in the earlier form or organization, the building club, but it seems likely that societies had never, even in their terminating days, been important sources of house-building finance for groups lower than artisan in status. This tendency was accentuated as the century progressed.[58] The same point is also made by Roberts. In Liverpool the societies predominantly funded the building industry, and in several cases had been established by Welsh builders specifically for this purpose.

This is particularly notable because it clearly contradicted societies' public descriptions of their activities and purposes which, Yeadell notes, have exercised some influence over earlier interpretations of their role. Societies' chosen public image seems to have been that of facilitating working-class self-help in progress towards property ownership. In fact they appear to have facilitated the maintenance of middle-class control of the rental market. The disparity between practice and protestation is interesting. So far as the working class were concerned, the real role of societies appears to have been to act as repositories for savings, which were then channelled to higher status groups for borrowing to finance building. Information on the characteristics of borrowers supports the historical convention that the main groups involved operated on a relatively small scale, although whether these characteristics changed significantly later in the century is unclear. As in the case of building firm sizes, the few large borrowers assumed an importance disproportionate to their numbers. Our limited information on specific builders' activities,[59] which confirms the importance of financial intermediaries such as solicitors, strongly suggests that such building society records substantially underestimate the extent to which their funds passed into builders' hands.

Yeadell also compares society advances and levels of building activity calculated from other sources, and finds a close relationship. His work on the levels of funds held by societies in the 1880s suggests that societies could not stimulate building, but only facilitate it, a point of wider significance in the study of the origins of building fluctuations. Yeadell's conclusions are of great value. Nonetheless, the evidence must not be pushed too far. The essay is necessarily restricted in its geographical scope, and a series of such studies would be required before nationally valid conclusions could be confidently advanced.

Questions of the finance of building are inevitably sensitive ones. Moreover, inherent difficulties in source availability exist. Despite such problems, the subject remains of crucial importance for the history of the building industry. A consensus seems to exist among historians and contemporary commentators that those who wished to build houses could always obtain capital to do so – that the industry was characterized by 'overbuilding in periods of easy money' rather than by 'underbuilding when money was tight'.[60] The sources of this capital and the fluctuations in its availability are of vital importance, not only in terms of the development of individual sites, but also to the relationship between investment in building and in other areas of the economy.

The expenditure side of the industry's financial operations has suffered from comparative neglect in recent years. Statistics of building costs have been available for some years, dealing in most detail with the period after 1845.[61] Although detailed differences between the series do exist, the overall trends of building costs have been satisfactorily established at national level. It is, however, essential to note that these indices are inferred from the price of inputs into the industry and are not based on prices actually paid for buildings. Evidence of the actual costs of houses is sporadic, and since the exact design of the houses to which it refers cannot be verified, and is unlikely to be precisely comparable, the information is vaguely defined and cannot provide the basis for valid generalization.[62] As with the assessment of land costs, substantial variations exist between available estimates, as a comparison of figures given in the essays in this book demonstrates. Thus any attempt to chart building costs in general is forced back upon the more easily obtained indices of the movement of prices of building material and of wages.

Recapitulation of the indices is unnecessary.[63] In general terms, after the 1840s the aggregate figures are reasonably stable. Odd peaks coincide with building booms, but no significant overall correlation between building costs and the building cycle can be demonstrated.[64] Since prices generally declined in the late nineteenth century, the relative price of building rose after 1870.[65] The general stability of the aggregate figures is not apparent if they are broken down into the components of wages and materials costs. Before 1845 wages fluctuated, but then rose steadily until by 1913 they had doubled. Materials costs fell substantially, so that wages, as a proportion of the total, advanced from around a third in mid century to a half in 1913, contributing to the stability of the aggregate figures.

The exploration of wage levels in building has largely fallen to historians of labour, although recent literature is relatively sparse.[66] Labour history, defined in what Price has called the 'heroic tradition' of industrial disputes and the growth of collective organization, is only relevant here to the extent that disputes can be shown to have affected the industry's output or organization, or to reveal details of working practices. Evidence exists at local levels linking disputes and building costs, and this can be shown to have influenced output.[67] At the national level, the generalization inherent in the figures obscures such phenomena, but all authorities are agreed that the introduction of orderly wage bargaining was stimulated by the desire to reduce the uncertainties created by less formalized methods.[68] Nationally, it seems likely that disputes *per se* were less important to overall costs or output than less specific but more extensive alterations in working practices.

13

The introduction of general contracting appears to deserve special emphasis in this respect. Price argues strongly that this change was central to labour relations in the industry, which were dominated by large general contractors in the same way that their output dominated that of the smaller firms.[69] General contracting and consequent subcontracting encouraged speeding up, 'sweating' or 'scamping' which seem to have been most noticeable in the earlier part of the century, perhaps because of the degree of innovation involved. At this time such developments may have largely offset the relative rise in the overall costs of building suggested by national indices. The nature of the indices, as inferred from input, rather than house prices, may mask the real trends operative in the industry.[70] The men seem to have recovered their position somewhat in the years after 1850 by the adoption and formalization of restrictive practices. Despite temporary fluctuations, restrictive practices resulted in a drop in the productivity of the industry during the nineteenth century. Regional variations bedevil comparisons, but to take the easily quantified example of bricklaying, there seems to have been an effective halving of the number of bricks laid per day by 1900. Other branches of the industry experienced similar developments.[71]

Such factors must have contributed to the increase in labour costs as a proportion of total building costs, but the decline in the costs of building materials was more significant. Building materials, as bulk commodities, were substantially affected by the reductions in transport costs resulting from nineteenth-century innovations, particularly the railway.[72] Less attention has been given to increased importation of materials, principally timber, from abroad. In this case, transport improvements combined with natural advantages or superior production methods to provide increasing supplies at decreasing cost as the century progressed.[73] Roberts explores some of the implications of such developments below, investigating all the major building materials. Liverpool's importance in the international timber trade needs little stress, but its Welsh builders were involved in other aspects as well.

The other major factor involved in the reduction of materials costs was improvement in domestic production methods, particularly the introduction of mechanization. The processes of building itself were not susceptible to mechanization, and the industry remained highly labour-intensive in the nineteenth century, as the employment figures, peaking at 1.2 million in 1901, testify.[74] The production of the materials themselves, however, offered much greater scope for mechanical assistance, although few developments seem to have taken place before 1850.[75] The woodworking trades experienced innovation earlier, and eventually more thoroughly than other areas. Certainly it was to the mechanization of joinery that the most dramatic savings in materials production costs in the latter years of the century were attributed.[76] Steam power must have been the major influence here, as in the production of stone and, especially, brick. Brickmaking also experienced major changes following the introduction of the Hoffman continuous kiln from the 1860s onwards. Nevertheless, ample evidence testifies to the widespread survival of hand production in all branches of the industry well into the twentieth century, though quantification of its importance is clearly impossible.

Whatever the precise extent of mechanization, the aesthetic impact of standardized materials in the later nineteenth century is perhaps the strongest impression to emerge from the work of architectural historians on the urban houses of the period.[77] The aesthetic and architectural implications of building materials are among the best explored aspects of the subject, and a wealth of literature exists on the erosion of local 'vernacular' styles by mass produced, railway transported, standardized components.[78] Urban historians have tended to ignore the detailed implications of such design developments for the urban environment, to the detriment of our understanding of the nature of life in the nineteenth century city.[79]

Trends in the production of building materials reinforced the pressure to greater standardization of the urban environment which resulted from the wider introduction of controls over building from the 1870s. Building had, however, been subject to legislative interference earlier in the century, through the taxation of building materials.[80] The impact of such taxes on building costs has not been analysed in any detail by historians, though contemporary estimates suggest it may have been considerable.[81] However, the indices of building materials prices do not demonstrate changes of the significance which might be expected after the dates of abolition of the various duties.

Whatever the impact of taxation, there is little controversy over the significance of the extension of legislative control over the standards of construction and amenity provision incorporated in new houses. Contemporaries certainly expected building costs to rise after regulation, and historians have agreed, although the relationships have rarely been systematically explored.[82] Naturally, the impact of regulation depended on the details of the legislation proposed, and each of the essays below contains information on this aspect. In general, the impact of regulation became more severe as the century progressed and the codes enforced became more effective. In Scotland, though, the regulations introduced in 1862 were unusually severe, and contributed greatly to the increase in builders' costs later in the century which is a central feature in Rodger's argument concerning the crisis in Scottish house-building before 1914.

The impact of bye-laws has also been investigated in relation to the physical form of nineteenth-century cities. An increasing volume of work is appearing on the architectural details and plan-forms of nineteenth-century working-class housing, as the inadequacies of the conventional dismissal of the 'monotonous bye-law terrace' are exposed.[83] Roberts' discussion of Liverpool building styles provides a valuable addition to such information, not least in its assessment of the importance of architect design of such houses.[84] Urban geographers have also posited the existence of 'bye-law cycles', created by the obsolescence of legislation as standards and attitudes changed, leading to the introduction of new controls. Investigation of such cycles has been confined to their morphological implications for house types and urban layouts.[85]

The introduction of higher constructional standards undoubtedly increased builders' costs during the years from around 1880 to 1914.[86] It may be, as Springett and others have suggested, that the increase in building project size apparent towards the end of the century reflects in part the influence of bye-laws, as builders sought to offset rising costs by economies of scale. It is, however, impossible to disentangle such influences from those of the increased labour costs of the period, which would have prompted similar attempts to cut costs elsewhere. The bye-laws have also been widely regarded as a significant factor in the decline in the profitability of working-class house construction which was evident at the end of the century, and thus to have contributed to the 'crisis' in housing before 1914.[87] Springett and Rodger provide detailed examples of the operation of such factors. While the existence of a permanent structural crisis in the Edwardian housing market has recently been questioned,[88] the interpretation is a credible one, and accords with the findings of those who have discussed the effects of legislative interference in other sectors of the economy.[89] Whether an unregulated market could have provided housing of acceptable standards which the poorer working class could have afforded remains unclear. The experience of the nineteenth century as a whole does not counsel optimism.

5

Many aspects of the history of speculative building in the nineteenth century await illumination. Our aggregate knowledge of the industry is remarkably limited and in many cases, as the account above makes clear, significant contradictions continue to require resolution. However, the achievements of recent years have made it possible to identify the challenges which face the subject more precisely.

Initially, there is the inevitable list of areas requiring further empirical research. Not only is our overall knowledge limited, but it is also heavily weighted towards the later nineteenth century. Yet all studies suggest that the structures and practices characteristic of the industry after 1850 had been developed and consolidated earlier in the century, if not before. The imbalance in the historical account obviously reflects the availability of source materials, but the essays in this book suggest that this problem is not insuperable, and each provides valuable additions to our knowledge and raises challenging new interpretations.

So far as the structure of the industry is concerned, even in the later period, detailed information is concentrated on only a handful of English cities, all predominantly leasehold areas. More regional studies are required. An area which might repay additional investigation is the north-west. Convention has it that this was the most advanced of the provincial regions, the area where general contracting was most highly developed, and where the structure of the industry (according to the employment data in the 1851 census) most closely approximated that of London. The north-west was essentially leasehold, and while the weight of evidence suggests that tenure had little influence on the industry, the absence of detailed evidence from a freehold area remains a serious gap in our information. In the issue of firm size, as far as the product of the industry (and thus its environmental impact) is concerned, the large firms, whose output was disproportionate to their numbers, form the most significant group. But the typical building firm operated on a much smaller scale. Our knowledge of both large and small firms is limited, and future research should not neglect either. There is still much work to be done on the structure of the industry before present analyses can be regarded as conclusive.

It would be easy to compile a substantial list of additional areas where our knowledge is similarly limited – indeed, this introduction is, in a sense, such a list. It does, however, seem necessary to stress the need for future studies to address the question of mutual comparability. If new work is to achieve its full potential, it is crucial that it should be designed and presented in a manner which allows direct comparison with other studies. Aspinall has demonstrated the value of statistical techniques, both within the study, in providing objective definitions of the significance of the findings, and externally in providing the basis for a range of objectively comparable studies. He remarked on the need for a standard methodology in 1977, and his observations remain equally pertinent today.[90]

It is particularly noticeable that until recently most historical attention has been concentrated on the supply side of the industry. Detailed attention to the demand for houses has been extraordinarily limited, and has tended to consider the volume rather than the structure of demand. Rodger's work on Scotland, in this volume and elsewhere, has demonstrated the extent to which a full appreciation of the demand for houses is essential if a balanced view of the circumstances in which the building industry functioned is to be obtained.[91] A number of notable discussions of such aspects have begun to appear, but the scope for additional research remains enormous.[92] However insensitive to demand speculative builders were, it was a crucial constraint on their activities, and until more effective assessments of it are available the foundations of many of our analyses of the industry will remain insecure.

Given the problems of source availability, it is unlikely that empirical research will provide answers to all questions about the building industry. Historical geographers have addressed the implications of this point more directly than historians, and have attempted to apply concepts derived from other disciplines to the study of urban development in the nineteenth century. Locational analyses, the value of which has been stressed by Springett, rest on such concepts, but more ambitious attempts have been made to integrate land factors, building cycles and processes of innovation into a general theory of urban development.[93] Historians have found it difficult to appreciate the utility of generalized theoretical propositions when faced with the task of explaining the complex information relevant to the development of a particular city or town.[94] This debate will no doubt continue. Nonetheless, if problems of source availability are to be surmounted, it may well be that historians could usefully adopt some of the theoretical armoury of other disciplines in their attempts to elucidate the labyrinthine world of the Victorian speculative builder.

NOTES

I should like to thank Derek Fraser and John Bentley for their advice on earlier drafts of this introduction.

1 A point demonstrated by surveys of the literature. See A.R. Sutcliffe, 'Working-class housing in nineteenth-century Britain: a review of recent research', *Bull. Soc. Study of Labour History*, xxiv (1972), and, more recently, K. Jackson, 'Housing standards of the English working-classes, 1837–1914' (Ph.D. thesis, University of Kent, 1977).
2 H.J. Dyos, 'The speculative builders and developers of Victorian London', *Victorian Studies*, xi (1968), 673–7, and, more generally, N. Jackson, 'The speculative house in London, c. 1832–1914' (Ph.D. thesis, Polytechnic of the South Bank, 1982), ch. 1.
3 H. Hobhouse, *Thomas Cubitt, Master Builder* (1970), 218.
4 H.W. Richardson and D.H. Aldcroft, *Building in the British Economy Between the Wars* (1968), 22.
5 H.A. Shannon, 'Bricks: a trade index, 1785–1849', *Economica*, n.s. i (1934); A.K. Cairncross, *Home and Foreign Investment, 1870–1913* (1953), containing a revised version of 'The Glasgow building industry (1870–1914)', *Rev. Economic Studies* (1934–5), 2; B. Weber, 'A new index of residential construction and long cycles in house-building in Great Britain, 1838–1950', *Scottish J. Political Economy* (1955), 2.
6 See the discussion in C.H. Feinstein, 'Capital formation in Great Britain', in *The Cambridge Economic History of Europe*, eds P. Mathias and M.M. Postan (1978), 73–8.
7 Feinstein, *op. cit.*, table 6, p. 40, for the early nineteenth century, and for 1861–1910, Feinstein, *National Income, Expenditure and Output of the United Kingdom, 1856–1965* (1972), table 40, T 88–9.

8 For the most recent discussion, E.W. Cooney, 'The building industry', in *The Dynamics of Victorian Business*, ed. R. Church (1980), 156.

9 The literature on such aspects is very extensive. For a recent account, which includes a full bibliographical survey, see F. Sheppard, V. Belcher and P. Cottrell, 'The Middlesex and Yorkshire Deeds Registries and the study of building fluctuations', *The London J.*, v, 2 (1979).

10 S.B. Saul, 'House Building in England, 1890–1914', *EcHR*, 2nd ser., xv (1962), 132–6.

11 Dyos, *op. cit.*, 648 n. 8; J. Summerson, *The London Building World of the Eighteen-Sixties* (1973), 11.

12 E.W. Cooney, 'The origins of the Victorian master builders', *EcHR*, 2nd ser., VIII (1955); Summerson, *op. cit.* Cubitt has attracted a full-length modern biography: Hobhouse, *op. cit.* Briefer accounts occur throughout the literature. See, for example, L. Wilkes and G. Dodds, *Tyneside Classical: the Newcastle of Grainger, Dobson and Clayton* (1964); Dyos, *op. cit.*, 646–7, 669–73; Dyos, *Victorian Suburb, A Study of the Growth of Camberwell* (1961), chs 4 and 5; Hobhouse, *op. cit.*; S.D. Chapman (ed.), *The History of Working Class Housing: A Symposium* (1971); M. W. Beresford 'The making of a townscape: Richard Paley in the east end of Leeds, 1771–1803', in *Rural Change and Urban Growth, 1500–1800*, eds C.W. Chalklin and M.A. Havinden (1974); R.G. Rodger, 'Speculative builders and the structure of the Scottish building industry, 1860–1914', *Business History*, XXI (1979), 236–7; D. Braithwaite, *Building in the Blood; the story of Dove Brothers of Islington, 1781–1981* (1981).

13 Dyos, 'Speculative builders', esp. 652; E.W. Cooney, 'The speculative builders and developers of Victorian London: a comment', *Victorian Studies*, XIII (1970), 355–7; P.J. Aspinall, 'The size structure of the house-building industry in Victorian Sheffield', Working Paper 49, The Centre for Urban and Regional Studies, University of Birmingham (1977), 1–2.

14 Cooney, 'Master builders', 167.

15 Hobhouse, *op. cit.*, 10–12, 27–9, 260–3.

16 Cooney, 'Master builders', 167–70; R. Price, *Masters, Unions and Men: Work Control in Building and the Rise of Labour, 1830–1914* (1980), 22–3. For earlier practices, C.W. Chalklin, *The Provincial Towns of Georgian England: A Study of the Building Process, 1740–1820* (1974), 168–9.

17 Hobhouse, *op. cit.*, 9–15; Price, *op. cit.*, 23–4.

18 Cooney, 'Building industry', 165.

19 Hobhouse, *op. cit.*, chs 3 and 4.

20 Price, *op. cit.*, 23–8.

21 Chalklin, *op. cit.*, 167–9; Sheppard *et al.*, *op. cit.*, 183.

22 Dyos, *Victorian Suburb*, 127–37. See also V. Belcher, 'The records of a London building firm', *Business Archives*, XLVIII (1982).

23 *Ibid.* 'Speculative builders', *op. cit.*

24 J.M. Imray, 'The Mercers' company and east London: an exercise in urban development', *East London Papers*, IX (1966); M.J. Daunton, *Coal Metropolis, Cardiff 1870–1914* (1977), 89–106; G. Crossick, *An artisan elite in Victorian society: Kentish London, 1840–1880* (1978), 54–8. P.J. Aspinall, *op. cit.*; Aspinall, 'Building applications and the building industry in nineteenth-century towns; the scope for statistical analysis', Research memo. 68, Centre for Urban and Regional Studies, Univ. of Birmingham (1978); Aspinall, 'The internal structure of the housebuilding industry in nineteenth-century cities', in *The Structure of Nineteenth-Century Cities*, eds J.H. Johnson and C.G. Pooley (1982); D. Cannadine, *Lords and landlords: the aristocracy and the towns, 1774–1967* (1980), 113–18, 260–3; J. Springett, 'Landowners and urban development: the Ramsden Estate and nineteenth-century Huddersfield', *J. Historical Geography*, VIII, 2 (1982); Rodger, *op. cit.*; see also G. Potts, 'The growth of Highfields', unpublished paper to the annual conference of the Urban History Group, Birmingham, 1969, quoted in R.M. Pritchard, *Housing and the Spatial Structure of the City* (1976), 39.

25 Especially in the case of Cardiff, Daunton, *op. cit.*, 95.
26 Aspinall, 'Size structure', 12.
27 Dyos, 'Speculative builders', 659–60, 678.
28 Aspinall, 'Size structure', 16. For Scotland, see also R.G. Rodger, 'The growth and transformation of Scottish towns: the role of the building cycle, 1860–1914', in I. Hammarstrom and T. Hall (eds), *Growth and Transformation of the Modern City* (Stockholm, 1979).
29 Saul, *op. cit.*, 132.
30 The mechanism is discussed in Aspinall, 'Size structure', 3, 10–11.
31 Rodger, 'Speculative builders', 237–8; Rodger, 'The invisible hand: market forces, housing and the urban form in Victorian cities', in *The Pursuit of Urban History*, eds D. Fraser and A.R. Sutcliffe (1983), 205–8.
32 For a concise discussion, Cannadine, *op. cit.*, 391–4.
33 *Ibid.*, 391–416; M.J. Daunton, *House and Home in the Victorian City: Working Class Housing, 1850–1914* (1983), 73–8.
34 R.G. Rodger, 'Rents and ground rents: housing and the land market in nineteenth-century Britain', in Johnson and Pooley (eds), *op. cit.*, 49–50.
35 M.J. Mortimore, 'Landownership and urban growth in Bradford and its environs in the West Riding conurbation', *Trans. Institute of British Geographers*, XLVI (1969), 109–17; S.M. Gaskell, 'Housing estate development 1840–1918 with particular reference to the Pennine towns' (Ph.D. thesis, University of Sheffield, 1974); D.J. Olsen, *The Growth of Victorian London* (1979 edn), 156; F.M.L. Thompson (ed.), *The rise of suburbia* (1982), 21–2.
36 Cannadine, *op. cit.*, 405.
37 Published figures vary from 'a traditional 5 to 10 per cent of overall cost' (Thompson (ed.), *op. cit.*, 6), through 15 to 20 per cent (Rodger, 'Rents', 39; Daunton, *House and Home*, 66). An estimate for an earlier period suggests 'between about 5 and 25 per cent of a builder's outlay' (Chalklin, *op. cit.*, 57). See also W.G. Rimmer, 'Working men's cottages in Leeds, 1770–1840', *Trans. Thoresby Society*, XLVI (1961), 190; E. Gauldie, *Cruel Habitations: a History of Working Class Housing, 1780–1918* (1974), 172; J. Burnett, *A Social History of Housing, 1815–1970* (1978), 22–3, 76; M.W. Beresford, 'The face of Leeds' in D. Fraser (ed.), *A History of Modern Leeds* (1980), 82. For a much more substantial estimate, see Springett, below. The problem is complicated by the lack of exact comparability in the figures and terminology.
38 Springett, *op. cit.*, 138–40.
39 D.A. Reeder, 'Capital investment in the western suburbs of Victorian London' (Ph.D. thesis, University of Leicester, 1965), 112.
40 Mortimore, *op. cit.*, 116–17.
41 M.W. Beresford, 'The back-to-back house in Leeds, 1787–1937', in Chapman (ed.), *op. cit.*, 119–21.
42 Huddersfield built back-to-backs on 999 year leases, see Springett, below and *op. cit.* For further examples see Daunton, *House and Home*, 64–77.
43 See also, R.G. Rodger, 'The law and urban change: some nineteenth-century Scottish evidence', *Urban History Yearbook* (1979).
44 Mortimore, *op. cit.*, 115–16.
45 Saul, *op. cit.*, 123. See also F. Trowell, 'Nineteenth-century speculative housing in Leeds, with special reference to the suburb of Headingley, 1838–1914' (Ph.D. thesis, University of York, 1982).
46 It is indicative of the state of research in the subject that assessments of the respective importance of freehold and leasehold tenures differ. See the interpretations of M.J. Daunton, 'The building cycle and the urban fringe in Victorian cities: a comment', *J. Historical Geography*, IV, 2 (1978), 178, and Cannadine, *op. cit.*, 401. More extensively, P.J. Aspinall, 'The evolution of urban tenure systems in 19th-century cities', Research Memo. 63, Centre for Urban and Regional Studies, Univ. of Birmingham (1978), 29–33, argues the predominance of freehold.

47 J.W.R. Whitehand, 'The building cycle and the urban fringe in Victorian cities: a reply', *J. Historical Geography*, IV, 2 (1978), 185.
48 Cannadine, *op. cit.*, 395, 401; Cannadine (ed.), *Patricians, Power and Politics in Nineteenth-Century Towns* (1982).
49 Cannadine, *Lords and Landlords*, 395–401; see also Daunton, *House and Home*, 76–7, 83–4.
50 Dyos, 'Speculative builders', 661–9.
51 The estate granted loans at 4 per cent to facilitate rebuilding on its London property, but provided no assistance in Sheffield. Olsen, *op. cit.*, 160; Aspinall, 'Size structure', 18.
52 Olsen, *op. cit.*, 159–60.
53 Dyos, *Victorian Suburb*, 114–18; S.D. Chapman and J.N. Bartlett, 'The contribution of building clubs and freehold land societies to working-class housing in Birmingham', in Chapman (ed.), *op. cit.*; Gauldie, *op. cit.*, ch. 18; Pritchard, *op. cit.*, 40.
54 S.J. Price, *Building Societies: their Origin and History* (1958); E.J. Cleary, *The Building Society Movement* (1965); Gauldie, *op cit.*, ch. 17.
55 Dyos, *Victorian Suburb*, 130.
56 Aspinall, 'Size structure', 18.
57 Pritchard's account of Leicester is similar, *op. cit.*, 76.
58 Similar, though less firmly supported conclusions are suggested in Chapman and Bartlett, *op. cit.* See also. R. Homan, 'The Kendal Union Building Societies', *Trans. Cumberland & Westmorland Archaeological Soc.*, LXXXII (1982).
59 See note 12 above. Trowell, *op. cit.*, vol. II, ch. 9, also contains relevant information.
60 Dyos, 'Speculative builders', 663; Aspinall, 'Size structure', 19.
61 G.T. Jones, *Increasing Return* (1933), 58–99 (index covering 1845–1913); K. Maiwald, 'An index of building costs in the United Kingdom, 1845–1938', *EcHR*, 2nd ser., VII (1954); Feinstein, 'Capital formation', 38 (index covering 1760–1860). See also Shannon, *op. cit.*; Cairncross, *Home and Foreign Investment* (index for Glasgow, 1862–1914).
62 For example, Rimmer, *op. cit.*, 190–1 and, more generally, Gauldie, *op. cit.*, 172; Burnett, *op. cit.*, 21–3, 76. Although it deals with a specialized building type, one uniquely detailed source for building costs has been uncovered: the account book of James Brandwood of Turton for 1794–1814. See W.J. Smith, 'The cost of building Lancashire loomhouses and weavers' workshops', *Textile History*, VIII (1977). Trowell, *op. cit.*, vol. II, 199–201, reviews selling prices in Leeds.
63 For a recent discussion, Cooney, 'Building industry', 148–9.
64 J.W.R. Whitehand, 'Building activity and the intensity of development at the urban fringe: the case of a London suburb in the nineteenth century', *J. Historical Geography*, I, 2 (1978), 212–13.
65 P. Deane and W.A. Cole, *British Economic Growth, 1688–1959: Trends and Structure* (1969), table 7; Daunton, *House and Home*, 36.
66 A.L. Bowley, 'The statistics of wages in the United Kingdom in the last hundred years', *J. Royal Statistical Soc.*, LXIV (1901); K. Burgess, *The Origins of British Industrial Relations* (1975), ch. 2; Price, *op. cit.*, Appendix B.
67 Cairncross, *Home and Foreign Investment*, 34–5.
68 Burgess, *op. cit.*, 112; Price, *op. cit.*, ch. 3; Rodger, below.
69 Price, *op. cit.*, ch. 1.
70 A more extensive discussion of the issue may be found in Cooney, 'Building industry', 149–50.
71 *Ibid.*, 154; Price, *op. cit.*, 77–8, 171.
72 For the effect of railways see C.G. Powell, *An Economic History of the British Building Industry, 1815–1979* (1980), 79.
73 Powell, *op. cit.*, 81. For timber statistics, E. W. Cooney, 'Long waves in building in the British economy of the nineteenth century', *EcHR*, 2nd ser., XIII (1960), 259–62, 268–9.

74 B.R. Mitchell and P. Deane, *Abstract of British Historical Statistics* (1962), 60.
75 The following discussion is based on: Jones, *op. cit.*; Hobhouse, *op. cit.*, 286–8, 291, 303–15, 490–1; K. Hudson, *Building Materials* (1972); R. Samuel, 'The workshop of the world: steam power and hand technology in mid-Victorian Britain', *History Workshop J.*, III (1977), 36–7; Samuel (ed.), *Miners, Quarrymen and Saltworkers* (1977), 3–97; Cooney, 'Building industry'; Price, *op. cit.*; N. Jackson, *op. cit.*, 236–47.
76 Jones, *op. cit.*, 97.
77 The major modern work is S. Muthesius, *The English Terraced House* (1982).
78 For example, A. Clifton-Taylor, *The Pattern of English Building* (1972 edn); D. Linstrum, *West Yorkshire, Architects and Architecture* (1978); R.W. Brunskill, *Houses* (1982), among others.
79 Daunton, *House and Home*, 5.
80 For general accounts see A.K. Cairncross and B. Weber, 'Fluctuations in building in Great Britain, 1785–1849', *EcHR*, 2nd ser., IX (1956), 283–5; Clifton-Taylor, *op. cit.*, 171, 228, 397; Burnett, *op. cit.*, 27–9.
81 Burnett, *op. cit.*, 21; K. Jackson, *op. cit.*, 134–8; N. Jackson, *op. cit.*, 236–46.
82 A clear example of the effect of proposals to introduce regulation of constructional standards was seen in the Liverpool building boom of 1844–6, prompted by discussions which resulted in the 1846 bye-laws: Cairncross and Weber, *op. cit.*, 290: J.H. Treble, 'Liverpool working class housing, 1801–51', in Chapman (ed.), *op. cit.*, 194, 210. A similar effect was observed in Hull, in advance of the 1893 bye-laws: C.A. Forster, *Court Housing in Kingston upon Hull: an Example of Cyclical Processes in the Morphological Development of Nineteenth-Century Bye-Law Housing*, Univ. of Hull Occasional Papers in Geography, 19 (1972), 38–43.
83 For an earlier account see J.N. Tarn, *Five Per Cent Philanthropy* (1973). For the most recent version, Muthesius, *op. cit.*
84 Trowell, *op. cit.*, argues this point strongly, especially in vol. II, ch. 10. See also N. Jackson, *op. cit.*
85 Forster, *op. cit.*
86 It is important to note that owing to the nature of the statistics as measuring the cost of inputs, rather than house prices, this rise is not evident in the indices of building costs discussed above.
87 Rodger, 'Rents', 68–9; Daunton, *House and Home*, 286–9.
88 M.J. Daunton (ed.), *Councillors and Tenants: local authority housing in English cities, 1919–1939* (1984), 2–8.
89 M.W. Doughty, *Merchant Shipping and War* (1982), ch. 1.
90 Aspinall, 'Size structure', 3.
91 Others have made the same point: see the implications of Yeadell's comments on the availability of finance in the 1880s being insufficient to stimulate building.
92 Pritchard, *op. cit.*; K. Jackson, *op. cit.*; A, Offer, *Property and Politics, 1870–1914. Landownership, Law, Ideology and Urban Development in England* (1981); D. Englander, *Landlord and Tenant in Urban Britain 1828–1918* (1983); Daunton, *House and Home*, 78–84, 286–307; Daunton (ed.), *Councillors*, 2–8.
93 J.W.R. Whitehand has led this enterprise. For a review of his many articles, see his 'Conzenian ideas: extension and development', in *The Urban Landscape: Historical Development and Management* (1981).
94 See Cannadine's comments in 'Urban development in England and America in the nineteenth century: some comparisons and contrasts', *EcHR*, 2nd ser., XXXIII (1980); also K. Jackson, *op. cit.*, 36.

Land development and house-building in Huddersfield, 1770–1911

JANE SPRINGETT

Land development and house-building in Huddersfield, 1770–1911

JANE SPRINGETT

1 Introduction

This present study, which focuses on house-building, forms part of a more comprehensive analysis of the land development process in Huddersfield between 1770 and 1911, undertaken for my doctoral thesis accepted by the University of Leeds in 1979. Following an established tradition of post-graduate research in hostorical geography at Leeds, the initial research focus was the role of the landowner in urban development, and in particular the decision-making behaviour of the dominant landowner in Huddersfield, the Ramsden Estate. It became increasingly apparent that the interrelationships in the decision-making process were such that any understanding of urban morphogenesis could only proceed from a detailed analysis of the actions of all landowners and builders in the land development process. The material presented below is taken directly from two chapters in the original study, but the analysis reflects a reassessment of the evidence and the development of thinking since 1979.

2 House-building as a locational decision – a conceptual framework

House-building can be studied from a number of perspectives. One approach is to characterize the production of living space as a behavioural decision-making process involving a number of key agents whose positive actions each contributed in varying degrees to the final housing package.[1] The individual decision-makers do not operate in a vacuum but in an environment created by other members involved in the building process, and adjust their behaviour accordingly. This makes the process a complex circular one of constant interaction. Each participant can initiate change or veto the change favoured by others, but with any innovation taking place in the broader context established by others. While the pricing mechanism plays an important role in the interaction between the large number of individuals involved in the building process, a behavioural perspective allows the identification of other factors which contributed to the way market forces did or did not operate.

The key decision-agents in the nineteenth century were the landowner, land developer, builder and potential building owner. These were supported by a number of secondary agents: solicitors, investors or mortgagors and, late in the century, real estate agents. The role of each category of decision-agent varied both with local circumstance and with time. With some exceptions the initiative usually came from the building undertaker (to distinguish from the profession itself), that is, the person who actually decided to build and brought together the factor inputs of land, labour, materials and capital. Most undertook house-building for rent, a few for owner-occupation. Considering the relative attractiveness at the time of other forms of investment it is surprising so many individuals did undertake building for rent. It was, however, the most popular source of investment amongst small savers, providing a low level of risk, a reliable repository of value and some promise for the future.[2]

The approach of the majority of house-building undertakers was that of satisfying a demand rather than a concern for maximization of profit. While house-building always contained an element of speculation, the amount of highly speculative building varied and in some towns building on a contractual basis was more common-place.[3] The housing undertaker's perception of the needs of market and consumer preference helped to determine the type of housing built, even if the response was not wholly perfect. Few resources were available to employ expertise and the jobbing builders who undertook most of the work operated on a small scale with a high level of risk and limited entrepreneurial skills. There is evidence that in a number of towns professional building contractors emerged towards the end of the century,[4] but on the whole judgment was undertaken by unskilled amateurs. Notwithstanding this, the building industry was surprisingly successful in terms of of quantity in housing the increased population consequent upon industrialization.

House-building not only involved a capital investment decision, it also involved a locational one. The changing morphology of the Victorian city was the collective result of the locational decisions of individual building undertakers. Uniqueness of location meant that each housing project was effectively a distinct unit of output and this had implications for both the markets in land and the housing package itself. As suburban living became fashionable, location acquired a social value in addition to that accruing from accessibility to workplace and town centre. Improvements in transport in the last decades of the century merely increased the choice available.

If house-building is seen as a decision-making process involving a locational dimension then land assumes importance as a factor input alongside other production inputs. Land has physical attributes, which affect the cost of development and the cost of land as a proportion of total development cost, but it also has abstract qualities which derive from the relative location of the land unit within a potential urban area. Circumstances such as the nature of population and economic growth, changes in transport technology and the locational requirements of industry as well as tastes and fashion will change these abstract attributes and therefore the decision-making context.

Land also has a third dimension which was particularly important in Victorian society. It has rights attached to it. House-building involved the appropriation and creation of landed property tenures and interests in one form or another. House-builders operated at the interface between the housing and land markets. The market in land and hence the market in housing was really a market in property rights.

Landed tenure in English law was, and is, given a primacy over all other forms of private property interests and became deeply embedded in the social and political institutions of Victorian society. Indeed the 'Man of property' came to typify the ideal late Victorian and Edwardian. While ownership of property alone was not a source of social prestige and political power, these could additionally accrue to those who held it. Thus its distribution was intimately bound up with the structure of society.

The effect of house-building was to create new property rights and interests out of existing ones. Their appropriation altered the structure of society and impinged on the relationship between land and capital by eroding the power of freehold landowners and giving rise to a new class of petty capitalists. This class was jealous of the continuing interests retained by landowners in urban development and posed a direct threat to the power of the landed aristocracy. The continuing interest varied from town to town,[5] but in those areas where the landowner retained some interests through the creation of leasehold rights, property relations had a different complexion from towns where freehold development predominated. In the former case, a commitment by landowners to an involvement in urban development created the potential for direct confrontation between landed and capitalist tenures. This was made manifest nationally at the turn of the twentieth century in calls for land nationalization and site value rating, but it also surfaced at the local urban level. Such was the position in Huddersfield in 1862 when the *Ramsden* v *Thornton* legal case was heard in the House of Lords. Huddersfield was one of a number of towns which developed on leasehold tenure. It became notorious for the dominance of one landed estate, the Ramsden Estate, although in reality this estate's monopoly was not absolute.[6] The situation developed, however, to create the classic conditions for confrontation: it consisted of, on the one hand, a large number of petty capitalists who had collectively enjoyed unchallenged for over half a century the fruits of urban growth by owning and building urban property and, on the other, an aristocratic landowner who sought rather belatedly to benefit also from the increased value consequent upon that growth by asserting his power as an owner of the superior interest of freehold.

Until 1854 a combination of lax management practices and the restrictions contained in wills and settlements encouraged house-building in Huddersfield on tenancy at will. This involved no written agreement or lease. An individual would build his property and surrender it to the landowner, becoming tenant at the will of the freehold owner from year to year at a nominal rent and in the full knowledge that he could be given notice to quit at any time. Ostensibly, therefore, a large number of inferior interests were created wholly dependent on the absolutism of the owner of the superior interest from which they derived. In practice the freehold landowner did not fully exploit his power by exerting control over these interests, so that not one tenant was given notice to quit for non-payment of rent. This curious reciprocal arrangement of non-intervention by the landowner in return for low rent was gradually eroded with the introduction of new personnel into the management of the Ramsden Estate in 1844 who attempted to enforce building standards and exercised greater control over the activities of builders. The creation of so many inferior interests without any controls over their formation had reduced the power of the landowner to determine the fate of the Ramsden Estate's landed interest. More seriously, the price the estate had paid for the failure to create more conventional leasehold rights was an inability to tap the inevitable rise in property and land values. The new management was aware of these inequities but saw fit not to disturb the established system, feeling that to do so would deter building. When a London solicitor took over stewardship in 1853 he sought to assert the landowner's authority. No new building on tenancy at will was to be allowed and tenants who had defaulted on the payment of rent were to be evicted. A test case was brought against a man called Swift which called into question the legality and security of all tenants at will. Confidence in the Ramsden Estate collapsed and all building ceased.[7] Eventually an Act of Parliament was obtained in 1859 (the Ramsden Estate Leasing Act) which converted all tenancies at will to 99-year leases, at the same time raising the rents to what was deemed an economic level. Alarmed at the impact such an increase in ground rent would have on their profits, a number of houseowners, solicitors and other interested parties, drawn mainly from the lower middle classes and led by a mill manager called Joseph Thornton, challenged the Act by refusing to apply for a lease.

The public posture Thornton adopted was that the decision to change the terms of tenure was detrimental to the interests of the thrifty working classes. Such people had saved for many years to invest in a house and since they were unable to pay the increased rent they would lose their life savings. He therefore was 'championing the cause of the working classes against the Tyranny of the aristocracy who were exploiting them'.[8] In reality the chief protagonists were the new property-owning classes and the old landed interest.

Legally the case was won, as would be expected, by the landed interests, but it symbolized the new form which property relations were taking. While the majority of tenants applied for 99-year leases few builders took up such leases for new building and the estate was forced to seek another Act of Parliament in 1867 which introduced 999-year leases. In the following year the Borough of Huddersfield was incorporated and for the first time the Ramsden Estate no longer had a say in the composition of local government, which became the collective bulwark of urban property interests.

The rest of this essay examines the building process which created the structure of property relations in Huddersfield and how they changed as the town developed. First, however, it is necessary to establish, in accordance with the model outlined, the general decision-making context in which building undertakers operated.

3   The decision-making context

a. *Economic and population change*

As a textile town Huddersfield's source of economic strength came from its role as a market centre for the cloth industry in the surrounding area. Industrial change took place slowly with domestic and factory production existing side by side for some time. While the bulk of factory construction took place between 1820 and 1850, some sectors such as the fancy trade operated almost entirely on a domestic basis until the late 1850s. Even as late as 1839 domestic production dominated Huddersfield's industrial structure.[9] With the advent of the factory system industry gravitated towards the valleys of the Colne and Holme and along the canal, not only in Huddersfield itself but also in the villages of Lockwood, Paddock and Mold-green. The dyeing and finishing processes that had been the mainstay of the embryonic town in the late eighteenth century developed into important chemical and engineering industries in the second half of the nineteenth century, confirming Huddersfield's maturity as a Victorian industrial city with some 158 factories ranging from those employing only 19 people to much larger ones employing 240.[10]

Commercial developments accompanied these advances. Office-building was encouraged by the advent of the railway in 1849 and the number of people employed in commerce and the service industries grew, although the professional and commercial classes still only accounted for 17–20,000 of the population in 1901.[11]

These economic changes had implications for the structure of both society and capital, which in turn had an impact on the building process. The late emergence of factory organization meant that the facility to accumulate capital was available to a larger number of individuals, thus creating a substantial number of small-scale capitalists, a long tradition of small-scale credit, and an only partially developed industrial proletariat. When factory organization did get established the textile industry developed a strict social hierarchy based on skill. As the century progressed higher wages accrued to those with the highest level of skill at the expense of the unskilled, swelling the ranks of the middle classes. Meanwhile the merchant manufacturers, many of whose wealth was based on a generation of investment in the cloth industry and who comprised the elite of the town, found the connection of the town with the national rail network removed the necessity to keep extensive stocks and released capital which some spent in conspicuous consumption rather than industrial investment.

b. *Population change and physical growth*

The demographic growth that accompanied economic change exhibited a high decennial increase between 1801 and 1851 and a declining rate of growth subsequently (table 1). Variations in the rate of increase reflected the character of economic activity in that decade. Huddersfield, like other textile towns, suffered a number of fluctuations in its economic growth, but to a lesser extent. Major depressions occurred: in the Napoleonic Wars; in 1847 when a general panic throughout the country was accompanied by a local reduction in demand for labour following the completion of the railway; in 1857 when the Crimean War ended; and in the 1890s when lower prices from increased foreign competition considerably reduced profits. This latter depression was the most severely felt and was reflected in the decennial decrease in population growth.

Differential rates of growth experienced by the individual townships which came to comprise the Borough of Huddersfield reflect the physical pattern of development rather than overall demand. In 1778 Huddersfield consisted almost entirely of one street and a few jumbled clusters of houses at bridging points on the river. The demand for space in which to house industry and commerce or for residential use was met by intensifying the utilization of existing buildings and of space in the tenter crofts behind. The main buildings consisted of the church, the George Hotel, the market and the Cloth Hall which symbolized the main function of the town. Outside the main township substantial weaving communities were found at Paddock, Lockwood, Berry Brow and Almondbury. Here too building was haphazard.

Early town development was concentrated round the central nucleus and on

Table 1   Population trends, Huddersfield district, 1801–1911

numbers date	townships Huddersfield	Almondbury	Dalton	Lockwood	Lindley	total
1801	7,268	3,751	1,222	1,253	1,377	14,871
1811	9,671	4,613	1,625	1,490	1,686	19,085
1821	13,284	5,679	2,289	1,881	2,040	25,173
1831	19,035	7,086	3,060	3,134	2,300	34,615
1841	22,744	8,828	3,906	4,182	2,881	42,541
1851	30,880	9,749	4,310	5,556	3,023	53,518
1861	34,877	10,361	4,692	6,755	4,259	60,944
1871	38,654	11,669	6,170	8,270	5,490	70,253
1881	42,234	13,977	8,019	10,446	7,284	81,960
1891	46,098	14,855	8,413	13,075	8,573	90,014
1901	44,921	14,436	8,521	13,365	8,445	89,688
1911	51,264	15,485	9,249	16,641	9,345	101,984
percentage increase						
1801	—	—	—	—	—	—
1811	33.06	22.98	32.97	22.45	22.44	28.34
1821	37.36	23.11	29.00	25.24	20.99	31.90
1831	43.29	24.77	33.68	66.60	13.04	37.51
1841	19.49	24.58	27.64	10.34	32.85	22.90
1851	35.77	10.43	10.34	32.85	4.93	28.34
1861	12.94	6.28	8.86	21.58	40.89	13.87
1871	10.82	12.62	31.50	22.42	28.90	15.27
1881	9.26	19.77	29.96	26.31	32.67	16.56
1891	9.14	6.28	4.91	15.59	17.69	9.83
1901	−2.55	−2.82	1.28	10.68	−1.49	−0.36
1911	14.12	7.26	8.44	24.51	10.66	13.70

Source: *Census Returns.*

those villages that were valley-orientated. By 1850 some differentiation in land use was emerging with a distinct sector on the north-west of the township of more substantial dwellings and an embryonic business district adjacent to the new railway station. The outward growth along the arterial roads from the central nucleus did not continue and most development between 1850 and 1880 took place in the out-lying industrial communities, provoking comment in the local press in 1871:

> The other townships exhibit as high a ratio of increase as any other centre in England . . . for the township proper the ungratifying fact of the absence of vigorous development has been noticed.[12]

In common with other Victorian towns, modern suburban development with its characteristic segregation of housing into homogeneous areas was initiated by the upper middle classes. Large villas with extensive grounds were built in 1855–75 at Upper Edgerton while smaller semi-detached villas with rather less land were built in the 1870s in Gledholt alongside Greenhead Park. Finally in the 1880s larger scale developments of inferior terraced and back-to-back houses were built along the arterial roads which the tram routes followed from 1883.

c. *Building activity*
Building activity fluctuated considerably in response to these changing demographic

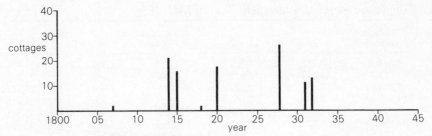

a. Cottages entered with Building Clubs, Ramsden Estate

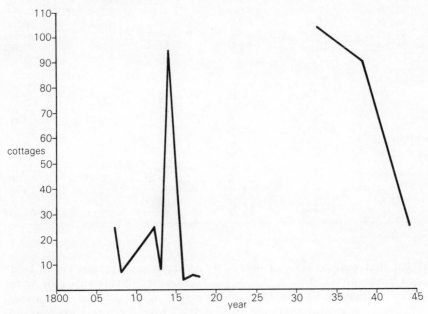

b. New additions in rentals, Ramsden Estate

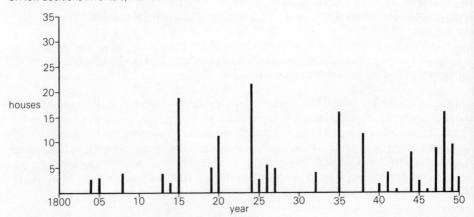

c. House-building on the Lockwood Proprietors' Estate

Land development and house-building in Huddersfield, 1770–1911
JANE SPRINGETT

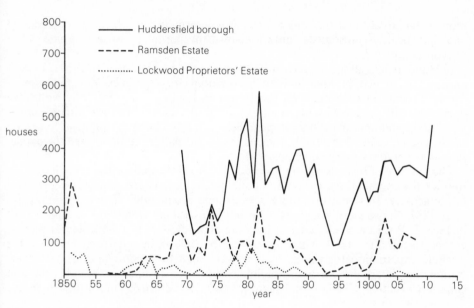

d. House-building in Huddersfield, 1850-1911

Figure 1.   The course of house-building in Huddersfield, 1800–1901. (Source for (c): HPL C/T/2/42.)

and economic conditions. Only fragmentary data are available for Huddersfield as a whole until 1868 when the first building plan registers were established.[13] Such data that are available reveal certain common trends in the collective response of building undertakers to demand (fig. 1). In the early years building took place continually in the central township and more sporadically in the surrounding districts where the timing and location of activity coincided closely with the building and extension of industrial mills. Thus in Moldgreen and Dalton, where most of the work was performed by outworkers no similar spurt in house-building was apparent. Discrepancies between national and local trends are also apparent. In the late 1840s, when Huddersfield central township experienced a steady rise in activity and only a minor cut-back in 1850 and a major peak in 1851, in Lockwood and elsewhere, the trend mirrored the national one except for a major peak in activity in 1847.

Nationally, the major features of the building cycle after 1850 were the peaks during the 1870s and the major slump of the 1890s, followed by a recovery which mirrored the recovery in the British economy as a whole. The Weber index[14] shows a generally low level of building during the mid 1850s with particularly marked slumps in 1857 and 1860 followed by a minor peak in 1863 and a general rise with peaks in 1872 and 1876. As already argued, and as Saul and Lewis have shown, the market for housing was largely imperfect and the role of overall demand such that the building industry was insensitive to marginal charges in market conditions, although sensitivity was greater where the building industry operated on a small scale. Lewis points to a strong association of the building cycle with the state of trade in the principal industry of any area. Saul, however, has argued

31

more persuasively that building activity was internally and positively determined and that local circumstances could influence the lag in response to a new wave of economic growth.[15]

In Huddersfield all the landed estates that were being developed in 1850–2 experienced a high level of building activity, in common with other West Yorkshire towns, towns, and an all time peak on the Ramsden Estate. The trend may well have been primarily dictated by the state of industrial activity, but local circumstances gave additional impetus. This comprised the general feeling of optimism following the traumatic years of the 1840s, the passing of the cholera epidemic and the expectations associated with the new railway link.

The absence of records for the Ramsden Estate in the mid 1850s makes it difficult to trace the course of the cycle but an analysis of various deeds indicates a general fall in activity. In Lockwood there was a slump around 1855–6 and a general rise after 1857. Subsequently activity followed the national trend with a minor peak in 1863–5. With the availability of building plan registers in 1868 a clearer picture can be traced after 1869. These reveal a rapid fall-off in activity in 1870–1. One possible explanation for this is that, as suggested by a contemporary observer, capital was diverted from house-building to finance an upsurge in industrial and commercial activity. Thus a local agent wrote in 1876 during a later peak in activity:

> The condition of trade is affecting building in a much more favourable way than it has been for some time in the past. Building is always slack when trade in the town is good, all capital that can then be secured, being absorbed in maintaining and operating businesses; but when trade languishes and men are unable to employ their money in business to ascertain them profit and have certain capital at their disposal, they turn to building both for the purpose of investment and also to provide either better dwellings for themselves or more suitable premises for their businesses.[16]

A more likely explanation was the projected introduction of bye-laws controlling the erection of houses under the 1871 Improvement Act which meant that builders held back on starting any new project. A high level of building activity took place subsequently and continued throughout the late 1870s and early 1880s, reaching a peak in 1882. The very wide fluctuations suggest it was highly speculative in nature. The slump of the 1890s occurred later in Huddersfield than elsewhere and the upturn did not accelerate until 1899. By 1903, however, trade was reported as being more active and building activity was stimulated by the expectation of rising living standards.

d. *The land market*
Levels of building activity such as those described were only possible if there was a readily available supply of land. In the early years of industrial development the operations of building undertakers evolved against the background of an imperfect freehold land market. Its structure was derived from the spatial distribution of pre-development landownership and reinforced by a number of institutional restrictions preventing its free operation and thus compounding the inherent monopoly position of the freehold pre-development landowner. In effect something approaching an oligopoly existed – a few individuals offering differentiated products in a market where there was a high demand. This limited competition gave land-

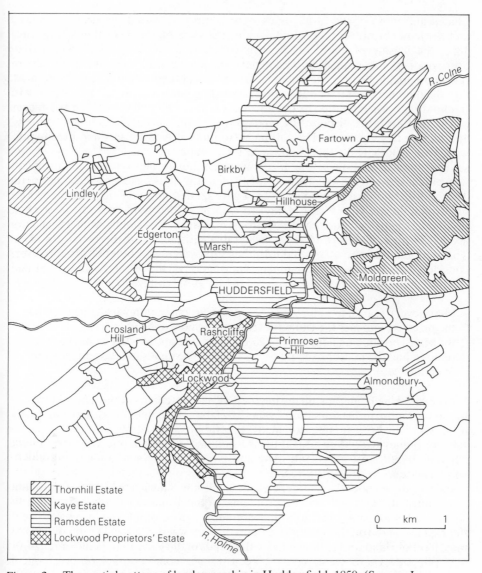

Figure 2. The spatial pattern of landownership in Huddersfield, 1850. (Source: J. Springett, 'Landowners and urban development. The Ramsden Estate and nineteenth-century Huddersfield', *J. Historical Geography*, VIII, 1982, 129–44.)

owners the opportunity to dictate the choice of tenure on which land would be made available for building.

In 1850 the spatial pattern of landownership was such that the Ramsden family owned most of the land in the immediate vicinity of the town centre while the Lockwood proprietors, a business consortium, and the Thornhill family dominated Lockwood and Lindley respectively (fig. 2). In the villages of Fartown, Birkby, Crosland Moor and Marsh landholdings were more fragmented. Some of the smaller

33

estates and most of the larger ones were subject to various restrictions in wills and settlements preventing sale, or as in the case of the Thornhill Estate until 1852, the leasing of land.[17] There was generally a low level of market activity even amongst the remaining landowners and the overall structure of ownership remained unchanged for the greater part of the century. Some inroads were made into the dominance of the large estates, providing limited opportunities to purchase freehold land for building. In the 1820s a number of small estates on the fringes of the built-up area disposed of land to merchants and manufacturers for villas and factory development. The former were built at Newhouse some five minutes walk from Cloth Hall; the latter were built along the canal.[18] The Kaye Estate sold off land in Dalton in the 1820s which, although laid out as building plots, was purchased for the creation of small mansion house estates. The sale of the Thornhill Estate land in Lindley in 1854 gave landed property rights to many local millowners in the village of Lindley. In contrast to freehold land sales elsewhere in Huddersfield, demand was very strong and the prices obtained at the auction artificially high. This was to the considerable satisfaction of the managers of the Thornhill Estate, who attributed it to the employment of Frederick Robert Jones, considered to be 'The most eminent land agent in the West Riding of York.[19] According to Christopher White, one of the Estates Trustees:

> I have every reason to believe that the judicious manner in which he lotted
> the property and met the claims of tenantry (a most difficult task) has secured
> for Miss Thornhill an addition of £20,000 over and above what would have been
> realised had the matter been placed as usual in the hands of a London firm
> of eminence.[20]

Pressure had been building up during the 1840s from tenants of the Thornhill Estate for better tenure terms than the 21 years available. A number of potential industrialists, who had been tenants for many generations, had applied to the estate for sums of money exceeding £2,000 for the building of mills and it was these tenants who purchased most of its land. Any house-building that subsequently took place was on leasehold rather than freehold terms.

Indeed, throughout the Huddersfield area, although during the 1850s estate agents were quick to capitalize on the problems of the Ramsden Estate and advertise small estates as being 'freehold and not subject to ground rent or chief rent or the expense and trouble consequent upon the renewal of lease on a term of years',[21] most freehold land sold either ended in the hands of the Ramsden Estate or remained undeveloped. There seems to have been, as one contemporary observer put it, 'not the slightest inclination amongst lessees to purchase ground rents – all the capital they command they prefer to apply in business which will probably realise a much greater return.'[22] Towards the end of the century, however, competition between landowners in supplying building land became intense as demand fell during the recession of the 1890s and transport improvements brought more land within the ambit of potential urban demand. While the older established estates responded by lowering ground rents, the prospects of long-term holding of freehold land became increasingly unattractive to the smaller landowner. The depression in agriculture and calls for land nationalization persuaded many of them to shed their landed property interests for other forms of investment. The mansion house estates created in the early 1800s were acquired by a new breed of speculative landowner

developer. Unconstrained by considerations of the perpetuations of property interests, these new landowners sought only to realize an immediate return on their
assets by benefiting from the improved value accorded to developed land. For
the first time freehold land was made available to builders in appropriate packages
and the changes that had taken place in the building process meant that the market
was ready to respond to the offer.

For the greater part of the century, however, the majority of landowners preferred
to retain some continued interest in landed urban property and let their land for
building on 999-year leasehold tenure. This enabled the builder to obtain a reasonable benefit from the capital employed but at a respectable return to the landowner.
As already indicated, the Ramsden Estate did not conform to this general pattern
until 1867. Before 1859 land was made available on 60-year renewable leases, renewable by uncertain fine between 1816 and 1845 and certain fine after 1845, tenancy
at will between 1800 and 1854, and 99-year lease between 1859 and 1867.[23]

The limited freehold land market and the predominance of leasehold land tenure
in various forms as the result of local landowning policy provided a set of priming
decisions within which the building undertaker had to operate and the following
sections will demonstrate how the interrelationship between landowner policy and
the building undertaker influenced the structure of the building process that
emerged.

4   The building process, 1770–1850

The papers presented as evidence by both the plaintiffs and defendants in the *Ramsden* v *Thornton* case provide a wealth of information on the early development
of the building process in Huddersfield. A striking picture emerges, supported
by other sources, of an imperfect system of development involving a large number
of small savers, who despite operating in an *ad hoc* manner nevertheless quite
adequately kept pace with the demand for living space quantitatively if not qualita-
tively.[24]

On none of the estates was any direction received from the landowner on the
nature of development, so builders were free to operate as they wished. As was
common elsewhere, builders, having selected their land, initially took out a building
agreement on the basis of which they assembled the necessary capital and personnel
and built the houses. When completed a lease was signed and backdated. Ground
rents tended to be fixed for certain locations and the builder was well aware of
their levels before committing himself to building. Few builders acquired freehold
land but where they did it was necessary to have a stronger capital base or at
least access to security. Building undertakers on freehold land came chiefly from
the wealthier echelons of society and restricted their activities to building houses
for members of their own class. A few were millowners and industrialists who
built mills and houses for key workers in the more isolated villages surrounding
the central township (table 2).

The situation of the Ramsden Estate differed substantially and because most
early development took place on Ramsden land, then the process pertaining on
that land was the predominant mode by which building took place. Estate management was the responsibility of a steward, John Bower, together with a local part-time
agent, Joseph Brook. Bower visited Huddersfield twice a year on rent day to audit

Table 2   The socio-economic status of building undertakers by percentage

source	industrialists/ manufacturers	merchant	small traders/ services	building trades	prof./ annuitants	workers/ unknown
LEASEHOLD/RENTAL						
1780 Ramsden survey	15.8	7.6	28.3	9.6	28.8	17.9
Ramsden rentals	11.2	7.5	11.2	4.2	3.3	62.6
Ramsden v Thornton case						
tenancies at will	4.4	2.0	22.2	13.7	12.3	45.4
Lockwood Estate Prop						
conveyance	24.3	16.7	10.6	6.1	21.1	21.2
Ingham/Dyson Deeds						
WRRD	57.4	0	5.7	0	7.1	28.6
Miscellanous Deeds						
WRRD	40	0	30	10	0	20
FREEHOLD SALES						
Kaye Estate	28.5	10.2	28.5	10.2	12.2	12.2
Lindley township	48.1	7.7	17.3	15.4	7.7	3.8
Fenton Estate	25	33.3	8.3	25	8.3	0
Ikin Estate	15.2	30.3	18.2	12.2	24.2	0
Miscellaneous sales						
Lockwood township	87.7	0	12.3	0	0	0

Source: *Deeds WRRD*

the accounts. In the meantime a person wishing to build would select a plot of land and report his choice to Joseph Brook, who on the receipt of an appropriate bribe would stake out the plot and agree a provisional rent which was usually approved when Bower paid his annual visit. In the interim period the applicant had already arranged capital and engaged builders in anticipation of a successful agreement. If the land was taken on tenancy at will, then security was provided by the builder's name in the rent book. If a lease was required then Bower would oblige for the cost of ten to fifteen guineas. Any vacant land could be built on, even land tenanted by someone else.[25] In this case the existing tenant received compensation for land taken. Thus entries were made in the rental book to the effect: '1829: Wm. Batley's widow £1 allowed for building . . . .John Tine paddock reduced for building.'[26] In the interests of securing the confidence for the continuance of investment, however, the tenant with any plot which had potential for investment was given first refusal when a request for building land was made. To take advantage of this many tenants took far more land than they needed in the first place.

Early building developments were undertaken on leasehold land. Because of restrictions on the leasing of the land imposed by legal settlements, only 60-year renewable leases were available, the first one recorded being granted in 1780. These leases were renewable on certain fine after 20 or 40 years and between 1780 and 1816, 138 such leases were granted, predominantly for industrial building but also for housing, the remaining building taking place on tenancy at will. In 1816 the terms of lease were changed to an uncertain fine of one year's improved value after 20 years, and 10 years improved value after 40 years. This was an attempt by the landowner to benefit from the increase in property values consequent upon urban growth. The response of builders was to ignore the leasehold facilities almost completely and restrict their activities to taking land on tenancy at will. Thus only 38 leases were granted between 1816 and 1840. The uptake did improve when certain fines were reintroduced in 1845 but again only for more substantial middle-class housing and industrial or commercial premises.

There were few restrictions laid down in these leases. The clauses contained in the earliest perpetuated the landlord-tenant relationships that prevailed under agrarian society. When a lease was granted to one John Holt in 1782 'in consideration of the expense incurred in building a house',[27] the covenants included performing suit at the Court Baron of the manor of Huddersfield and the need to grind corn at the Lord's Mill. The lease was not entirely archaic because a clause was included to the effect that the landowner would have the right to acquire any building erected should street improvements be necessary and in such a case the compensation payable would be fixed by arbitration.

The system of tenancy at will which became the prevailing system of land tenure also had many of the vestiges of a pre-industrial society. It was a system of tenure associated with agricultural land which emerged during the medieval period following the commutation of services to money rents. As an inferior interest in land it was similar to copyhold but this latter tenure, used in some towns in the south-west for building, was in fact legally more secure. Notwithstanding, the system in Huddersfield achieved its own status as a secure tenure, and confidence in that security was such that money for building was advanced on the strength of a tenant's name in the rental book. It meant that land was not only easy to obtain but also cheap (table 3).

Table 3   Comparison of land costs on leasehold, tenancy at will and freehold, Huddersfield, 1846

	leasehold		tenancy at will		freehold	
	RENT		RENT		SALE PRICE	
	per		per		per	
location	sq yd	per annum	sq yd	per annum	sq yd	total per plot
Spring Street	3½d.	£3 12s. 10d.	1¾d.	£1 16s. 7d.	7s. 0d.	£87 7s. 0d.
Snoddle Hill						
Marsh	2¾d.	£2 19s. 11d.	1½d.	£1 11s. 3d.	4s. 2d.	£52 0s. 0d.

Source: Ramsden Estate Expectation Leases (granted to allow tenants to receive compensation from the railway).

Readily available small amounts of cheap land on which building could take place meant that building was undertaken on a very small scale. Nearly three-quarters of building projects consisted of less than three houses and were undertaken by ordinary working people, and small traders and capitalists (table 2). This resulted in a highly dispersed form of housing capital sufficiently apparent to be remarked upon by the Commissioners investigating the proposed Improvement Bill, who visited the town in 1846.

There is a peculiarity to be observed in Huddersfield that workmen pride themselves in being able to build and have a home of their own. More cottage dwellings belong to workmen than in any other town.

This participation was made possible by the availability of facilities for the accumulation of capital by small savers through the medium of building clubs: 'There is a large proportion of building societies to the population: they put their money in building clubs.'[28] These building clubs display many of the features of similar clubs in other parts of the West Riding. They were based in local inns from which they derived their names and were only temporary in nature. The sole record of their existence that survives is the name of the club against a tenant's name in the Ramsden Estate rentals.

The first such entry was in 1798 when reference was made to Paddock Club Houses. This was followed in 1807 by reference to the Cherry Tree Club. By 1815 a number of tenants had the name of a club or a club secretary entered alongside their name. Most club secretaries were members of the lower middle classes and at one time included the local agents of the Ramsden Estate itself. Membership varied from the Angel Inn Club, Paddock, with 120 members to J. Pollard's with 12. Quite small sums of money were saved, considerably below those normally quoted for building societies. Individuals saved on average £100 over 20 years, 4 shillings a week in the summer, 2 shillings in the winter, and most of the cottages built on this system ranged in value from £50–£200. Typical of a building club was the Angel Inn which lasted for 14 years until each member had expended a total of £90. Typical of a building club saver was one Joseph Moore, a cloth finisher of Paddock who:

having saved money by my labours entered the King's Head Club and Tam O'Shanters for £50 each drew out £100 for a piece of building ground but he refused to let me have the field I wanted unless others would also build. I found two others, James Barber and Abraham Beaumont both working men and who saved a little money. Brook marked out the sites but he would not fix rents until he knew how much land was occupied.[29]

Women as well as men were savers and not all savers built only for themselves. Additional houses were often added after a considerable interval, sometimes up to 30 years, although on average an interval of between 5 and 10 years was normal. If the property was sold a similar time interval took place before disposal occurred.

Cooperation of the kind indicated in the quotation required considerable faith not only in the landowner for security of tenure but also in other members of the club. This faith was not always justified. It was reported in the rental of 1812 that Martin Collis, who had started building a cottage in Upperhead Row, had run away after drawing £25 out of the club. 'Mr Marshall and Joe Heywood have found wood, stone and workmanship for the same and drawn £75 more making £100 from the club. Lindley Moor Club must stand tenants for the same and pay all bills against building.' Again this quote gives some hint of the extraordinary level of cooperation and the complex distribution of capital in house-building. It also illustrates how the activities of any building club in financing the erection of houses were not restricted to a particular location. There was only one instance where people combined in a club to build property in a specific street. In 1822 the Union Row Club was formed to build Union Street which eventually comprised 30 pairs of back-to-back houses. Fifteen owners were listed in the Ratebook of 1847, ten of whom were the original builders and two owner-occupiers.[30]

Building clubs were closely associated with tenancy at will. Elsewhere in the area more traditional sources of mortgage capital were used but nearly all were locally based. Doctors, solicitors, merchants, industrialists and landowners all contributed to house-building.

The actual building itself was undertaken by jobbing builders. The building industry did not play a substantial role in primary decision-making although the contribution was greater on long-term leasehold and freehold land (table 2). There were some master builders. George Scarlett gave evidence in 1862 that he had been a builder for over 30 years and that he employed 20–30 men in different trades.[31] The largest master builder in the district was Joseph Kaye who built both domestic and public buildings but never himself owned property. He told a Royal Commission in 1842 that he had built about a third of Huddersfield and employed at any one time between 250 and 1,100 men. Despite this boast he worked like other builders by rule-of-thumb methods. Issac Hordern, cashier to the Ramsden Estate, later wrote: 'Joseph Kaye was a funny old man. He was known to say after taking a contract for a church that he had forgotten the estimate at the tower end. I never heard of him getting paid extra.'[32]

Many builders went bankrupt and there was a large turnover in personnel in the trade. Often each trade was engaged separately by a building undertaker or group of undertakers. With middle-class housing the architect often acted as the contractor. Thus Joseph Thornton's own house in Paddock was built by the firm Beaumont and Haigh of Paddock with James Leech, Thornton's managing clerk, acting as architect and contractor.[33]

For the majority of houses, the combination of small saver and jobbing builder meant tight economic margins and inevitably corners were cut. The result was extremely poorly built property. The houses had: 'scarce a sash or pane that will open and ventilation flues for cottages are almost unknown.'[34] Sanitary provision was also poor, thus when a building undertaker had:

> accumulated perhaps fifty pounds, they will go and build a house that costs perhaps seventy or eighty pounds but are unable to complete it . . . the privees are the last thing to be erected and they are generally very badly done. They have no capital to go farther.[35]

It is not surprising therefore that the Improvement Commission Inquiry[36] found a lot to be desired in the level of sanitary provision in Huddersfield which exhibited many of the characteristics of other Victorian towns of the period:

> Huddersfield is by no means a well built town. The houses inhabited by the working classes, until very recently have been constructed back to back or rather as a double house . . . . According to a Government report the new houses were built on ill-constructed sewers. In courts and alleys especially the abodes of the poor there can scarcely be any attempt at draining.[37]

The very limited spatial horizon of many building undertakers contributed to the *ad hoc* nature by which house-building was undertaken. A high percentage of owner-occupiers who built houses for other people, as well as other undertakers, built in close proximity to their own houses. Of such owners identified in the 1847 Ratebook, 216 show a surprising degree of inertia in their ownership pattern, having built their property 10 to 20 years previously or at least being relatives of the original builder. This is despite a heavy turnover of property generally within five years of building.[38]

In total over 10 per cent of the house property in Huddersfield was owner-occupied. It was concentrated amongst the newest built houses in the lowest rental classes, levels decreasing over time as property became older. A number of owners were actually residents of the cellars of their houses, deriving income from letting the main house, demonstrating an indifference to poor living conditions in general.[39] Indeed a number of attempts to obtain support from local ratepayers for an Improvement Act in the early 1840s met with apathy and sometimes downright opposition.[40] It was not until the cholera outbreaks of 1847 and 1849 that there was any incentive to improve social capital. Even then the enthusiasm for improvement was short-lived and, as a local agent of the Ramsden Estate remarked, most property owners were soon 'lulled into former apathy and lamentable indifference.'[41]

The imperfect manner in which the housing market operated is confirmed by the land rent profile of 1834.[42] Rents varied within streets, according to the amount of land taken and the whim of estate managers. That owners preferred to deal directly with the landowner and his management in itself contributed to imperfect knowledge. When the Ramsden Estate attempted to auction lots of land around the railway station in 1851 there were no bidders for what was prime development land. The estate was forced to revert to the old system of letting land despite the fact that the rent was finally fixed at a higher level than the original reserved price.

In essence this symbolized the nature of property relations for the first part of the nineteenth century. Fostered by the attitude of the landowner and the management, patriarchal pre-industrial modes of operation were perpetuated, reinforcing the *ad hoc* nature of the building process which existed uneasily with the new economic order.

In 1844 a new management structure was initiated on the Ramsden Estate which was more appropriate to maintaining and developing an urban estate. This went some way to promoting a more organized approach to urban development but did little to undermine the building process as it had been established. In 1845 Engels, that critic of the Victorian city, wrote: 'The charming situation and modern style of building in Huddersfield have made it the most beautiful of factory towns in Lancashire and Yorkshire',[43] suggesting that despite the small scale and haphazard nature of development that took place, Huddersfield was better built than other similar towns.

5   The building process, 1850–1911

In the transition of Huddersfield to a mature industrial town during the second half of the nineteenth century house-building undertakers became increasingly subject to constraints imposed by external agencies. They also had to respond to a new pattern of demand and this combination of circumstances generated subtle changes in the structure of the building process itself and property relations.

From mid-century onwards, middle-class interests came to dominate the housing market. The advent of the railway in 1849, which engendered a feeling of high expectation of the benefits that would accrue from linkages with the national network, and the movement in income which investments would produce in the foreseeable future, encouraged property development of all kinds. The so-called 'New Town of Huddersfield' symbolized this change and heralded the new era. Imposing buildings housing office and warehouse accommodation were built around St George's Square adjacent to the railway station and in Kirkgate and West Gate. The impact on any visitor was impressive:

> The first impression of a stranger in Huddersfield as he approaches the town from our noble railway station is that Huddersfield is one of the most splendid towns in the kingdom. The beautiful designs of the new erections for warehouses, shops, hotels etc. which there meet the eye, the wide well-paved streets, the fine open square and the beautiful colour and quality of stone give to the vista a 'toute ensemble' rarely to be equalled, coupled with a feeling that all erections are sound reality not mere effects produced by plaster and paint. Even those who ten years ago possessed an intimate knowledge of Huddersfield are struck by the wonderful change which that short space of time has effected on the general appearance of the town and its rapid extension.[44]

Merchants and manufacturers found that they no longer needed to invest in large stocks and the more prominent members of the community sought to capitalize on the fruits of the early century and turned their minds to personal conspicuous consumption in the form of increasing living space.

Contemporary advertisements give some indication of what they sought. These refer to elevated sites with rolling vistas in harmony with nature away from the smoke and the grime that was the source of their wealth but in reasonable proximity to allow a watchful eye to be maintained over the business.[45] Much was made of access to the railway station, 15 minutes walk being considered the optimum distance people were willing to travel. Fashion further dictated that the ideal dwelling consisted of a large gothic villa set in grounds of its own with a lodge at the gate to keep the 'masses' at bay, a miniature replica reminiscent of the mansion house estates surrounding the town at the time.

The upper middle classes were not the only section of the community to benefit from a rise in personal income. The middle class as a whole from mill manager to small shopkeeper experienced a rise in real wages and sought improved living space, thus increasing housing expenditure. Developments in commerce and the increasing involvement of the local state in everyday living swelled the ranks of those with the ability to command a steady income with white-collar workers such as clerks and cashiers.[46] In addition, the more skilled trades in the textile and newly developed engineering industry increased their income relative to other workers. A pattern designer who in the early 1840s earned 37s.6d. was earning over 60s. a week by 1880.[47] The economic power of this group of elite workers was limited by their susceptibility to downsavings in the trade cycle, although in terms of the average income there was little separating them from the lower middle classes. For the majority of the working class, now a fully established industrial proletariat, there was no longer the opportunity to accumulate wealth by the fruits of one's labour such as had existed in domestic production prevalent in the early part of the century. Thus their role in housing demand diminished.

The new lower middle classes were also distinguishable from their working-class rivals in their pattern of working and journey to work. As already indicated, contemporary property advertisements bore frequent reference to a house's location in relation to the railway station.[48] The introduction of first the horsebus and then the tram must be seen as a liberating influence increasing the distance it was possible to cover in 15 minutes, especially since fare levels and timing were ideal for shop and office workers. Even before this, the journey to work of many of the middle class had increased (table 4). After 1880 they were joined by clerks and cashiers whose preferences further reinforced the trend towards social segregation and suburbanization.

Table 4   Journey to work of middle classes, Huddersfield, 1864 and 1881 (figures given as percentages of middle class identified in directory)

| date | distance in miles | | | | | | | |
	$\frac{1}{4}$	$\frac{1}{2}$	$\frac{3}{4}$	1	$1\frac{1}{4}$	$1\frac{1}{2}$	$1\frac{3}{4}$	2
1864	17.16	17.59	15.87	21.03	9.44	11.15	0.53	6.93
1881	2.35	31.31	3.03	21.21	18.51	13.80	1.68	8.08

Source: R.J. Charlton and C. Anderson, *Directory of the Woollen Districts of Leeds, Huddersfield, Dewsbury and the surrounding districts* (1864); W. White, *History, Directory and Gazeteer of the West Riding of Yorkshire* (1881).

The lower middle class became a major force in urban development, for not only were they important consumers of housing, they also were substantial contributors to the building process as building undertakers and owners on the new estates which sprang up along the tram routes (table 5). The distribution of owner occupation in 1896 reinforces this picture with owner-occupation highest amongst the lower rental groups and concentrated in the newly developing areas and old established middle-class districts.[49] A distinct sectoral pattern was produced, but one that deviates slightly from that which would be expected. For in those very areas where lower middle-class houseownership was highest owner-occupation was less than average. This suggests that some of the better off of this sector of society were using their economic power to ensure preservation of the status quo by the provision of rented accommodation for members of the same class who were less financially well endowed. There is no concrete evidence to support such a view or to show that it was a conscious decision on the part of this particular social group. However, property ownership and a house in the suburbs increasingly became the mark of Victorian social status which the highly class-conscious lower middle classes were concerned to acquire. As the group who would feel most insecure they were probably the most eager to preserve their position in society with the outward symbols of success.

Landowners keen to benefit from middle-class demand sought to satisfy their desire for preservation of the status quo with the use of restrictive covenants in their leases in the hope of encouraging well-built and substantial properties. The existence of a general plan of an estate's development for the protection and guidance of all parties concerned also helped to induce stability in the market. A landowner who made no attempt to safeguard the interests of the middle classes did so at the risk of his future income. Frances Battye found it increasingly difficult to let land on her estate for superior villas after she had attempted to exploit the potential of land adjacent to Marsh for terraced houses. Tenants on her estate even petitioned the council about terraced houses being built behind their properties.[50]

Table 5 Socio-economic characteristics of building undertakers in Huddersfield, 1850–1911

area/estate	merchants wholesalers	manufacturers	professions/ gents	builders	small traders shopkeepers	others/ industrials	clerks/ cashiers
1850–75							
Primrose Hill (freehold)	11.11	11.11	8.33	0	30.55	38.88	—
Bay Hall (freehold)	13.79	10.34	31.03	17.24	27.58	—	—
Lindley (leasehold)	7.54	15.09	—	24.53	22.63	30.08	—
Crosland Moor	2.94	17.64	—	11.76	8.82	58.82	—
North Green Armitage Lock-wood	0	45.45	18.18	9.09	27.27	—	—
Brook, Moldgreen	0	16.66	4.76	33.33	19.04	26.19	—
Edgerton	42.85	9.52	38.09	0	9.52	—	—
March	8.69	0	21.73	4.34	65.21	—	—
1875–1911							
Crosland Moor Bottom Thornton Lodge/Springdale	1.36	1.36	4.08	36.73	29.25	18.36	7.78
Yew Green/Lockwood	0	1.75	1.75	21.05	42.10	31.57	1.75
Marsh	5.55	0	2.77	18.05	48.61	16.66	8.33
Birkby	3.37	2.24	14.60	19.10	49.94	21.34	1.12
Fartown	10.00	0	7.50	7.50	43.75	16.12	12.50

Source: REP Register of Application for Leases, 1859–83, 1883–97; Statement of Application for Leases 1896–1911; Deeds at WRRD relating to land in Huddersfield.

43

The nature and content of covenants varied from estate to estate. The most wide-ranging restricted use to residential only and a defined level of maintainance. Some controlled house type by stipulating the value of the house to be built. Back-to-back houses were controlled by clauses specifying the location of windows. Sometimes specific types of houses were excluded. Thus leases granted on land belonging to G.W. Marsh specifically stipulated that no cottage with only one room on the ground floor should be built.[51]

The closest control of development on estates other than Ramsden was undertaken by the managers of the Thornhill Estate. Under a deed of dedication attached to the Thornhill Estate Act of 1852 detailed covenants were laid down for the leases granted in each of three areas of development identified. This ensured that building followed the course stipulated by the Act. All plans and elevations were subject to close scrutiny by the agents of the Trustees and any change in use or ownership was with their consent.[52]

For the Edgerton area, destined to be the most fashionable in Huddersfield, the covenant stipulated that no trade of any kind would be allowed and the only properties to be created would be villas. In the other two areas, at Lindley and Hillhouse, no offensive trade was to be allowed unless first sanctioned by the lessor and a penalty of £10 was to be exacted if such a trade was practised without consent. Villas in the Edgerton area were to be erected only when their exact location and architectural quality had been agreed by the agents of the estate. In Hillhouse the forecourt of each house was to be 'kept entirely as garden', while for houses in Lindley restrictions were placed on the construction of cellars. The range of covenants selected for each area was ideally suited for the market and largely the result of the expertise of F.R. Jones.[53] The success of a covenant depended on its enforcement and continual surveillance of building was necessary. Only the Thornhill and Ramsden Estates maintained a high level of enforcement. Often landowners depended on professional surveyors rather than their own agents and in the final decade of the century found it difficult to impose covenants to ensure that only middle-class housing was built. The growing practice of offering either leasehold or freehold also reduced any effectiveness of a covenant.

The imposition of covenants reflected an attempt by landowners to take a more positive role in urban development through restrictions on builders' behaviour. In doing so they hoped to preserve or increase the value of their assets by attempting to exert some control over the output in the production process. The power of the landowner to dictate the terms of contract was dependent on the continuance of a monopoly in the supply of land or at least an agreement amongst potential development landowners that they would act in a similar manner. The mobility of the middle class increased competition amongst landowners by providing the opportunity for choice in location. It also allowed choice between landowners concerning the terms of tenure offered. During the period 1859–67 when the Ramsden Estate only offered leasehold on 99 years, builders sought land from other landowners who offered 999 year terms. A property relationship which was weighted in favour of the landowner was not acceptable, despite a number of attempts by Sir John Ramsden to stimulate development.[54] This was most strikingly illustrated at Hillhouse where builders chose land solely from the Thornhill Estate during this period despite more accessible land made available by the Ramsden Estate. The heyday of landowner control was the mid century when the spatial horizons of builders were still limited but the demand for land high. Changes in management on the Ramsden Estate in 1844 imposed a new regime on the building monitoring process and even tenant at will builders were subject to close scrutiny.[55] New back-to-back houses and cellar dwellings were forbidden, building lines enforced, materials and building standards rigorously supervised. Quality was maintained by the regulation of individuals since the covenants imposed in the Ramsden leases were sufficiently flexible to give the landowner considerable scope for action if he so chose. Reciprocity in the new property relationship came in the provision of social capital by the landowner. Although streetage charges were made, this provided a useful service to the building undertaker and facilitated development generally. The initial outlay could be considerable. Three roads in the Thornhill Estate, for example, cost a total of £1,498 12s.3d. in 1863.[56] While builders were willing to tolerate restrictions that would increase their building costs in the 1850s, the rise in ground rents and the introduction of 99-year and then 999-year leases increased their sensitivity to such restrictions and charges and they gravitated towards landowners who did not impose them. Mention has already been made of the extent to which this was apparent to contemporaries and it was continually remarked upon by local agents in their correspondence with Sir John William Ramsden.[57] In the depression of the 1890s all landowners stopped streetage charges.[58]

Restrictions on builders' behaviour came from other directions too. In 1868 the Borough of Huddersfield was incorporated and all building plans had to be submitted to the council for approval. Since many members of the council were also building undertakers themselves, this requirement must be seen as an attempt by building undertakers to monitor each others' activities. Bye-laws were introduced in 1872. Although their scope was limited and substantially less restrictive on builder behaviour than the controls imposed by the Ramsden Estate, their impact on the type of development undertaken was quite dramatic, leading to a substantial reduction in the numbers of working-class cottages built, if not on the total quantity of houses built.

The corporation played a role in the provision of social capital, although it placed the onus for providing drains and roads on the landowner, restricting its activities to setting street lines and street improvements. It also owned the tramway system, running it at a loss amounting to ½d. on the rates. It even extended the tramway into developing districts rather than confining the network to well-established areas. For example, a three-mile line was built to Crosland Moor at a cost of £1,400, running at a serious loss of 11s.9d. a mile during its first years. The corporation explained to a Royal Commission in 1894:

a corporation can afford to look to the future better than a private company can ... the new tramway will develop considerably the property it is run into, to the advantage of the owners of the property who are private individuals.[59]

Those private individuals were also property-owning councillors.

The Incorporation of Huddersfield marked the final demise of political dominance of the Ramsden Estate in local government and the emergence of a more complex structure of property relations.[60] The corporation's activities directly impinged on those of the estate and an uneasy relationship developed. Occasionally the two protagonists worked together towards an agreed end as they did in 1876 when the Westgate-Kirkgate area was redeveloped. Sometimes there was direct confrontation, as in 1889 when the corporation told Sir John William to complete Claremont

Street. In retaliation Sir John erected 'private' notices at the end of the street and prevented all but residents from using it. On the whole, cooperation tended to work to the advantage of the corporation. Sir John specifically built St Andrew's Road at the request of the corporation and a cost to himself of £11,163, expecting some repayment from the corporation within 5 years. That obligation was never fulfilled so when the corporation requested the building of St Thomas Road for the relief of traffic congestion, they were asked to lease a large part of the land along the road to obviate any further failure to fulfil obligations.[61] An uneasy truce existed between the new collective interests comprising the local state and the aristocratic landowner. The purchase of the Ramsden Estate by the former in 1920 symbolized the demise of the latter and the eventual dominance of the collective will of property interests over those of the landowning interests.[62]

For the individual builder the imposition of building standards, from whatever quarter, increased building costs thereby compounding an associated general rise in building and material costs. Builders could and did respond in a number of ways. One way to offset the increased costs was to seek economies of scale through an increase in building project size. A building undertaker's ability to do this depended upon the capital resources to which he had access. Without a tradition of large-scale building few undertakers had the ability to expand their activities sufficiently (table 6). Some categories withdrew completely from the building process while others increased the scope of their activities, particularly the building profession (table 4). By 1900 some substantial building contractors had become active participators.[63] Nevertheless, the average size of building project did not increase markedly although some individual projects were substantially larger than any undertaken in the mid century when the Ramsden Estate actively discouraged speculative building. The scale of building operations had yet to reach the proportions found in other cities. The largest single project was that undertaken by the building firm Garforth and Day who built 69 back-to-back houses in Aspley in 1902.[64]

The ability to expand was limited by the capital structure. Up until the 1870s building clubs continued to be a major source of capital. They were gradually replaced by permanent building societies. In 1864 the Huddersfield Equitable Benefit Building Society was constituted and along with the Halifax Building Society took over the business of many localized societies such as the Moldgreen Freehold and Leasehold Benefit Building Society which financed house-building on an estate developed and purchased by Richard Brook.

In its first year, the Huddersfield lent a mere £3,953. 14s.10d. to six members but by 1897 record advances of £69,000 were made. Mortgagees were allowed to repay their loans over a generous 24 years at an interest of 3½ per cent in 1895. The extent of the society's operations were such that in the depression year of 1894 mortgage lending dropped by £10,000. Most of the property mortgaged was of less than £500 in value. The policy of the society was such that it was wary of speculative builders. Members of the building industry nevertheless had close connections with the society and in 1870 Joseph Radcliffe, of the building firm Radcliffe and Son, became its director. It was noted in 1877 that John Kirk, the society's surveyor, created substantial amounts of business for the society through the activities of Radcliffe and Son. The strength of the society's power in influencing the building process was such that it was able in 1906 to bring pressure to bear on the Ramsden Estate, forcing it to convert all 99-year leases to 999-year leases.[65]

Table 6   Building project size, Huddersfield, 1850–1911

(a) *Building project size 1850–75 (project size in houses)*

	1	2	3	4	5	6	7 or more
RAMSDEN ESTATE							
1851–3							
% of builders	69.65	22.06	3.44	1.83	0.45	2.06	0.45
% of houses built	46.47	29.44	6.90	4.90	1.53	8.28	2.45
1858–67							
% of builders	67.83	22.22	3.50	2.33	0.58	2.30	1.16
% of houses built	41.87	27.43	6.49	5.77	1.80	8.66	7.94
1867–75							
% of builders	53.89	31.13	2.69	3.59	0	3.59	5.08
% of houses built	23.90	27.62	3.58	6.37	0	9.56	28.95
LOCKWOOD PROPRIETORS' ESTATE							
1851–7							
% of builders	7.69	7.69	0	23.07	7.69	11.53	42.30
% of houses built	0.98	1.97	0	11.82	4.92	8.86	71.42
1858–67							
% of builders	6.00	12.00	6.00	42.00	4.00	8.00	22.00
% of houses built	1.20	4.93	3.70	34.56	4.11	9.87	41.56
1867–75							
% of builders	11.11	38.88	0	16.66	11.11	5.55	16.66
% of houses built	2.73	19.17	0	16.43	13.69	8.21	38.72

(b) *Building unit project 1875–1911 Ramsden Estate (% size of project in houses)*

		1	2	3	4	5	6	7 or more
1876–80	Builders	54.87	21.95	6.09	7.92	2.43	1.82	4.87
	houses	25.00	20.00	8.33	14.44	5.55	5.00	21.66
1881–5	Builders	66.44	17.10	3.94	5.26	0.65	2.63	3.94
	houses	34.58	17.80	6.16	10.95	1.17	8.21	20.54
1886–90	Builders	65.07	17.98	4.23	3.70	0.52	4.23	4.22
	houses	31.94	17.66	6.23	7.27	1.29	12.46	23.11
1891–5	Builders	68.05	12.50	6.94	8.33	0	2.77	1.38
	houses	37.69	13.84	11.53	18.46	0	9.23	9.23
1896–1900	Builders	69.64	19.64	1.78	1.78	0	1.78	5.35
	houses	34.82	19.64	2.67	3.57	0	5.35	33.92
1901–5	Builders	39.79	26.88	0	30.10	0	0	3.22
	houses	14.97	20.24	0	45.34	0	0	19.43
1906–11	Builders	59.34	14.28	2.19	17.03	1.09	1.09	4.94
	houses	25.96	12.50	2.88	29.80	2.40	2.88	23.55

(c) *All building applications 1869–1911 (project size in houses)*

	1	2	3	4	5	6	7 or more
% of builders	43.44	27.93	9.82	8.10	3.10	1.03	6.55
% of houses built	17.30	22.25	11.73	12.91	6.18	2.47	27.12

Sources: REP, Applications for leaseholds and tenancies at will, 1845–53; Register of leases, 1859–83; 1883–1908. Lockwood Estate conveyancing deed, 1954, C/T/2/42. Huddersfield Council Minutes building plan lists, C/T/C/M/1–63.

An alternative solution for the builder in the face of rising building costs was to reduce the land cost element in the housing package. This could be achieved in two ways, either by increasing the intensity of development or by seeking land from those offering cheaper ground rents, usually on the urban fringe.

The scope for site intensification was limited by the restrictions placed on builders by both local authority and landowner. On the Ramsden Estate, for instance, back-to-back houses were actually banned until 1899.[66] Elsewhere, site intensification was chosen as an option on more expensive land close to industrial centres and when it was possible to provide for the lower end of the market.

Builders increasingly made a positive decision and chose the second option of cheaper land in the suburbs. It was those landlords who offered the lowest ground rents and the least restrictive tenure terms who experienced the most rapid uptake of plots when opening up new estates (fig. 3). The result was a considerable change in the land rent profile (fig. 4). Such landowners usually comprised the new breed of speculative landowner/developer who became more common after 1870. Concerned only with short-term economic gain, these developers were a fundamental necessity in a building process dominated by petty capitalists. Throughout the century wherever there was a demand for housing and only freehold land was available, middlemen had to intervene to produce suitable land packages. At the Thornhill Estate Sales in 1854 and 1855 only one builder was directly involved and the mill-owners who purchased the land subsequently leased and sold it in small plots in the 1860s. Richard Brook, referred to previously, purchased a block of lots from the Kaye Estate in 1857 and, having built a house himself, leased the remainder to building undertakers in small lots, financing their operations with the Moldgreen Permanent Benefit Building Society, of which he was secretary.[67]

Nearly all of the new landowner/developers of the post-1870s had some previous connection with the building industry or estate development. George Crowther, a local surveyor, from 1880 onwards gradually acquired various shares in the Ashworth Estate at Row and in 1893 opened it for development.[68] Most active and dominant of all was J.A. Armitage, who initially gained experience in land development as a trustee of an estate at Crossland Hill in 1879. He entered into partnership with John Henry Hanson of a local firm of surveyors, Abbey and Hanson. In 1857 they purchased an estate at Thornton Lodge, laid out streets and drains, made the land available on 999-year leasehold at a bargain rent of 1d. per square yard and imposed no streetage charges. The extremely rapid uptake of plots, mostly for back-to-back houses, meant that within 10 years nearly all twenty acres were covered with buildings. In 1890 Armitage collaborated with one Sarah Martha Grove Grady in the purchase and development of an estate at Moldgreen. This time the option of either freehold or leasehold tenure was given. Finally, in 1897, again in partnership with Hanson, Armitage purchased forty-five acres at Clough House. Here again leasehold and freehold terms were offered to the builder.[69]

In a sense a new professionalism was emerging in the building process. Unconstrained by the mores of a previous age – the aristocratic notions of estate continuity, the role of landowner and the reciprocal relationship between landowner and tenant – such entrepreneurs, in seeking maximum short-term profit from estate development, were more flexible to the needs of the time. The sale of land as freehold allowed the landowner to defray the expense incurred in laying out streets for which no charge was made, and enabled land to be supplied with leasehold or freehold at the price the market would bear. Landowners who fixed their rents

Land development and house-building in Huddersfield, 1770–1911
JANE SPRINGETT

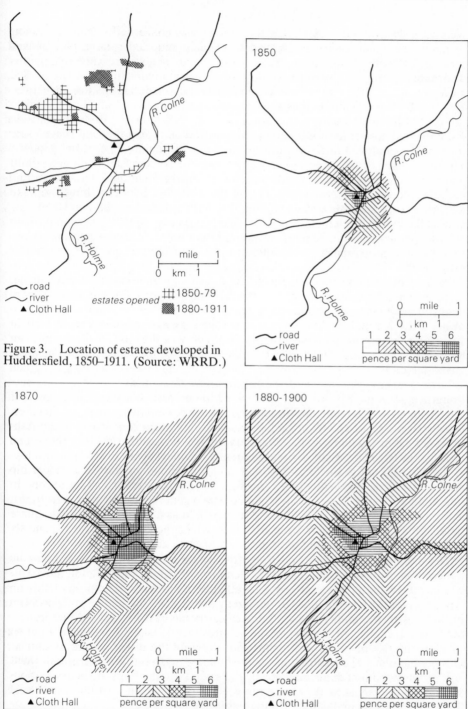

Figure 3.   Location of estates developed in Huddersfield, 1850–1911. (Source: WRRD.)

Figure 4.   Land rent profile, Huddersfield, 1850–1900. (Source: WRRD; Ramsden Estate Papers.)

were at a disadvantage. As far as the builder was concerned substantial savings in land costs could only be achieved if a tenant required a large plot of land. Thus a plot comprising 3,000 square yards at 2d. per square yard (charged on Thornhill Estate at Edgerton) would cost £25 per annum in ground rent. Such a plot would probably have erected on it a house which had a value of between £80 and £100 per annum, thus the land cost element would amount to over 25 per cent of the total value. A site closer to Huddersfield leased from the Ramsden Estate would cost at least 4d. per square yard[70] thus raising the land cost element to between one-third and one-half the total annual rental value of the property. For the builder of the large middle-class house the trade-off between accessibility and travel cost would be a significant element in the locational decision and this alone would be an incentive to build on the Thornhill Estate without the added advantage of restrictive covenants and long-term leases. For the builder of small houses the land cost element was a less significant proportion of the total package, but as costs increased in general and competition for middle-class consumers grew they became more sensitive to differences in land rents charged as the century progressed.

Perhaps more important was the ability to attract high rents and a stable investment income. Thus location in the suburbs itself was as important as the cheaper land obtainable there. Middle-class demand was not infinite and some building owners saw a rapid decline in property values as new additions were made to stock on the periphery of the urban area. Such was the case of the homes built by Lewis Starkey near St Thomas Church, Longroyd, for which records have survived (table 7).

Lewis Starkey was owner of the firm Starkey Bros. who had been resident at Longroyd Mills in 1818. In 1884 he decided to enter the housing market and built the 13 homes which made up Woodthorpe Terrace, employing local architects and masons at a cost of £4,669.15s.4d. J. Radcliffe, the firm of masons, hired all the necessary labour, while water and sanitary services were undertaken by the Council under contract. The houses were subsequently occupied by the lower middle classes. Although adjacent to the imposing church of St Thomas and part of a middle-class enclave the terrace was close to the town centre and industry, and adjacent property housed the working classes. This, coupled with a general decline in property values and the overproduction of homes in Huddersfield as a whole in the 1890s, contributed to a decline in rents from £101–£26 while the cost of upkeep increased. In 1898 the property was sold off, reportedly to small investors.[71]

This example not only demonstrated the actual mechanics of how building was undertaken at this time but also the dilemma with which the building undertaker was faced. Increased building costs, together with more restrictions on quality and type, coupled with rising inner urban land values forced the builder to concentrate on those with the ability to pay the necessarily increased rents and the desire to take the advantages of a house in the suburbs. At the same time this market was smaller, the risk involved was higher and therefore the return sought was higher. Despite the removal of restrictions on the building of back-to-back houses in 1899,[72] and an almost immediate increase in the supply of this type of housing, house rents in Huddersfield in 1910 were reported to be higher in relation to real wages than anywhere else in the West Riding (table 8).

The consequences were most severe for the poorer classes, who not only had seen a diminution in real wages relative to the rest of the population but also

Table 7   Starkey Estate: extracts from accounts relating to Huddersfield property, 1888

Woodthorpe Terrace
1. List of accounts for the erection of 13 dwelling houses near Bankfield Terrace for L.R. Starkey, J.P., John Kirk and Sons, Architects, Huddersfield and Dewsbury. October 1888.

Trade	*Builder's name*	*Account*		
Masons	J. Radcliffe and Sons	£2,733	10	5d.
Joiners	Hampshire and Armitage	£914	1	2d.
Plasterers	D. Tunnacliffe and Sons	£225	0	0d.
Plumbers	J.J. Taylor and Co.	£192	10	7d.
Painter	Joseph Preston	£42	16	4d.
Slater	Pickles Bros.	£128	14	0d.
Whitesmith	T.A. Heaps and Co.	£188	0	6d.
Water service	Huddersfield Corporation	£30	19	3d.
Gas works and fittings	Huddersfield Corporation	£18	15	10d.
Sanitary	Huddersfield Corporation	£9	15	0d.
		Total: £4,484	3	1d.
Architects	J. Kirk and Sons	£185	12	3d.
		£4,669	15	4d.

2. *Rental charged*

10 houses at £16 10s.
 2 houses at £22
 1 house at £19 10s. per annum = total £128 per annum

3. *Rental collected*

1888	£101 13 3d.	1891	£84 18 2d.	1894	£70 7 0d.		
1889	£94 16 6d.	1892	£92 16 5d.	1895	£58 13 5d.		
1890	£98 17 10d.	1893	£85 13 8d.	1896	£26 0 2d.		

Residents of property in 1890 (extracted from Directory)

Commercial traveller	Tea and sugar merchant	Designer	Gentleman
Manufacturer	Minister	Designer	Warehouseman
Superintendent of police	Widow	Engineer	Manager

Source: Starkey Papers, DD/Sn/Vc/2; DD/Sn/IVd/2/11, Nottingham County Record Office.

Table 8   House rents, Huddersfield, 1908 and 1910

1910

187 through houses	6s. 0d.
21 back-to-back with side vents	6s. 8d.
109 without side vents	4s. 11d.

1908

2 rooms	3s. 0d. to 3s. 9d.
3 rooms	4s. 6d. to 5s. 6d.
4 rooms	5s. 0d. to 5s. 9d.
5 rooms	7s. 0d. to 9s. 0d.

The cheapest accommodation was found in the inner city yards where there were dwellings of two or three rooms and perhaps a scullery. In 1847 such cottages had cost between 1s.9d. and 2s.3d. to rent and the cellar beneath 1s.3d. to 1s.6d.

Source: L.W. Darra Moir, *Report on back-to-back houses* (1910), Cmnd 5314, Appendix.

a restriction in housing choice. Income and the need to live in proximity to their work meant they had to be satisfied with a filtered-down housing stock built chiefly before 1853. The trend towards pricing the working class out of the market for new housing was one common to all late Victorian towns but it was exacerbated by Ramsden Estate policy. The local agent to the estate predicted the consequences in 1852:

> when a builder takes a piece in that way he will erect a certain number of houses for the poorest classes. What they do is build the first two and then a back house . . . . However, in the last three years . . . I have refused in many cases back houses and made sure I only accept sites that provide through ventilation and a separate outlet. However, it has meant that rents rose to £12 rather than £6.[73]

He could not predict the consequences of tenure policy in the late 1850s and 1860s but the result was to reduce the supply of housing in the inner township. In 1867 the Rivers Commission reported: 'There is a lack of dwelling houses for the labouring classes in this neighbourhood with two or three families to one home',[74] and the 1871 census confirms the picture of overcrowding in central and southern districts where the average number of persons per inhabited house was as high as 5.78 compared with 4.5 in Lockwood and Moldgreen. While the building industry kept pace with household formation and population growth as a whole there was a maldistribution of housing space amongst the classes. Overcrowding and over production existed side by side and conditions if anything became worse at the turn of the century. The Medical Officer of Health reported the existence of some 335 cellar dwellings in 1899 and intimated what was required was a house of two rooms at a rent of 2s. or 2s.6d.[75] The artisan houses built by the corporation in St Andrew's Road did nothing to improve supply. The MOH wrote in 1890 that these houses 'since their erection have been constantly occupied, but unfortunately by a class of people in a grade of society above those for which they were intended'.[76] This is not surprising since rents ranged from 3s.–4s. a week. The Council charged economic rents to pay off the interest on money borrowed and other expenses including £190 ground rent and £70 10s.2d. for repairs. On the surface little had changed in the building process. It was still small-scale, involved chiefly petty capitalists and took place largely on a contractual basis for returns that were not dramatic: 'Building here does not present to the capitalist any particular inducement to lead them to speculative operations.'[77] Although it was claimed in some property advertisements for working-class cottages that returns of 6.5–7.5 per cent could be expected, this was unusual.

Subtle changes were, however, apparent. Economic reality had introduced a new professionalism to house-building and members of the building industry, whether building society, architect, builder, surveyor or estate agent had a much larger role to play as intermediary than hitherto. Although to some extent this was an inevitable consequence of urban expansion and size, it reflected the more sophisticated nature of the building process in general, albeit still a substantially imperfect system. Ultimately, however, it was the collective will of the petty bourgeoisie who having brought the Ramsden Estate to heel in mid century, determined the complexion of the late Victorian city and the structure and outcome of the building production process.

6 House-building and the locational decision-making process

The period 1770–1911 saw a transformation of the house-building process. Early development took place on a small-scale *ad hoc* informal manner founded on personal relationships and against a background of paternalistic property relations fostered by the Ramsden Estate. The process of house-building itself, however, carried with it the seeds of its own transformation. Urbanization created new property interests. These undermined the established order which was slow to respond to new urban economic forces. Only in the mid century did landowners belatedly attempt to reassert their position by seeking a better return on their assets and controlling the output of the production process. Already the rules of the game were changing. Spatial constraints imposed by fashion and necessity were gradually removed, effectively increasing the supply of potential building land. Thus the basis of the monopoly power of the landowner was removed and a new set of relations evolved based on a more economically sensitive response to market conditions. Meanwhile the power of control of the building process was transferred into the hands of the new collection of property interests through the medium of the local state and increasingly the building industry concentrated on satisfying the demands of the new urban middle class it had created. The result was the emergence of a more complex and professional production building process geared to short-term economic gain and involving a range of new agents including developers, building society and estate agents as well as the building profession itself.

The changes seen in Huddersfield mirror those found in other Victorian towns. Huddersfield confirms Aspinall's findings on the long-term trends in the size structure of the building industry.[78] It also illustrates the demise of the landowner as highlighted by Offer and others.[79] In particular it demonstrates the importance of including the spatial factor in any analysis of house-building. The house-building undertaker's decision on what to build and how also included a decision on where, and this latter factor became more important as the nineteenth century progressed. More fundamentally, the nature of the house-building process which emerged had its roots in the spatial pattern of pre-development freehold landownership, which provided the basis of the early monopoly power of the Ramsden Estate and the way property relations subsequently developed.

It is in the context of the property relations which the house-building process created that we may get nearer to understanding the relationship between shapes on the ground and shapes in society.

NOTES

1 F.S. Chapin, S.F. Weiss and T.G. Donnelly, *Factors Influencing Land Development* (1962).
2 A. Offer, *Property and Politics, 1870–1914: Landownership, Law, Ideology and Urban Development in England* (1981).
3 P.J. Aspinall, *The Size Structure of the House-building Industry in Victorian Sheffield* (1977); M.J. Daunton, *Coal Metropolis: Cardiff 1870–1914* (1977); M.J. Daunton, *House and Home in the Victorian City: Working-class Housing 1850–1914* (1983).
4 E.W. Cooney, 'The speculative builders and developers of Victorian London – a comment', *Victorian Studies*, VIII (1969), 355–8; Aspinall, *op. cit.*

5 *Select Committee on Town Holdings,* PP, 1886 (213) XII, 1887 (260), XIII; 1888 (313), XXII; 1889 (251), XV; P.J. Aspinall, *The Evolution of Urban Tenure Systems in Nineteenth Century Cities* (1978).
6 J. Springett, 'Landowners and urban development. The Ramsden Estate and nineteenth-century Huddersfield', *J. Historical Geography,* VIII, 2 (1982), 129–44.
7 Ramsden Estate Papers (REP), Miscellaneous documents relating to the tenant-right case received from Mr Nelson, 1874, Box 12 Huddersfield Public Library (HPL). Case filed in Chancery 6 June 1862 between Joseph Thornton and Lee Dyson and Sir John William Ramsden, 2 vols, HPL.
8 *Ibid.*
9 F.S. Hudson, 'The wool textile industry in Huddersfield district', *International Dyer and Textile Printer,* Dec. (1965) and Jan. (1966), 951. *Factory Inspectors Report* (1839).
10 *Return of Factories,* pp, 1904, LXXXVII, 109.
11 *Report of an Enquiry by the Board of Trade into Working Class Rents, Housing and Retail Prices,* PP, 1908 CD, 364 CVII; Town Report, Huddersfield, 223.
12 *Huddersfield Examiner,* 19 Mar. 1871.
13 Most data came from an analysis of deeds pertaining to Huddersfield in the West Riding Registry of Deeds (WRRD). Lockwood Estate Conveyancing Deed 1954, C/T/Z/42, HPL; Ramsden Estate Leasing Act 1859, HPL and Building Plan Registers, HPL.
14 B. Weber, 'A new index of residential construction 1838–1950', *Brit. J.Political Economy,* II (1955), 104–32.
15 J. Parry Lewis, *Building Cycles and Britain's Growth* (1965); S.B. Saul, 'Housebuilding in England 1890–1914', *EcHR.,* 2nd ser., XV (1962).
16 REP, RA/DD/27/5, HPL.
17 Thornhill Estate Papers (TEP) Thornhill Estate Act 1852.
18 WRRD, ME/553/681 1820; HE 592/678 1820; HE 593/679 1820; HC 700/749 1820; HC 702/750 1820; HF 453/501 1820; HG 48/51 1820; HN 214/218 1821; GY 510/526 1821; IZ 587/562 1827.
19 Thornhill Estate Papers, Affidavit of Christopher White, 2 Jan. 1853, HPL.
20 TEP, Court in Chancery Proceedings, Affidavit of Christopher White, 1855.
21 *Huddersfield Chronicle,* 16 Mar. 1861.
22 REP, Mr Beasley's Report. DD/R Box 24, HPL.
23 REP, case filed in Chancery *op cit.,* Mr Beasley's report *op cit.,* Ramsden Estate Leasing Act 1867.
24 J. Springett, 'The mechanics of urban land development in Huddersfield, 1770–1911' (Ph.D. thesis, University of Leeds, 1979), 293.
25 REP, Rough Draft of Report to the Ramsden Trustees by George Loch, 1 June 1844, Box 24, HPL.
26 REP, Ramsden Estate Rentals, Box 24, HPL.
27 REP, Miscellaneous bundle of old leases, Box 12, HPL.
28 House of Lords Record Office, Report of the Commissioners of Her Majesty's Woods, Forests, Land Revenue, Works and Public Building, Local Acts, Huddersfield Improvement Bill – unpublished minutes.
29 *Thornton* v *Ramsden* case, *op. cit.,* affidavit of Joseph Moore.
30 REP, Rental 1812–13.
31 *Thornton* v *Ramsden* case, *op. cit.,* affidavit of George Scarlett.
32 REP, Issac Hordern's notebook 1866–1911, HPL.
33 *Thornton* v *Ramsden* case, *op. cit.,* affidavit of Joseph Thornton.
34 *Appendix to the First Report of the Commission of Inquiry into the State of Large Towns and Populous Districts,* PP, 1844 (572), XVII, 177–8.
35 *Ibid.*
36 H of LRO, Woods and Forests, *op. cit.*
37 Angus Bethune (1849), letter to the *Morning Chronicle* 3 Dec., in C. Aspin, *The Yorkshire Textile Districts in 1849* (1975).

38 HPL, Huddersfield Township Poor Ratebook 1847 C/F/TH/V/7; REP Rentals.
39 According to the unprinted Census Enumerators' books, 1851.
40 Woods and Forests, *op. cit.*
41 REP, Correspondence Halthorn to Lock, Nov. 1849, DD/RE/C/65.
42 Springett, 'Landowners and development', 134.
43 F. Engels, *Condition of the Working Class in England in 1844*, translated by W.O. Henderson and W.H. Chaloner (1959), 49–50.
44 *Huddersfield Chronicle*, 11 Mar. 1857.
45 *Huddersfield Chronicle*, 26 Apr. 1851, 17 Jan. 1857, 14 Mar. 1863, 10 May 1863, 26 May 1863.
46 J. Burnett, *A History of the Cost of Living* (1969), 218–19; G. Crossick (ed.), *The Lower Middle Class in Britain 1870–1914* (1977).
47 *Labour Statistics,* Cmnd 5172, 1887.
48 *Huddersfield Chronicle.*
49 HPL, Huddersfield Township Poor Ratebook, 1896.
50 Huddersfield Council Minutes, Committee for Marsh Ward, 4 June 1889.
51 WRRD, 37/88/49, 1894.
52 TEP, Correspondence of George Crowther; Deed of Dedication relating to Thornhill Estate Act 1852; Court in Chancery Records PRO.
53 *Ibid.*
54 Springett, *op. cit.,* 142.
55 REP, Correspondence 1844–53, DD/RE/C/1–104.
56 TEP, Outlay and Income 1858–68, DD/T/33, HPL.
57 See note 12.
58 REP, DD/RA/21/9, HPL.
59 *Huddersfield Examiner,* 7 Feb. 1891.
60 Hitherto the Ramsden Estate had some control over appointments to the Council and had a direct say in the decision-making where it impinged on the estate.
61 REP, Correspondence DD/RA/27/7; DD/RA/20/10; DD/RA/14/5, DD/RA/22/7.
62 REP, Dawson File.
63 REP, Register of Applications for Leases 1859–97; Huddersfield Council District Highways and Improvement Committee C/T/CF/M/ST, *et. seq.*
64 REP, List of Leases for Execution 1897–1909. Box 70, HPL.
65 T.H. Hall, *The Early Years of the Huddersfield Building Society* (1974).
66 REP, Sir J.W. Ramsden's Interview and Memorandum Book vol. 7, 1899–1909, Box 5. See also Springett, *op. cit.*
67 WRRD, W.G. 453/485 1861; 42/8/62 1865; 844/80/87 1880.
68 WRRD, 834/376/446 1879.
69 WRRD, 32/275/148 1887; 13/287/149 1888; 27/822/49 1890; 26/1029/488 1890; 25/426/223 1890; 26/10441/492 1890; 28/653/313 1891; 2/44/208 1897; 2/436/206 1868; 2/439/207 1898.
70 A rent that was fixed as most appropriate for villa land. Land immediately adjacent on Frances Battye's estate had a rent of only 2d. per square yard.
71 Starkey Papers, DD/Sn/IVd/12/11; DD/SL/IX/6—7; DD/Sn/IVd/2, Nottingham County Record Office.
72 REP, Memorandum book *op. cit.*
73 REP, DD/RE/C/102.
74 Third Report of the Commission appointed to inquire into the best means of preventing the pollution of Rivers (Rivers Aire and Calder) vol. 2, Minutes of Evidence and Index, pp, 1867 (3850–1), xxxiii, 293.
75 *Huddersfield Examiner,* 9 Sept. 1891.
76 Report of the Medical Officer of Health, Huddersfield Council Proceedings, Minutes 1890–1899.
77 *Huddersfield Chronicle,* 28 Apr. 1877.

78 Aspinall, *Size Structure, op. cit.*
79 Offer, *op. cit.*, D. Cannadine (ed.), *Patricians, Power and Politics in Nineteenth-Century Towns* (1982).

Building societies in the West Riding of Yorkshire and their contribution to housing provision in the nineteenth century

M.H. YEADELL

Building societies in the West Riding of Yorkshire and their contribution to housing provision in the nineteenth century

M.H. YEADELL

1 Introduction

The material in this contribution formed part of a study of the building industry and of fluctuations in levels of building activity in the woollen cloth district of the West Riding of Yorkshire. Building society advances were used as an index of building activity to supplement information already available in the figures of building plans for several West Riding towns. They had the advantages that they extended the information to towns not covered by plan figures, and that they reflected ex-post demand for housing rather than ex-ante demand in the shape of plans submitted as requests for building permission. The building booms indicated by building plans were confirmed by building society advanced figures, and an extra increase in spending on building was indicated in the last years of peace before 1914, a boom not seen in the figures for building plans because the houses built were generally larger properties. The increased quality of the dwellings was not reflected in the quantitative plan figures.

Before the statistics from building societies could be used it was important to assess their scope and significance, especially in the West Riding. There was some material available on building societies but it tended to be either eulogistic, written by or for societies themselves, or generalized, and it was deemed necessary to include in the original thesis a discussion of the growth, development and contribution of building societies in the West Riding from a more analytical point of view before information from them was used in the wider context of building activity levels.

At the time when the majority of the work for this material was done four of the largest ten societies in the country had their head offices in the West Yorkshire area, and these held slightly under half of the total assets of the ten. The area has been one in which building societies flourished from the earliest years of the movement and a study of the development of societies in the region gives us an opportunity to approach them with the view of an economic historian rather than that of a business or institutional historian, puting them into the wider context of the building industry in the area. Conclusions drawn here are relevant in other areas where societies grew.

I received tremendous help from many people in the societies, especially from the staffs of the Bradford and Bingley, the West Yorkshire, the Leeds Permanent, the National and Provincial, the Otley Building Society, the Hull branch and head office of the Halifax, the Huddersfield and Bradford, the then Wakefield Building Society (now that town's branch of the Halifax), and the Skipton society. In addition the Registry of Friendly Societies, Bradford City Library and the County Records Office in Wakefield gave valuable assistance. Finally, I must express my debt of gratitude to Professor John Saville without whose guidance and encouragement this work would never have been started or carried through.

2 The development of building societies in the West Riding woollen towns

The towns in the area discussed by Heaton in his study of the Yorkshire woollen and worsted industry all grew prodigiously throughout the nineteenth century.[1] Leeds had a population growth of some 34 per cent in the 1820s, and of 47 per cent in the 1830s. Bradford had a decennial growth rate of over 60 per cent 1811–31 and in excess of 50 per cent 1831–51. Elsewhere, Halifax and Huddersfield both grew by about 30 per cent per decade to 1841, while Dewsbury and Wakefield both grew at about 20 per cent each decade up to mid century. After 1850 the percentage growth rates were less impressive over existing large populations, but population increases in absolute terms remained large. The average decennial population growth in Leeds in the second half of the nineteenth century was over 51,000, while that in Bradford was over 22,500 (despite a very small increase 1851–61). Halifax grew by an average of 8,300 each ten years, Wakefield by almost 2,700. Huddersfield and Dewsbury grew by over 9,200 and over 4,600 per decade respectively until 1891.

The amount of building generated by these population increases obviously varied with the fluctuations in building caused by changes in levels of economic prosperity. According to figures put forward by J. Parry Lewis of building plans accepted, house plans in Bradford exceeded 1,700 in all but two years from 1867–78 and they were over 1,000 a year from 1898–1904.[2] Leeds plans never fell below 1,000 a year from the start of the series of figures in 1876 until after the turn of the century and twice exceeded 3,000.[3] The sums of money spent on property, both existing and newly-built, were very large.

The growth in industrial prosperity in the region ran chronologically hand in hand with the growth in *laissez-faire* and individualism. Within this compass came the friendly societies, the burial clubs, the savings clubs, and the like. It has been estimated that by 1801 there were over 7,000 such bodies in the country.[4] They were an attempt by the working classes to improve their lot by collective action in an increasingly individualistic and insecure world. In particular, the feature of the savings club was regular subscriptions to save for some larger item that the member would otherwise be unable to afford. It is more than likely that one such larger item may well have been a house.[5] Certainly there is no reason to believe that saving for a house by regular subscriptions to a society was a new thing when building societies first appeared in Birmingham about 1775. Not only savings clubs need have been so engaged. The Loyal Georgian Friendly Society in Halifax, founded in 1779, which met in the Old Cock Inn, early developed the practice of lending money to its members for building houses,[6] and several of its later members formed the nucleus of the Halifax Permanent in 1853. Banks must have been carrying out a similar role for the landed and merchant classes for some time, and building society development may well be seen at its outset as an attempt by the working classes to find a practical method of accumulating capital.

Sometime around 1775 Ketley's Building Society was formed in Birmingham, and another followed in Dudley in February 1779. These are the earliest societies for which records have been found, and it has been assumed that they were the first.[7] There are records of several more in the East Midlands area in the 1780s,[8] and by this time the idea seems to have spread to Lancashire and Yorkshire. In Leeds, on 3 November 1787, articles of agreement were drawn up for the Crackenthorpe Gardens Building Club. Land was purchased between Vicar Lane and Sheepscar Beck, an open sewer running through the city, and divided into 52 plots on which were to be built back-to-back houses and some separate cellar dwellings. The density of the housing was increased by only building half of it on front roads, the other half being erected on back alleys which were narrower. It is likely that these properties were the first back-to-back houses in Leeds.[9] The society built Union Street, Ebenezer Street, George Street and Nelson Street. In the next century these were constantly reappearing as bad health risks. In 1865 the Leeds Medical Officer of Health thought Ebenezer Street was the filthiest street in the town, and all of these streets were dirty and confined.[10]

On 27 February 1788 articles were signed for the Hill House Bank Building Club to build 42 back-to-back houses in what became known as King Street and Queen Street. An advertisement in the *Leeds Intelligencer* dated 20 April 1790 stated that three club houses were to be put up for sale by auction. Obviously the club had decided to take some action over members whose subscriptions were in arrears.[11] Several other Leeds societies began building in 1789.[12] St James Street Building Club was one, though its land purchases went back to 1787, making it one of the earliest societies in the West Riding. It built back-to-backs, as did one of a pair of 1786 societies. These were the Greater and the Lesser Building Societies which purchased land on Boggard Closes, Quarry Hill in 1787. The former built Regency-style through houses in St Peter's Square, while the latter erected back-to-backs on adjacent land in High Street. The Greater Building Society property was meant to be high class, and was completed some time before 1815, but it was poorly sited and quickly degenerated into slums.[13] Also established about 1786 was the Union Row Building Association which purchased land in that year on Quarry Hill for 22 houses (probably half-backs, or a single row of back-to-back type houses) which were completed by 1796.[14] If time were needed to acquire capital for purchasing land this society may date from 1785 or earlier and this would make it the earliest building society in the Riding so far discovered.

These early building clubs were 'building' societies in the literal sense of the word. They did build, as a general rule. Today building societies do not construct property themselves (indeed, it is illegal for them to do so) but in the early years this was the practice.

Generally, the early societies took the form of several men, often tradesmen, meeting in a local room, usually the local public house, who decided to buy themselves a house each. They wrote rules, formed a society of normally a dozen or two dozen members, held meetings, collected subscriptions, bought a piece of land, built several houses thereon as funds permitted, drew lots for order of occupation and, when all the houses were completed and all the members satisfied, disbanded the society. For these early societies were terminating societies, and when the object for which the society was formed, say to build 20 houses on a plot of land, had been fulfilled, there was no further need for the body and it ceased to exist.

These societies depended to a large extent on fines to maintain discipline, and they usually met in public houses, the most convenient local meeting places. Some people who felt strongly about the drink connection did form societies meeting in church halls, school rooms or mechanics' institutes, and vestiges of these lasted well into the present century as temperance building societies. Some inn-keepers obviously encouraged the formation of societies in their inns. Mr James Patchett of the Coach and Horses, Bradford, provided accommodation for the three Bradford Moor Union Building Societies between 7 February and 14 March 1825, and George Lumb of the Crown Inn, Ivygate, Bradford, played host to the Bradford Trades-man's Building Society and the Bradford Commercial Building Society from 1825, and the Bradford Improved Commercial from 1838 (probably on the termination of the first Commercial).[15] It was not uncommon for these societies to include a requirement that members drank at least fourpence worth of beer (about 1½p.) at each meeting in their rules, though this usually excluded women and young members. In addition, George Lumb was a stone and marble mason, and he prob-ably gained business by attracting societies to his inn.[16] Fines were considered necess-ary to enforce rules which stipulated modes of conduct at meetings, payments of subscriptions, and so on. They varied to some extent but followed a generally similar pattern. A fine of sixpence (2½p.) was imposed for drunkenness, of a shilling (5p.) for the use of insulting language, and of five shillings (25p.) or thereabouts for fighting. These transgressions were no doubt encouraged by the customary meeting place, but there were other fines which dealt with problems other than behaviour. If a society operated a rota system and a member refused to act as chairman he could be fined 2s. 6d. (12½p.), and arrears were usually discouraged by a sliding scale of fines which could become excessive. In the final event, if back payments were not paid up, members could often be expelled without rights, losing all money paid so far. The high level of fines helped to keep members aware of their responsibilities, but another advantage was that the proceeds from fines (and the retained payments from expelled members) helped, sometimes signifi-cantly, to swell the funds of the society.[17]

A share in these early societies was a house, and members paid an entrance fee (usually a small sum of threepence or about 1½p.), and weekly subscriptions of around 2s. 6d. (12½p.). The most usual figure later on was a monthly fee of 10s. 6d. (52½p.). On top of this was the rent once a member occupied a society's house, and this could be six to ten shillings (30p. to 50p.) a week.[18] Clearly, with a likely cost to the member of 12s. 6d. (62½p.) a month, and with the heavy fines (and danger of complete loss of a share if non-payment continued too long) seen against a backcloth of economic instability, building societies were not for the ordin-ary labourer or factory operative. Rather they were for the upper working class, or the lower middle class wanting to move out of their way. Security of employment and continuity of income were necessary for the likely duration of a society, and the ordinary worker could not usually guarantee that. Societies usually lasted 14 years and often longer and this was a long period over which to commit any future income which could not be guaranteed, at least to some extent.

Figure 5.   Clubhouses Yard, Horbury, in 1971; some of the properties built by the Horbury Building Society established in June 1793. There were 29 members, but it seems unlikely that many houses were built. They were straight-through houses, surrounded by brick- and stone-built back-to-backs. The inhabitant of No. 31, the property at the end of the yard, aged about 70 when interviewed in 1971, could remember when the society houses continued down to the main Wakefield-Huddersfield Road; when photographed they stood some 40 yards back behind a police house. (See Horbury Building Club, *Rules and Orders for the Government Thereof*, an article of agreement dated 1 June 1793, which was held by the then Horbury Urban District Council in 1971.)

Figure 6a. and b.   Kings and Queens Streets, Skipton. None of this property was back-to-back. It was built by the Harts Head Building Society 1825–40; this society had several members in common with the Skipton Tradesman's Building Society, including John Kendal and Forster Horner.

Figure 7. Victoria Street, Bradford. Not all the houses in this street were built by the Improved Commercial, but the styles of the houses do not differ; in fact most of the rest of the street was built by other societies. (See E. Naylor, *Bradford Building Societies from 1823*, 1908.)

There were further societies, in Mirfield and in Bingley in 1806, in Skipton from 1807, and in Holbeck about 1810.[19] There were certain disadvantages inherent in the early type of building club which erected its own houses on a piece of land purchased for the purpose. Not all the members wished to live in the same place, while some had ambitions to be rentiers and desired property near their present home. Others found different areas, or existing houses, which they preferred. It was clear, too, that increasingly members were appearing who did not want to occupy or rent houses, but merely to invest money in a more liquid form than a purchased house. In addition, there was the problem of equating the value of the dwellings themselves. Society officials went to some lengths to make the houses comply to a standard, but this was usually difficult, and almost invariably some bickering seems to have taken place over the comparative merits and demerits of each property. These were not the main problems of the terminating society, but they were the easiest to overcome. By the beginning of the 1820s, as Britain climbed out of the post-Napoleonic War depression, the building society was ceasing to build, and was reverting to the form that friendly societies and savings clubs must have taken before 1775, in which, instead of building houses as each share, a sum of money was forwarded. With this, the member could buy any freehold or leasehold land or (more usually) property that he wished, this providing the security for the advance, and the deeds being held by the society in the normal way until the loan was repaid. An investor could now subscribe for a late advance, using existing personal property as security if the advance was made before the termination of the society.

The first recorded building society in Bradford was the Bradford Union Building Society, established on 7 January 1823.[20] Among its rules was one which stipulated that subscriptions, 10s. 6d. (52½p.) every four weeks, were 'to continue till the purpose of the society shall be fully accomplished.'[21] This underlined another problem of the terminating society, because to set a particular date on which the society would end required a level of clairvoyance which few men possessed. There were too many imponderables. Costs could be higher than originally estimated, or delays might encourage several members to leave, reducing the long-term income of the society to offset windfall gains from sacrificed subscriptions. Societies which set out to build a certain number of dwellings and bought sufficient land at the outset sometimes found it necessary to sell off part of it, or to complete the planned number of houses and then divide the proceeds of their sale to the members.[22] If the latter course were adopted, the house construction had to be financed by a smaller number of subscribers, which obviously took longer. It was common, therefore, for the termination date to be couched in vague terms, but there was then no way of knowing one's commitment at the outset.

The need to maintain membership meant that most societies discouraged their subscribers from leaving or, as in the case of the Bradford Union, banned withdrawal. Even if a member died, his heirs were encouraged to keep up payments, and if they tried to sell the interest in the society to another party there was the high cost of joining late with the payment of back subscriptions, and perhaps fines also, and this probably meant selling at some discount to find a purchaser.

The Bradford Union asked workmen for tenders, and once arrangements had been settled and a dwelling started the rent was fixed. At this point balloting would take place to see which of the members with an unadvanced share would move into the house on completion. Balloting was, in fact, the least popular method of settling order of occupation.[23] Far more commonly used was allocation by bidding where members hopeful of obtaining an advance competed for it by offering higher discounts. A £120 share which should have been discounted to a little over £60 in the first year might well have led to an advance as small as £30–£40. This was obviously to the advantage of the society's funds, and hence its popularity. Allocation by rotation was also used. These alternatives were not open to a society with houses as shares which could not be discounted. The Bradford Union had 25 members, including three women (presumably widows), and 33 houses were constructed in George Street, Ebenezer Street and Vicar Lane, Bradford, the completed dwellings being conveyed to the owners on 4 and 5 March 1833. The society thus took just 10 years to run its course, a fairly rapid passage. Obviously some members took more than one house, even assuming that there were no members sharing a house with someone else, a habit which was seen in some societies, and which was, no doubt, a way of investing in a society the end result of which could officially only be bricks and mortar to the value of £120.

This dual and double share ownership was well illustrated by the Skipton Tradesman's Building Society established in 1823. An indenture between John Dewhurst, a trustee of the society, and Robert Wildman, a member, dated 1 July 1836 gave details of the society 'lately existing in Skipton', and referred to 'Houses in Commercial Street in Skipton . . . erected by the same society.' Fifty-four houses were built in the life of the society, and it terminated at the conveyance of the property to the members, of whom there were 37, on 29 and 30 June 1836, an existence of over 13 years. In the conveyance indentures available for several houses in Commercial Street details of the members are given.[24]

Table 9   Membership of the Skipton Tradesman's Building Society, 1836

name	address	occu-pation	number of houses	remarks
1 William Oldfield	1 Commercial St Skipton	Yeoman	1	Addresses given are probably for 1836
2 Elizabeth Demaine	Skipton	Widow	2	It is not known whether Skipton refers to Commercial St
3 Peter Jowett & wife Mary	Baildon, Nr Shipley	Yeoman	3	At termination it appears Peter Jowett was dead. The house was conveyed to Mary
4 John Gill	4 Commercial St	Shopkeeper	4	
5 John Burton Birtwhistle	Richmond	Clerk	5	
6 Robert Wildman John Robinson	Gargrave Skipton	Gentleman Silk mercer	6	Robinson took over his part of the share by the will of a Wm Cliffe
7 Jane Wharton	Skipton	Innkeeper	7	
8 Thomas Cockshot	Shipley	Grocer	8	
9 Jonathan Birch	Skipton	Clogger	9, 21	
10 William Parkinson	Commercial Inn, Commercial St	Innkeeper	10, 11, 12	
11 Storey Watkinson	Skipton	Innkeeper	13	
12 Thomas Baynes Preston	Skipton	Gentleman	14 to 18	

Table 9 (contd)

name	address	occupation	number of houses	remarks
13 Forster Horner	Skipton	Currier	19	Jn Tasker got his part
Thomas Tasker	Skipton	Shoemaker		share by the will of
John Tasker (trustee)	Skipton	Printer		Robt Tasker shoemaker
14 Forster Horner	Skipton	Currier	20, 34	2nd listing
15 Thomas Little	Skipton	Draper	22	
16 Mary Philip	Skipton	Widow	23, 24	
17 John Dewhurst (trustee)	Skipton	Cotton spinner	25, 26	
				Numbers 27 and 28 were not built
18 John Bonny	Blackpool	Stone merchant	29, 30	
19 Isaac Dewhurst (trustee)	Skipton	Cotton spinner	31	
20 John Sharp	Idle	Gentleman	32, 33	
21 William Laycock	Skipton	Grocer	35	
22 Joseph Thornton	North Bierley, Bradford	Innkeeper	36	
23 Samuel Thornton	Skipton	Shoemaker	37	
24 John Watson	Skipton	Shoemaker	38	
25 Dodsworth Dixon	Skipton	Shoemaker	39	
26 George Petty	Skipton	Lodging-house keeper	40	
27 Robinson Lockwood (trustee)	Skipton	Grocer	41, 42	
28 William Robinson	Skipton	Mechanic	43, 44, 45	
29 Robert Wildman	Gargrave	Gentleman	46	2nd listing
30 Hannah Wikeley	Skipton	Grocer	47	
31 Forster Horner	Skipton	Currier	48	Horner's 3rd listing.
John Hall	Colne	?		Eliz. Bentley inherited
Elizabeth Bentley	Skipton	Widow		part share from husband, Wm
32 John Brown	Skipton	Joiner	49	
33 John Aitkin	Otterburn	Yeoman	50	
34 Rachel Holdsworth	Oulton (Rothwell)	Widow	51	
35 Samuel Cockshot	Addingham	Gentleman	52, 53	
36 William Read	Bolton Bridge, Skipton	Yeoman	54	
37 Francis Road	Bolton Bridge, Skipton	Yeoman	55, 56	Also received in deeds a rivulet running along-side the land
38 John Sidgwick	Stone Gap, Carlton	Gentleman	—	It seems that Sidgwick may have represented the members in some way at termination. As the last member he may have got an advance without security

Source: Indentures held by the Skipton Building Society.

There are several comments which may be made on the above list.

1. The simple one man-one share situation, or even one man-one or more shares, was not as invariable as may be expected. Although the shares were constructed houses, several people held parts of shares with others. Perhaps they shared rents, or perhaps the part shares were sold to one of the joint holders after construction and conveyance.
2. The investment motive is obviously present. Thirteen members bought more than one house.
3. The trustees of the society could join the society. Two had two shares each, one had a single share, and one, the printer, had a nominal third share by inheritance. John Kendal, the retired innkeeper, however, had no shares.
4. All the members were skilled men, or men with not insignificant incomes. Presumably the widows had private incomes. The main trades or occupations were yeoman (5), innkeepers (4), shoemakers (5, counting a clogger), grocers (4), and gentlemen (5).
5. Family connections seem to have been important in spreading the word of the society. One could perhaps make allowance for local names, but even so, six names are common to more than one member.
6. No conclusions can be made about the geographical distribution of the members. The addresses are those, presumably, of the members at termination, this being the date of the conveyances. Yet, if this is the case, then very few of the members seem to have moved into Commercial Street. Even allowing that those living in Skipton were inhabitants of the houses built (and this is by no means certain), of those 22 members with only one house each, eight were not living in them at termination. Only three members were actually given addresses in Commercial Street.

Attempts to overcome two further difficulties of the early terminating societies can be seen in the formation of the Bradford Improved Commercial Building Society in 1838. It met in the same premises as had the 1825 Bradford Commercial, the Crown Inn. The Commercial was probably just about to terminate, and there was room for another society to take its place. The expense of joining a society late could be avoided by the formation of another society, on the same basis as the older successful society and even with the same rules and officials. The second difficulty involved finance early in the life of a new society when its credit standing was poor and its income (as yet not augmented by rents) was low. A second, and subsequent societies could perhaps lean on the reputation and finance of an earlier society with which it had connections. Whether or not this happened in the case of the Commercial and the Improved Commercial is not known, but the latter was certainly in a position to provide 'a second generation' society if one was required. This was undoubtedly what happened with the series of terminating societies which were the antecedents of the present Leeds and Holbeck Building Society. Samuel Smiles wrote of the first in 1846.[25] It was the Leeds Union Operative Land and Building Society, and it ran from the Old School Room in Holbeck, Leeds, between 1845 and 1857. It was followed by four other terminating societies, the Second Leeds Union Operative Benefit Building Society (1852–64), the Leeds Union Operative Benefit Society (1857–70), the Holbeck Benefit Building Society (1864–79), and the Leeds Union Operative (1870–83).[26]

The step to a permanent building society was now a small one. There may have been examples of an interim type where completely separate series of share issues were made by one society the holders of which left the society when their shares were fully paid up. One possible example was the Leeds Commercial Building Society established in 1845. Its name appears on the list of friendly society rules kept by magistrates in Wakefield under the Building Societies Act of 1836. Its rules were altered as late as 1873, a long (but not impossible) life for a terminating society. The Wakefield list ends in 1874 after the Building Societies Act of that year, but in July 1853 the fourth series of the Leeds Commercial was registered as a permanent society which existed until 1913. Another possible example was the West Riding of Yorkshire Benefit Building Society, Leeds, enrolled under the 1836 Act in August 1849.

The advantages of the permanent mode of organization were several. Societies organized under it did not suffer from the difficulties of the old terminating type. New members could join at any time, without the obstruction of back subscriptions. There was no difficulty about lack of finance in the early stages, and the resultant slow start. If a member became unemployed or suffered from financial embarrassment for some other reason, then in a permanent society he could suspend his subscriptions, or withdraw (unless he had received an advance), without destroying its financial balance. It was also considered important in Yorkshire that there was no uncertainty over the timing of termination, for the final paying off of an advance depended only upon the member's own regularity in paying subscriptions. He was no longer dependent upon the failures and arrears of other people.

There were, besides the advantages, some basic features which helped to change the face of the building society when the permanents appeared. Up to this time, investors and house-purchasers had to all intents and purposes been regarded as the same sort of person by the societies. Admittedly some had borrowed money on a fairly large scale, but shareholders were not distinguished as to their motives for taking up subscriptions. In the permanent societies this was altered, and investors and borrowers became more distinct. While one individual could be both, it was the case that borrowers received no profits (except in a few cases, for example the Leeds Permanent), while investors did. The permanent societies ceased to be mutual aid organizations, and became rather more finance houses for property dealings and places for investment of small savings. Reflecting this change in emphasis was a change in personnel. The old terminating societies had been run by the artisan working classes or lower middle classes. The permanents attracted career men to run them, very often with working-class backgrounds, but with financial talents far beyond those of the average weaver or joiner. The job of a building society administrator became a profession, for which a salary, albeit usually a low one, was paid. The profit motive, tempered by a real and genuine wish to encourage self-help doctrines among the working classes, became important. The introduction of the permanent society acted as a great stimulus to development.

The country's first permanent society appeared in 1845, probably in Essex or London,[27] but for a year or so the Yorkshire woollen towns were happy to develop the terminating society. Several appeared, in Leeds, Bradford, Bingley, Otley and Wakefield, as well as in other towns. While they varied in size, the important new feature was their increased scale and professionalism. As an example, the Leeds Building and Investment Society terminated in 1858, having, in its first 10 years, advanced $178\frac{1}{2}$ shares to 51 members, these having a value of £10,207. The Wakefield Benefit Building Society, founded in July 1846, changed its rules to become permanent in 1850. The Wharfedale Investment and Building Society, Otley, established in July 1848, similarly converted itself in June 1850. Elsewhere completely new permanent societies grew alongside the older terminating bodies, the Permanent Second Leeds Benefit Building Society (the Leeds Permanent, 1848), the Bingley, Morton and Shipley Permanent (now part of the Bradford and Bingley, 1851), and the Bradford Second and Third Equitables (1851, 1853). Further significant formations were the Leeds Provincial (1849, now with the Bradford Third and the Burnley as the National and Provincial), the Halifax Permanent (1853), and other societies which still have existence in some form in Huddersfield, Skipton, Keighley and Dewsbury.

All the major formations had been made by 1875. There then followed a rash of commercially sponsored societies, the best known of which were the Starr–Bowkett societies. Over a thousand of these were established around the country, and they had many emulators. In the main they were lacking in the self-help or philanthropy found in earlier societies, and their financial workings were questionable. The basic pattern of building society structure had been laid down by the 1850s and any subsequent societies that strayed from the pattern were moving up blind alleys.

Initially building societies had no legal recognition or control, though some registered as friendly societies. The Bradford Union Building Society and the Barkerend Union Building Society in Bradford both took this course in 1824. In the early 1830s society leaders around the country went into paroxysms of anxiety at the threat of stamp duty being levied on building society shares, and petitions and representatives arrived in Westminster in large numbers. As a result of the lobbying the Chancellor of the Exchequer agreed to introduce building society legislation which would make the position of such organizations clearer.

In the event the Building Societies Act of 1836 did not achieve its objective. It was badly drafted. To begin with it codified much that was already accepted practice. For example share denominations were restricted to £150 and monthly subscriptions to £1 per share, though the normal figures were below this. Confusion arose because the law made no stipulation over how many shares a member could have so that an investment of £300 could be undertaken simply by taking up two shares. Further confusion arose in the fourth section of the Act which stated that the provisions of the Friendly Societies Acts of 1829 and 1834 could be applied to building societies where they were suitable, though no guidance was given as to which provisions these might be. Some were obviously irrelevant, such as sections on sickness benefit, while others were clearly appropriate, for example those relating to meetings, misappropriation of funds, preparation of annual accounts, and the like. There were clearly some sections, however, where relevance was highly debatable. Minors could join friendly societies and take part in their proceedings, yet minors could not undertake mortgages. (Although their membership was in doubt, many minors joined building societies to encourage thrift.[28]) The Friendly Societies Acts were altered in 1846 and repealed in 1850, yet they remained as part of the 1836 Act specifically for building societies until 1874.

Further regulations gave registered society rules legal backing, and society interest rates were exempted from the usury laws. Conveyancing of mortgaged property was eased, and building societies were given an assurance that their shares would not become subject to stamp duty. Building societies thus achieved legal status, and there was a useful bonus in the barrister appointed to register societies, J. Tidd Pratt. Holding office until his death in 1870, Tidd Pratt did more than anyone else to standardize building society procedures, refusing to register rules to which he objected and issuing books with model rules, forms and conveyances.

Concern over the legal position of building societies arose anew in the later 1860s with the Liberal government considering the possibility of applying joint stock company legislation to them. A royal commission was appointed to look at the question of friendly and building societies in 1870, and its report led to the Building Societies Act of 1874. This repealed the 1836 Act, though any societies enrolled under the earlier law could continue to operate under its regulation. They could also incorporate under the new law. A clear distinction was made between terminating and permanent societies (the latter had not appeared at the time of the 1836 Act), and a proper procedure was laid down for the dissolution of both types. The Registrar in London was now to keep all rules of societies rather than the local clerks of the peace. No restrictions were placed on the size of shares or subscriptions as in 1836, but the role to the building society was more clearly defined. It was to be a body which provided a fund made up from subscriptions and other payments from which loans on property could be made, but it could not now own property apart from its own offices. If any foreclosures took place the property obtained as security had to be sold as soon as was practicable.[29] The importance of this section of the Act was that it made the original form of self-building society illegal.

The 1874 law allowed societies to adopt corporate status. This did away with the need for trustees and made societies liable for debts. It was therefore possible to introduce limited liability in line with that given to joint stock companies in 1856 with which building societies were in competition for funds. Further restrictions were introduced covering borrowing powers, and societies were barred from lending or investing surplus funds in anything other than public securities.

The 1874 Act was amended in 1894 following the failure of the giant Liberator Building Society in 1892. This came about largely because the Liberator moved into the speculative business of financing building being carried on by a company belonging to its manager, J.S. Balfour. Projects included luxury flats, hotels, and even a light railway. The 1894 legislation was designed to fill the loopholes of the 1874 Act. For example, the earlier legislation had allowed societies established before 1874 to remain outside the restrictions of the new law. Under the 1894 Act this was only possible for societies established prior to 1856, all later societies now being forced to incorporate under the 1874 law. New regulations about the style of annual reports from societies were included, societies now having to give details of property in hand and of the sizes of mortgages being given.[30] Balloting of advances was made illegal and this effectively killed off the commercial terminating building society.

3 The contribution of building societies in the quantity and class of housing provision

It has proved impossible to form any kind of accurate estimate of the proportion of total housing financed by building societies, but it is likely to have been considerable if only because of the large number of societies and the size of their business.

When asked how many of the houses in Bradford inhabited by the working classes (though not necessarily owned by them) had been built through the agency of building societies, J.A. Binns, president of the Bradford Third Equitable Building Society, replied 'an exceeding large number'.[31] H.J. Dyos thought building societies were the principal means of financing housing through advances to builders and owner-occupiers in Camberwell.[32] The alternative methods of house finance, personal capital, bank loans, and loans from family and friends, were of limited use to the majority of people. According to Dyos, property being erected was mortgaged to building societies, banks, or money-lending solicitors, and buyers took over any mortgage commitments,[33] but most London banks at least were unwilling to lend on mortgage except to the upper and professional classes and building societies 'were certainly of great importance.'[34] Dyos maintained that the solicitor 'may well have been the real fulcrum for the bulk of the capital movements' in the industry,[35] but he spoke of them several times as 'channels' for money[36] or as trustees 'apparently acting on their own behalf.'[37] The indication is that solicitors obtained finance for builders from other sources and there is no shortage of evidence that they had numerous and close contacts with building societies. Wherever credit was obtained by builders, it is an obvious truth that it had to be repaid eventually with money obtained from purchasers of completed property. Consequently, however builders got their working capital, it was the source of the money coming into the industry from outside, from house purchasers, which was important, and they were less likely to have access to the alternatives to building societies than builders.

The membership of building societies was restricted to the upper working classes or middle classes as much by the duration of share repayment periods as by the cost. Repayments on a £120 share of 10s. (50p.) a lunar month initially seem quite feasible compared with the wages of a building labourer in the 1820s and 1830s when they stood at about 2s.6d. (12½p.) a day, or probably 15s. (75p.) a week,[38] though obviously ease of repayment depended on what other commitments the worker had. There was then the cost of rent or society excess on top of the subscriptions, in the latter case putting total payments up to £1 every four weeks, or something over a week's pay, and this was probably prohibitive to many workers. The real restriction became apparent over 14 years, however, bearing in mind the heavy sanctions invoked by societies to deal with arrears. The sanctions were cumulative, too. A spell of unemployment during which no payments could be made would leave the society member with a heavy burden of present payments, past payments, and fines. So an all-important aspect of building society membership must have been long-term security of employment and income. The building societies would have seen to that for their own security, even if prospective house purchasers were over-optimistic. Even building craftsmen were only on some 4s. a day in the 1830s, or about £1 4s.0d. a week (20p.; £1.20),[39] and subscriptions and excess together would still have taken a sizeable share of total income, but at least security of occupation was greater. There were other disadvantages for the working man below the level of the really skilled. It was, for example, important for all members to be able to read and write, and they had to be able to attend meetings regularly on payment of fines. Yet the working day of the ordinary factory hand or labourer was very long, leaving little time for such activities after eating, rest and entertainment. Labouring members must have been the exception rather than the rule, and even skilled workers, perhaps, not too common.

The Royal Commission on Friendly and Benefit Building Societies which reported in 1872 looked at the membership of contemporary societies, particularly of the permanents. In the small Lancashire towns (where societies were still largely of the terminating type) the bulk of the members apparently still consisted of working men and 'the number of genuinely working men in the better class of permanent societies in Birmingham, in Lancashire and Yorkshire, seem evidently to be very considerable, such members being indifferently either borrowers or investors.'[40] In evidence to the 1872 commission, J.W. Middleton, solicitor of the Leeds Permanent, said that all classes in Leeds used the society, but that the bulk were 'working men'.[41] 'Many higher classes avail themselves of the advantages', but five-sixths of borrowing members borrowed under £400. Members 'of superior means' were becoming more common in northern societies.[42] This was taken to mean that five-sixths of the Permanent's borrowing members were working class,[43] but £400 was a considerable sum of money when purchasing a house in the mid 1850s, and it was not worth much less by 1872.[44] Certainly more than one house or cottage could be purchased with it, and this does not seem to match the probable aspirations of the ordinary working man.[45] From Liverpool, statistics showed that 'working men' seldom borrowed, but deposited a large proportion of the capital used by societies,[46] which suggests that the middle classes were in fact using money supplied by the poorer sections of society. Certainly there was no danger of loss if building societies were used only as savings facilities or banks by workers who would nevertheless not feel secure enough to take out a mortgage. John Fisher, first president of the Halifax Permanent, expressed the view that working men believed banks were only for the rich. Also manager of the Halifax Joint Stock Banking Company, he believed building societies to be the bankers of the poor.[47] In London working men formed only a minority of society membership (except with the Birkbeck Building Society, a giant and badly run body which went bankrupt in 1911).[48] The commissioners heard from a Mr Peacock, representing several London societies, who said that permanents were used by all classes, and that Bowketts and Starr–Bowketts (the long-term, small-subscription commercially sponsored societies then beginning to spring up around the country), were almost entirely for the working classes. This was to be expected with their very low subscriptions and slow return. It was said that middle-class speculators took part in those commercial terminating societies which made a feature of balloting and selling advances,[49] again no doubt making money from the poorer and perhaps less financially aware working class.

The commissioners concluded that 'the proportion may vary, [but] it is safe to say that the English middle class now enter into the building society movement in much larger numbers, take a much larger share in its direction, and derive much greater benefit from it, than they did 30–35 years ago.'[50]

The middle-class interest in building societies was reflected in building society literature and publicity, though they nearly all emphasized the usefulness of saving in such societies for safety in times of sickness, bad trade or old age, problems besetting all classes, but which were more serious for workers because they had no way of making suitable provision. The preambles of older terminating societies maintained that such bodies had been set up 'principally among the working classes', but this was merely an echoing of the misconception in the 1836 Act, and a fairly restricted idea of who made up the working class. This idea was not really surprising. Given Victorian values, the working classes supposedly consisted of those who tried and were successful, and those who did not try. Only the former were expected to join building societies. It would have been unusual to hold the view that the latter could not join, rather than that they would not. Victorians would tend to see what they expected to see. They created in their own minds the ideal that there was progress for all who wished to benefit from it, and building societies were expected to benefit all classes.

The permanents sounded a truer philanthropic proposition. For instance, in the third report of the Bingley, Morton and Shipley, local men were encouraged to make loans to the society, saying that 'we confess the society is established for the benefit of the humbler classes' and wealthy neighbours could help the society to 'radically change the condition of the humbler classes.'[51] The following year it was impossible for the 'industrial classes' to save because of bad trade, but whether this affected the loans by the society or not, advances and property thus financed covered a similar class of business to the year covered by the third report. Eighty-nine shares were advanced to twenty-three members, and of these, only three and a half shares and four members were concerned with single dwellinghouses. The others varied from two to fourteen houses (the average number of houses per loan, including the single houses, fell just slightly below four), and there were eight shares advanced on a chapel.[52] The purchase of more than one house was an investment decision which the ordinary working-class man was unlikely to take.

In Leeds, an 1848 Leeds Permanent handbill pointed out, erroneously, that the ideas of building societies were spreading from London and Manchester. 'Leeds, with its influence and population, ought not to be behind in advancing the interests of the industrious classes.' And in 1860, when 151 members received advances, 66 (or only just over 40 per cent) obtained under £200. This still did not include any deposit (which was usually 25 per cent) and, in any case, £200 was more than sufficient for several properties to be purchased. Nevertheless, the board said that 'we confidently hope that the habits of forethought, frugality and temperance, encouraged and diffused by [building] societies, will greatly assist by elevating the working classes.'[53] Running right through all this literature is the belief that working men could improve themselves by adopting middle-class ideals and modes of behaviour.

The call on the working classes was usually that of 'Why pay rent?'. For the outlay of just a little more than a weekly rent, one could eventually own one's own house. More than this, if you bought more than one property, the income from rents of the houses you let helped to pay the subscriptions to the society. It was not an aim of the building societies to make the working classes better off, saving them from landlords and the like. What they wanted to do was to lift members out of the masses into the middle classes. In 1847 an advertisement from the terminating Leeds Building and Investment Society setting out the advantages of joining a building society recounted how one member in Holbeck had taken three shares with an advance made of £270 with which he had purchased four cottages producing a weekly rental of 9s.6d. (47½p.). His weekly payment to the society was 10s.6d. (52½p.).[54] It is not clear if this 9s.6d. was obtained from three cottages while the member lived in the fourth, or whether all four cottages were let. Either way, this was encouraging very obvious middle-class, rentier aspirations. While societies saw the waste of their members paying rent, they were happy to see them gain from payments of rent made by others outside the society. As late as 1907, the Leeds Permanent was encouraging the working classes to become middle-class rentiers. The society issued a handbill aimed at the industrial class.

WORKING MEN!

Help yourselves to become landlords by
joining this society. It is the best
thing you can do.[55]

More detailed information is available on membership from two societies, the Otley and Wharfedale and the Provincial of Leeds. In a register of members, the Otley society made an undated record of occupations from 1853 (though not for all members) covering the years up to the 1870s (table 10). With any list like this, there is the difficulty of deciding whether a trade denotes an employer or an employee. Labourers were obviously working class, and professional people obviously middle class. Tradesmen were probably, at the least, self-employed artisans. Taking the labourers and the woolcomber as working class, and perhaps including in this category the boatman, 88 per cent of the Otley's members for whom occupations were given were not in the lowest social stratum. The fact that the occupations were noted makes this a selected sample, but the inclusion of labourers and other working-class occupations suggests that it may be a significant sample.

Table 10   Otley and Wharfedale Permanent Investment and Building Society: occupations of those members whose occupations were recorded 1853 onwards

Farmer	7	Fuller	1	Minister	3
Farm labourer	1	Boatman	1	Sadler	1
Grocer	1	Mechanic	1	Bookbinder	1
Labourer	1	Gamekeeper	1	Woolcomber	1
Draper	1	Art student	1	Widow	4
Miller	1	Tailor	3	Spinster	8
Overlooker	3	Solicitor	1	Minor	3
Plumber and glazier	1	Joiner	3		

Source: Otley B.S. Register of Members.

Far more important was the enrolment book which the Leeds Provincial kept, from which three years' membership was studied (1849, 54 and 63).[56] Again the problem of seeing class by a mere job description presents many difficulties, but only 10 per cent of members were found in the obvious lower working-class occupations and those which are perhaps doubtful – the labourers, quarryman, lamp lighter, miners, powerloom operators, the weavers and spinners, the groom, and the furnaceman. Those members who were definitely in the professional classes, the dentists, the bookkeepers, the solicitors, the teachers, the opticians, the architect and so on, constituted something like 9 per cent. A careful and conservative list of tradesmen and dealers, middle-class or upper working-class members, the hairdressers, the tailors, the printers, the shoemakers, the cloth manufacturers, the shopkeepers, the butcher, and similar groups, made up 36 per cent of the membership. A quick glance at the full lists is all that is required to see the preponderance of farmers, joiners and carpenters (artisan trades), overlookers and foremen, tailors and drapers (artisans at least), butchers, merchants, shoemakers, manufacturers, and other trades and professions. The working-class members, the nine miners, the powerloom operator, the nine forgemen, perhaps some of the bricklayers and the paver, and certainly the seven labourers, are obviously exceptions to a fairly general rule.

Information is also available on the types of property involved in mortgages. It confirms the middle-class investment interest as of great importance. The Bingley, Morton and Shipley Permanent left details of advances made between March 1851 and March 1852, between March 1853 and 1855, and in the twelve months from March 1856.[57] All monetary figures given were the actual advances and did not include deposits, so that they represented approximately 75 per cent of the total cost of the properties.

Over the four years covered by the Bingley schedules, the average number of houses per advance made fell slightly short of four. In 1851–2 it was just below six, in 1853–4 it fell to four and three-quarters, in 1854–5 it was just below four, and in 1856–7 it was almost two and a half. (This should not be taken to indicate a falling trend over these years. Four years is too small a sample even spread over six years in time, and these four were near the start of the society. The average may have been settling to a norm.) In any event, there were only 11 of the advances in those four years which involved the purchase of only one house, and 83 per cent of the advances involving houses were for multi-house purchase. The middle-class rentier involvement is certainly confirmed for this group.

We may look similarly at another society in the same area, the terminating Bingley Building and Investment Society. Very little information is available here, there being only two schedules, one for 1852–3, and the other for 1855–6, but in the first, besides five and half additional shares, two shares worth £112 were advanced upon three dwelling houses, and in the latter there were two additional advances, plus two advances of £200, each for four houses.[58] At the foot of the 1856 schedule it was stated that 51 members had received total advances worth £10,207, an average advance to each member of almost exactly £200. This, plus the 25 per cent deposit, was more than enough for two or three houses. It could have been that some advances were made to groups of people rather than to single members. This was suggested by evidence in Skipton.[59] However, wider evidence from advances and minute books studied over the Riding suggests that this was not common by 1850. On occasions two or three people did unite in a partnership but this was usually for large advances sometimes of several thousand pounds. There was no real advantage in (say) four people clubbing together to purchase four houses. The repayments were still the same divided between the four. In addition, there was the increased danger that one of the four would not keep up his payments, in which case the load on the other three would be increased, a positive disadvantage. It is unlikely then, that the working classes used building societies in this way, and multiple house purchase must have been for letting.

The Leeds Permanent also left details of mortgage securities,[60] confirming that this degree of multiple house purchase was not confined to Bingley, but further, that even when single houses were purchased they were far too big and expensive to be anything but middle-class residences in many cases. In the financial year which fell almost completely in 1849, the average number of houses purchased with each advance was almost exactly three (in fact, a shade under), and in the year ending in 1853 the figure was again almost exactly three (very slightly higher). Of the 50 advances made in 1849 which included dwellings as part of their security, as many as 22 were for only one house (ten of these had other property included as well, such as a shop or land, but the house could still have been for owner-occupation). This was considerably more than in Bingley, but there was an important difference. In Bingley, the single house mortgages had been for figures of from

£59 to £74. In Leeds in 1849 the single house mortgages were somewhat bigger. Excluding any mortgages on single houses which included other property, they sometimes ran up to well over £100, and in one instance rose to £729. Bearing in mind that the mortgage figure was only three-quarters of the price of the house, it seems fair to assume that an ordinary working-class house could be purchased with a mortgage of under £100, giving a total cost to the house of around £130, but of the twelve mortgages on single houses and nothing extra, only three were below £100 in value. Similar findings can be made in 1852–3. In that year thirty-two mortgages were for single houses, but nine included other property the value of which we are not concerned with. Of the remaining twenty-three only eight were below £100, and there were several over £300. At first sight, the greater number of single house purchases found in Leeds would tend to negate the findings in Bingley, but it would seem on closer inspection that in fact they support them in that when single houses were purchased, they tended to be to a large extent (24 out of 35 solely on houses) quite big, and in some cases, probably very extensive. A mortgage of £729, plus a third for the deposit, would give a value to the 'dwelling house' of about £972. Of all the advances on security including housing, 63 per cent were for multi-house purchase in the two years, 67 per cent in 1853 alone.

The first two reports of the Halifax Permanent showed 77 per cent of securities, including houses, being for multi-house purchase in 1853–4, and 80 per cent in 1854–5.[61] In 1853–4 the average number of dwellings per mortgage (excluding those advances which did not include a dwelling as part of their security) was only just below 4.7, and for 1854–5 the figure was just above 4.7. In 1853–4 only five advances concerned single dwellings, and of these, two included other property the value of which is not known. Of the other three single houses, one was given an advance of £120 and two received £300 each. The former would compute to a total price for the house of something like £160, and the two latter would probably have cost £400. In 1854–5 there were eight single house mortgages, of which four included no other security. The lowest of these four advances was £300, while two were £480 each (making a total cost of something in the region of £640 each), and the fourth was £600 (making the total cost of the house about £800).

As well as these records of advances, it is possible to take a wider view by looking at the sums of money given on mortgage by societies so that we can get an idea of the proportions of mortgages which were small or moderate, or which were too large to be contemplated by the ordinary owner-occupier. Using the advance details from the Bingley societies in the 1850s, those of the Leeds Permanent in the late 1840s and early 1850s, and those of the Halifax Permanent from 1853 to 1855 it is possible to calculate an average price for houses. This has to be used with care. It is only an average, and actual prices varied considerably. The houses were not described or classified (beyond the distinction between dwelling houses and cottages, the usual term for back-to-backs, in Leeds and Halifax) so that we cannot know what sort of houses they were. Clearly some houses were large, and this would inflate the averages slightly. Lastly, it might be the case that some deposits varied from the normal 25 per cent. It has been assumed here that all mortgages were 75 per cent of the purchase price of the house. By including all those mortgages where dwellings alone were used for security, and excluding those on chapels and public houses, those including warehouses or land, those on property said to be in course of erection (full advances may not have been made), additional advances (which would increase the average price very slightly), and an advance of £17 in

Bingley in 1854–5 on two houses which must be a mistake, we can arrive at likely prices for houses which would be relevant for the whole of the nineteenth century given that prices did not vary much. The average price in Bingley was £79.30, in Leeds £98.10, and in Halifax £109.20. As it was clearly possible to purchase houses for as little as £50 or £60 it seems safe to assume that one could buy a house suitable for a working-class family for less than £100. The Bingley, Morton and Shipley Permanent left details of 61 advances given during the 1850s. The average size of advance was £287, but this disguised a variation (excluding additional advances and those on property in course of erection) from £60 up to two advances of £1,800. In purely numerical terms, that is ignoring the amounts of money involved, 23 per cent of the mortgages were for sums of under £100. Another 33 per cent were for amounts up to £199, 56 per cent in all for mortgages quite big enough in their day for houses, and 14 per cent of the mortgages were for sums between £200 and £299. Anything above £300 could be interpreted as a very generous mortgage for a single house, and more probably for a multi-house purchase, and 30 per cent of the 61 mortgages were within this category. Indeed, 5 per cent were above £1,000. In monetary terms, 65 per cent of the finance advanced by the Bingley during the period between 1852 and 1858 went on mortgages of over £300, and 27 per cent on those over £1,000.

The Leeds Permanent left details during its early years, and its first year and the last for which details were available were analysed, 1849 and 1853. In those two years £38,170 was advanced in 151 mortgages, an average of £253. There were no amounts over £1,000, though one advance in 1853 was for £987. There was one down as low as £60. Numerically, only 14 per cent of the Leeds Permanent's mortgages in these two years were for sums of under £100, with another 39 per cent between that figure and £199. Mortgages between £200 and £299 were 16.5 per cent of the total, and those above £300 were 30.5 per cent. Of the money advanced in these years 56 per cent went in mortgages of £300 or over.

Available details from the Halifax give the impression of even greater emphasis on the higher advance. During the 1850s the society had an average mortgage of about £430, only a few dropping below three figures but several being in four. Only 4 per cent of mortgages granted were for sums beneath £100, and there were another 25 per cent over that figure but not exceeding £199. Mortgages between £200 and £299 were 12.5 per cent of the total. Those above £300 amounted to 49 per cent of the mortgages given, and those above £1,000 were 8.5 per cent. The Halifax Permanent thus advanced some 29 per cent of its mortgages for sums of under £200 which could be expected to be used for individual owner-occupation purchases, and 57.5 per cent on mortgages of over £300. This latter involved a commitment of 84 per cent of the money advanced by the society, 28 per cent of the total advances going to the 8.5 per cent of advances above £1,000.

The Leeds Provincial left extensive details of mortgages granted in its minutes, and a random sample was used to establish the mortgage commitments in the society. In all, over 100 mortgage advances were used over a period from the 1870s to 1907. Months were picked at random, and the advances for those months recorded. The total advances included amounted to £74,702, and averaged out to £673, though this did include by chance a board meeting on 29 August 1893, which sanctioned several very large advances which were clearly above the norm.[62] Without these, the average mortgage was somewhat more conservative, though still on the high side, at £406. Mortgages below £100 were 4.5 per cent of the total, and between there and £199, 14.5 per cent. Those between £200 and £299 were 21.5 per cent of the total. Of the mortgages advanced in the sample 43 per cent were for figures between £300 and £999, and 16 per cent were for sums in excess of £1,000. In monetary terms, the Provincial committed something in the region of 88.5 per cent of its advances to those over £300, and 67 per cent to those over £1,000. Even if the August 1893 mortgages are left out, the shares are still 80 per cent and 45 per cent respectively.

In the 1894 building societies legislation it was stipulated that annual reports should set out society mortgage commitments according to size. The graduations were laid down in the Act, and introduced five categories. The first was for mortgages up to £500. This was already above the arbitrary level of owner-occupier mortgages set at £300 above, but even at this higher level the findings are striking. The very fact that the registrar felt it necessary to have graduations which started only at £500 and which then went much higher (rather than having, say, a lower category of up to £300, and a high category of over £2,000 which would have been by the house prices of the day a considerable sum of money) was indicative of the leaning within the building society movement towards larger advances. Above £500, the groups were to £1,000, from £1,000 to £3,000, from £3,000 to £5,000, and above £5,000.

The Provincial of Leeds produced its 1895 report in the new form.[63] The details showed that numerically mortgages above £500 amounted to over a quarter of all advances, and that those above £1,000 were one in ten of the total. Subsequent annual reports showed that between 20 and 25 per cent of advances numerically exceeded £500 in the years to 1914, while those over £1,000 were between 6 and 8 per cent of the totals.[64] This displayed a smaller commitment to larger advances than the computed shares based on a random sample of shares including earlier years. It may be that the Provincial decided to follow a rather more cautious policy after a severe financial crisis in the years from 1892 after the Liberator collapse, or perhaps the society may have followed a policy of moving towards smaller mortgage activities. In any case a numerical analysis hides the financial details, and the 6 to 8 per cent of mortgages over £1,000 could well have absorbed something like a third of the available finance.

The transfer of money from small savers to large borrowers was confirmed by other societies. Following the introduction of the new style of reports in 1893 (pre-empting the statutory compulsion) the Leeds Permanent claimed that 32 per cent of advances exceeded £500 and 13 per cent exceeded £1,000. These accounted for 72.5 per cent and 49 per cent of advanced money respectively.[65] Later reports confirmed that something over a half, and on occasions approaching three-quarters, of the money lent by the Leeds Permanent went on mortgages in excess of £500, and between a third and a half went on those above £1,000.[66] A quarter of all advances from the Halifax Equitable in 1896 were above £500, 17 per cent above £1,000.[67] The Bradford Third Equitable had between 25 and 28.5 per cent of its advances above £500, 69 to 71 per cent of the money lent, between 1896 and 1914. In the same period 12 to 13.5 per cent of advances exceeded £1,000, 49 to 51 per cent of the money lent.[68]

The mortgage structure of building societies up to the First World War is clear. In monetary terms, West Riding societies invested more of the funds at their disposal in larger advances than they wished to admit. Something like two-thirds to three-quarters of available finance went to mortgages above £500, and perhaps four-fifths or so could have gone on those above £300 as in the Provincial or the Halifax Permanent. Between a third and a half of the money went on mortgages in excess of £1,000. About one in three or one in four of all mortgages were generous enough to be defined as large (taking that definition to be anything above £300 or £500), and about one in eight were very big, above £1,000 (though this varied rather more from society to society, for example the Leeds Permanent which apparently gave none, and the Halifax Equitable or the Provincial which gave such big mortgages as about one in six of their business). Yet the majority of societies denied this feature or at least played it down. In the 1901 report, the chairman of the Halifax Equitable stated that the society had 248 mortgages where the debt did not exceed £500, 'showing that they did a very large business with small borrowers, and this was the business they decidedly wished to cultivate'.[69] The Bradford Third had had a rule which banned any advances over £720, though Charles Lund had admitted to an advance of £15,000 to a builder in 1869 or 1870.[70] All societies claimed, to a greater or lesser extent, to be assisting the working, industrious or labouring classes to acquire their own property. A measure of the stress laid upon this aim was the proportion of available finance channelled into mortgages small enough to be afforded by those classes.

This evidence is confirmed by findings elsewhere.[71] In Birmingham 'scattered evidence offers some confirmation that building societies ... catered only for the artisan elite and the middle classes'.[72] While Birmingham societies were not exclusive, 'their subscription rates clearly excluded all but those whose incomes consistently allowed a comfortable margin above subsistence'.[73] There is also confirmation that 'many members' built more than one house, sometimes building a front house to live in, and other back street blind-backs (the Birmingham term for a Leeds 'cottage' back-to-back house) for letting.[74]

4 The economic organization and effects of building societies

The earliest terminating societies were as fundamentally simple as any financial organization involving a number of individuals could be. People contributed to a fund regularly, each receiving a share of the fund at some time during the life of the body. There was no distinction between those who invested and those who loaned money; indeed, there were probably very few men who were purely investors in the early years, in the Midlands and in Leeds in the 1770s and 1780s. Only when the building society was seen to work was it likely that people would invest for profit, for until then the risks were indeterminate. Even those who became investors by the accident of bad luck, those who received an advance near to the end of a society's life, got nothing extra to recompense them for their longer wait. By the very nature of the share when it was advanced, a dwelling which had to be as closely as possible similar to those before and after it to avoid jealousy and discord, there could be no interest paid. Societies at this early stage were little more than convenient places to keep savings for a house, and an institutional framework to encourage regularity of thrift and perhaps allow for economies of scale when building.

There were other sources of income for societies. Firstly, they encouraged the necessary regularity of thrift by fines, sometimes quite heavy, and fines also helped to guarantee self-discipline. In addition, because houses were not transferred to the ownership of the members until termination, societies had possession of houses over several years which were rented to the inhabitants. This gave societies an increasing income as the number of completed houses rose. All members paid subscriptions regularly, but in addition, and augmented by receipts from fines, those members who moved into society houses paid an excess in the form of rent which was usually (but not always) equal to the subscriptions already being paid.

The situation had not really altered very much by the 1820s when societies ceased to build. The usual £120 share representing the approximate value of the sort of houses built by societies at the time, and maintained by the use of commercially available tables based on that figure, stood in exactly the same place in the society system as had the society house. It was undiscounted, and all members received the same amount irrespective of when their share was advanced. There was still no payment of interest to investors. Societies of the type found in Bradford in the mid 1820s were no more complicated than the early constructing building clubs.

An example helps to explain the operation of the society thus far developed (table 11). The usual subscription was 10s. (50p.) a month. (In fact this was usually a lunar month making annual subscriptions £6 10s., £6.50, a year, but for ease it has been assumed here that payments were every calendar month, giving a round figure of £6 subscription a year.) The model society has 20 members and the rent for the society house (if that is what the £120 advance represents) or the excess paid after the advance is received (if it is cash) has been fixed at a sum equal to the subscription. In the model a further four months would see the final share advanced and the society terminated; in most societies the higher annual subscriptions usually meant that they completed after rather more than $13\frac{1}{2}$ years. The recipient of the first share paid £166 for it, £86 in subscriptions and £80 in excess; the recipient of the last share paid £86 in subscriptions only. As both got shares worth £120 it is obvious that those obtaining early advances made greater contributions to their society, while those who waited until the end received more than they put in. The first member to get a share paid £46 towards the general fund which financed those shares advanced later, while the last member to have a share advanced got £34 from the fund.

Table 11   Society operation: an example

year	subscriptions £	excesses £	brought forward £	total £	advances
1	120	—	—	120	1
2	120	6	0	126	1
3	120	12	6	138	1
4	120	18	18	156	1
5	120	24	36	180	1
6	120	30	60	210	1
7	120	36	90	246	2
8	120	48	6	174	1
9	120	54	54	228	1
10	120	60	108	288	2
11	120	72	48	240	2
12	120	84	0	204	1
13	120	90	84	294	2
14	120	102	54	276	2
			36		19

It is tempting to look upon this gain by those who received later advances as interest but this is misleading. The £46 paid by the earlier borrowers above the £120 received was part of a payment of £80 rent, either for a society house, or for property purchased by the society. The member who received the last advance (perhaps only because of bad luck in the ballot) got an apparent bonus of £34 but this merely compensated for the rent he had presumably been paying elsewhere. He was, in the final analysis, no better off financially having loaned his subscriptions to the society for 13–14 years, and if the society had tried to keep rents low to members he may have been worse off. Even after societies ceased to build, the distinction between rent for a house and interest for a cash advance is a nice one, given that in organizational terms the societies hardly altered.

Investment for monetary return was difficult in a society which built (though it was perhaps possible to receive a cash advance without organized collateral right at the end of a society's life immediately before termination, as John Sidgwick of the Skipton Tradesman's Society might have done). Most societies could force members to accept shares and become borrowers if their name came up in a ballot, so investment could be something of a lottery, but if a member were lucky and avoided an early advance his bonus of £34 was interest. The nature of the reward depended upon the motive of the member, and in this case the rate was about 4 to 5 per cent. It is still difficult to show that a borrower paid interest.

The more sophisticated terminating societies found by the 1840s turned the process around by introducing the concept of discounting. The distinction had been made between investors and borrowers, and they were mutual benefit organizations wherein those members with money (investors) could lend money to those members who needed it (borrowers). The former earned interest, the later paid it. The share was usually of a nominal value of £120, but neither investors nor borrowers in fact paid that much. In the following examples figures are close approximations of actual values as they may have appeared in vari~us members' accounts. Shares are taken to be £120, and subscriptions 10s. (50p.) a month, or £6 per annum.

Payments were worked out round the 5 per cent interest rate. A subscription of £6 a year when paid a compound rate of 5 per cent amounts to the sum of over £116 over 14 years, at that time the normal duration of societies. (With an extra month or two over the 14 years this made up the £120.) Subscriptions, however, only amounted to £86. On the other hand, this principal sum of £120, discounted over 14 years, was worth roughly £60. An investor, then, paid his £86 over 14 years, and received £120 as his advance at the end of the society. A borrower wishing to have his money in the first year received £60 and then paid back £86 during the life of the society. A member paying money to the society for about 7 years and then obtaining an advance found himself both paying and receiving about £86. The important feature of this system was that the money received, the share advanced, was different to the two types of member, but both made identical contributions. There were no payments of rent for society houses. Instead borrowers received a reduced, discounted share for a given sum of money, and did not pay any form of excess for any additional service (such as early accommodation) provided by the society. Indeed, borrowers got less from the society for their contribution, and there was now no doubt that the extra paid over receipts was not payment for extra or early benefit. There was no other payment warranted except one of interest.

Although permanent societies stayed in existence, at least in theory, for ever, for many years the main ones continued the practice of running terminating shares of £120 lasting over 13 years or so. Various amounts of money could be borrowed or invested, depending on the multiples of £120 shares and fifths thereof. An advance of about £300, for example, could be obtained by contributing for either two and two-fifths shares (£288) or two and three-fifths shares (£312), but the repayment period under this system could be nothing but 13–14 years. Though the system was not adopted by all societies, nor at the same time by those that did, it became the practice to run more than one share denomination. We can take as an example the Provincial Building Society of Leeds. By 1877 this society ran three share denominations, now known by their discounted value, so that the old-established £120 share (that figure having little relevance to a borrower who neither received nor paid that amount) became the £66 3s.6d. (£66.17½) share. This original share was still paid back at 2s.6d. (12½p.) a week over 13¼ years which at £6 10s. a year amounted to about £87 15s. (£87.75). The first new share was that of £82, introduced in 1873, where repayments were still 2s.6d. (12½p.) a week, but over 18½ years, so that final payments totalled £120 5s. (£120.25). The second new denomination, brought in in 1877, was for £100, repaid at 2s.6d. (12½p.) a week over 26 years, bringing total repayments to £169. With these three shares borrowers could obtain advances to be repaid over 13¼, 18½ or 26 years for virtually any sum which was a multiple of a fifth of £66, £82 or £100. If we take the example of a member wishing to borrow the sum of between £90 and £100, it will be seen that he can now borrow this to be repaid over any one of the three periods. Detailing the three possibilities, they are as follows:

Possibility A
About £92 borrowed under the old denomination of £66 3s.6d. To achieve the required sum one and two-fifths shares will be needed. Repayments will be 3s.6d. (17½p., i.e. 2s.6d. per one share and 6d. per fifth of a share) per week, or £9 2s. (£9.10) per year, over 13¼ years, totalling £122 17s. (£122.85).
Possibility B
£98 borrowed under the £82 denomination. One and one-fifth shares will be needed to achieve the required sum. Repayments will be 3s. (15p., 2s.6d. per share plus 6d. for the extra fifth) per week, or £7 16s. (£7.80) per year over 18½ years, totalling £139 10s. (£139.50).
Possibility C
£100 borrowed in one complete £100 share. Repayments will be 2s.6d. (12½p.) per week, or £6 10s. (£6.50) a year over 26 years, totalling the usual £169.

Bearing in mind the slight differences in the amounts borrowed, borrowing a roughly equal sum over a shorter period does, as would be expected, work out to be somewhat cheaper. It was possible to transfer a loan from one period to another, extending or decreasing the length of time over which repayment was being made, virtually by repaying the loan still outstanding and taking out another to the value of the loan still outstanding in another denomination.

The Provincial's system had not altered by 1885, but in that year, as a result of slight changes in the periods of repayment which increased the overall cost of each advance, six new tables were introduced, all calculated at 4.5 per cent. There was now complete separation between the investing members and borrowers, each operating on different tables.

Table 1. This was for investment shares, subscriptions being the usual 10s. (50p.) per lunar month (2s.6d., 12½p. a week). At the end of 206¾ lunar months total payments amounted to £120 17s.6d. (£120.87½), and the interest to £47 2s.6d. (£47.12½) giving the total value of £150.

Table 2. This concerned paid-up shares. The present value (i.e. the eventual value discounted to the first month), was £82, and this was the amount invested. After 176 lunar months this was worth £150.

Table 3. A borrowing table for advances of £66 3s.6d. (66.17½). Total payments, £88 10s. (£88.50).

Table 4. A borrowing table for advances of £82. Total payments, £121.

Table 5. A borrowing table for advances of £100 repaid over 26 years. Total payments, £170.

Table 6. A borrowing table for advances of £100 repaid over 39 years in half-yearly amounts. Total payments, £214 10s. (£214.50).

The changes displayed a growing sophistication, with greater emphasis in providing distinctly different services, not only for investors and borrowers, but within one or other of the fields. Investors did not have to subscribe (or deposit a lump sum which, of course, did not require such tables because no share values were involved), but could now invest lump sums in paid-up share accounts. Borrowers taking £100 advances could choose over which period and in what manner they wished to repay. Three years later, in 1888, the Provincial took another step towards the modern system when a single table was devised (calculated at 4 per cent, a reduction) on which different amounts could be borrowed over different periods. It was basically a table for a £130 share, not all of which was utilized if a smaller share was required. There were six possible periods for shares on what was known, following on from the tables it partially replaced, as Table 7 (table 12). Tables 1 and 2, for investors, remained in force. Nine years later, another series of tables was introduced, calculated at 3.5 per cent. Repayments were still 2s.6d. (12½p.) a week, or £6 10s. (£6.50) a year.

Table 12   Provincial Building Society, Leeds: Table 7, 1888

period	(years: lunar months)	advance	payments
1	7:1	£40	£46
2	11:7	£60	£75
3	17	£80	£110 10s. (£110.50)
4	23:12	£100	£155 10s. (£155.50)
5	33:7	£120	£218
6	40:2	£130	£261

Table A
Advance £50.   Period 9 years, 1⅘ weeks.
Table B
Advance £75.   Period 14 years, 48 weeks.
Total payments, £97.

Table C
Advance £100.   Period 22 years, 16⅘ weeks.
Total payments £145 2s. (£145.10).
Table D
Advance £125.   Period 32 years, 18⅖ weeks.
Total payments £210 6s. (£210.30).
Table E
Advance £150.   Period 47 years, 45 weeks.
Total payments £311 2s.6d. (£311.12½).

The old system was still applicable in that these share denominations denoted periods rather than amounts. For example, £300 could be borrowed as:

(a) 6 £50 shares.   Total payments over 9 years, £352.
(b) 4 £75 shares.   Total paid over 15 years, £388.
(c) 3 £100 shares.   Total paid over 22⅓ years, £435.
(d) 2⅖ £125 shares.   Total paid over 32⅓ years, £505.
(e) 2 £150 shares.   Total paid over 48 years, £622.

There was only one investors' table, Table 2B, which stipulated subscriptions of 2s.6d. (12½p.) a week, or 10s. (50p.) a lunar month. At the end of 228¼ lunar months subscriptions were £114 2s.6d. (£114.12½) and interest £35 17s.6d. (£35.87½), totalling £150. The Leeds Provincial was slow to make the final change, when instead of lending shares and parts of shares, actual sums of money were advanced and interest worked out according to the amount and the required period of the loan. In the main this was a twentieth-century development, although the Bradford Third adopted this system as early as 1858.

The commercial building societies of the late 1870s and the 1880s were not insignificant despite their ultimate demise, largely under pressure from the 1894 building society legislation which made balloting for advances illegal, an important feature of the type. There were 1,013 Starr–Bowkett societies alone around Britain, though only 13 in the Yorkshire clothing region. In the main the West Riding attracted the emulators, 5 Self-Help societies, 10 Perfect Thrift, 29 Model and 7 Richmond commercial societies, in all some 67 between 1878 and 1890. This was undoubtedly a smaller number than in other areas because of the dominance of the established permanents.

T.E. Bowkett had to appear before the royal commission on building societies in 1871, before the style of society had become established. Dr Bowkett had invented the workings of the society and had then included modifications suggested by R.B. Starr. He claimed in his evidence that Starr–Bowketts, which he went around the country sponsoring for a fee and for which he prepared all the stationery which he then sold, were based on 'intricate mathematics little understood'.[75] There were no interest payments and all that was entailed was that a working man loaned a small amount to the society for a long time and borrowed a large amount over a short period. Bowkett used a model to explain the scheme, in which he assumed there were 100 members each paying annual subscriptions of £2 1s.2d. (£2.06). He also said that in the 10 years after the advance of £200 was received by each member 10 per cent (or £20) was repaid annually. The total subscriptions over the period of the society, 31 years for each member, were £62. (The extra 1s.2d.

a year covered 'expenses'.) The society's total subscription income was £6,200, but in practice those who received later advances, having waited 25–30 years, were allowed a reduction in their subscriptions which made the total subscription income rather more like £5,000 than £6,200. At the termination of the society, subscription were returned to each member. In the intervening 40 years the society would have purchased 100 houses at £200 each, or £20,000 worth of property.

In short each society with £5,000 subscribed purchases £20,000 worth of property, and having purchased the £20,000 worth of property, returns the £5,000 to those who had subscribed it, they being in possession of the £20,000 worth of property. The money is turned over four times, the accumulation of compound interest is remarkable, and was never dreamt of, and is not perceived by people now.[76]

Further, Bowkett pointed out that in his model society rents from the property reached a maximum in the twenty-fifth year when total income for that year was £1,000: £800 rent and £200 subscriptions. If each man paid subscriptions for 25 years, the total amount paid by the 100 members would be £5,000, and

one tenth of £5,000 would only bring in £500 a year income from subscriptions; but because it is compound interest, the rent for repayment is £800 a year instead of £500 a year. You will perceive that there is an intricacy in which we do not wonder at the world in general not understanding.[77]

The quickness of the velocity of circulation deceiveth the eye! In fact, having mentioned the repayments of £20 a year for 10 years completely repaying the £200 advance, Bowkett ignored this feature of the society's income, apart from the passing rather vague mention of 'rents', which in fact had nothing whatsoever to do with being a tenth of £5,000 subscriptions subjected to compound interest. In the twenty-fifth year of the society, 40 members would be paying back their advances, there having been 66 advances made but 26 having already completed their repayments. £20 a year (one-tenth of the advance repaid each year) from 40 members is £800. There is no mystery with these societies about compound interest and mathematics not to be understood by ordinary mortals outside the royal commission. Bowkett's approach to it is reminiscent of Hans Christian Andersen's two tricksters in the 'Emperor's New Clothes'.

Stated simply, the societies worked as ordinary very long-term societies without interest, so that each member paid in £200 in ten annual payments (which were probably broken down still further into monthly payments), and received an advance of £200. It was as easy as that. The subscriptions were necessary at the outset only to provide the first few advances so that income could begin to flow in (repayments of £20 only beginning after advance), and after this they remained only as extra lubrication. The last 10 years of the society (in fact they lasted longer than Bowkett's 25–30 years by some 10 years) saw the last recipients of advances repaying the £20 annually, subscriptions having ceased, and in about the fortieth year these repayments would have built up to equal the total of subscriptions, £5,000 or £6,200, and these could then be repaid. The subscriptions were only required because there was no interest charged to borrowers. If there had been, capital could initially have been borrowed.[78] The last man to receive his advance was the first to have his £62 (or less) subscriptions returned, and this helped to pay off the £200 advance, but in the final analysis, each member had paid £262, received £200 to buy a house, and then had £62 returned.

The weaknesses of this type of society were obvious. They were certainly open to speculation. If you drew an early advance you could, if you wished, sell it at a premium. If you drew a late one you had lost very little – a few low subscriptions – and could withdraw. It was poor people who wished to buy houses who lost out. They probably had to pay handsomely for an early advance, and then pay subscriptions for the next 30 years, or they had to pay the subscriptions for 30 years before they even managed to buy the house. According to the evidence of W.J. Prangnell, the secretary of the thirty-eighth Starr–Bowkett Building Society, it was 'customary' for members to sell their rights of advance, usually at a premium of some £50.[79] People joined Starr–Bowkett societies expressly in the hope of getting an early advance, a speculative gamble with little risk of loss. Some societies sold advances directly rather than balloting them. In a sense, this converted them into ordinary terminating societies charging interest. There was little practical difference between subscribing some £84 over a period in return for an advance of £60 as in a conventional society, and receiving an advance of £84 nominal value in a ballot and sale society for which one had to give a premium of £24. In a conventional society, however, the interest was fixed by a society rule, whereas the 'interest' in a ballot and sale society was fixed by the competition met by the bidder. Some societies seem to have bid against their members to keep premiums up. Members also had to make the £200 repayments over the next 10 years. If a man joined a Bowkett society when he was 21 he could be about 52 before he received his advance, and 62 before he finished paying for it. No doubt the returned £62 was useful in retirement. The vast majority of Bowkett, Starr–Bowkett, and other such societies seemed to have struggled on with people leaving (losing their payments so far which provided a welcome bonus to those members remaining[80]); and members who had already received their advances and paid back the £200 ceasing their subscription payments.

The interest paid by borrowers of mortgages did not vary as much as might be expected, nor was it excessively high despite the fact that the 1836 Building Societies Act excluded it from the usury laws. As we have seen, early terminating societies did not charge interest, even after cash advances became the norm. However, it did become common for advances to be sold by societies. There were several methods of deciding on the order of allocation, but the 'first come, first served' technique was not appropriate because all the members usually joined at the same time and balloting or draws earned no money for the society. The sale of advances was open to obvious abuse, but it did have certain advantages in economic logic. When the society had amassed enough money by the collection of subscriptions and the extraction of fines, it put an advance up, virtually, for auction. Members bid for the share, so that if one offered £30 for a share he would obtain the £120 share less his offer, or £90. Obviously the member who bid the highest amount, the highest discount, got the share, and this benefited the society. Abuses crept in when societies bid against their own members to keep discounts up, but the system was based on the principle that those who desired an advance most were likely to be willing to pay most for it. A society member who wanted only to invest would not bid at all; one who wanted an early advance very much would bid a great deal. This was, in principle, interest, for there was little difference in subscribing to a more sophisticated society for a £120 share and receiving an early advance discounted to £66, and subscribing to a sale society for a similar share and receiving an early advance by offering to 'pay' £54. The important distinction came in the fact that the effective rate of interest was fixed in the sophisticated society's rules, whereas that in the sale society was fixed by the effectiveness of attempts to put up counter bids, the availability of property for security which would make more members bid (whether or not it was the first or a subsequent advance), and a good deal of chance. There is not enough evidence available to give a clear picture of the usual rate of interest paid in the sale societies, but if the discounts were something in the order of £40 or £50, then the rate was something like 4 or 5 per cent.

This was the usual level of interest in the late terminating and early permanent societies. The Bradford Freehold Land Society gave and charged 5 per cent,[81] the Bradford Third initially gave 5 per cent (dropping to 4.5 per cent in 1860),[82] the Skipton Building Society gave its investors 4.5 per cent,[83] and the Haworth, Lees, Cullingworth and Keighley gave 5 per cent. This society operated with shares worth £80, and stipulated a 'bonus to the society' of £15 at least for an advance in the first year, 1846–7. Members had to bid above this figure, starting at £16, and the member who bid the highest got as many shares as he required. At a minimum discount, this was low as an equivalent rate of interest, though it was undoubtedly usually higher, but in addition to any discount at the outset borrowers paid 5 per cent extra per annum once shares were advanced.[84] The Leeds Permanent charged 5 per cent initially, reduced to 4.5 per cent in 1853.[85] The Wakefield charged 5 per cent. Rates for subscription and paid-up shares, for loan deposits and advances in the Leeds Provincial were very stable, remaining unchanged for periods of over 20 years, and in the case of subscription shares for over 35 years.[86] The obvious conclusion to be drawn from this, and it is confirmed by data collected from all of the building societies, was that they did not vary interest rates either eagerly or often. The Provincial could maintain a stable rate of 4.5 per cent on advances for 30 years, and on subscription shares for nearer 40, and it was by no means individual in this respect. In the early years of building societies rates of interest were fixed by society rules, and any changes had to be sanctioned by the Chief Registrar. This was an inconvenient and a cumbersome way of regulating income or advance business, especially as managers were sometimes unsophisticated and could not always tell if movements in receipts or advances were going to be temporary, or if they were part of a longer term trend. There were changes in rates but they were usually part of a very long trend, certainly not in the shape of monetary manipulation. A change in interest rates required completely new investors' and borrowers' tables, and administrative changes for all society members, extending loan periods or increasing subscriptions if interest rates were raised. Rules were eventually altered. The Bradford Second ended fixed interest rates in 1895,[87] and the Provincial adopted rules allowing the free variation of rates in the later 1880s.[88]

Until then, alternative methods of keeping down receipts or using up idle funds had to be found. The problem of attracting funds in periods of high economic activity was not common in the second half of the nineteenth century. Various societies augmented a steady drop in interest rates by closing down deposit departments or finding alternative investments to housing. Here, care had to be taken. Societies were always very aware of the distinction between themselves and joint stock companies on the Stock Exchange. The distinction between a building society share with a fixed value, and the shares of public companies, or even Government stock, which varied in value, had been emphasized in the discussion over controlling legislation in the late 1860s and early 1870s. Few society leaders would have welcomed suggestions to invest society funds in assets with variable values; the reputation for safety and integrity had been hard-won. Consequently, investments acceptable as alternatives to property on mortgage were limited, largely to loans to local authorities.

Evidence from all the established permanents is similar, showing both the stability of the various rates charged and given by societies on their accounts and advances, and the continuing falling trend in rates. Where more than one rate was charged the society set certain conditions, perhaps giving a higher rate to existing lenders than to new ones.[89] Complaints of idle balances, closure of loan account departments, reductions in bonuses (given on top of interest, and one method of by-passing the inflexibility of rates fixed by society rule), and investments in local corporations – all were seen from the mid 1870s, through the 1880s and into the 1890s. The Bradford Third Equitable's need to discourage investment in 1886 was such that some of its directors established a company to lend money on the security of property in the United States.[90]

From an organizational point of view, this failure to use interest rates positively is fascinating in itself, but the failure is significant in two other ways. Firstly, it is clear that societies did not suffer any shortages of money in the 1880s or 1890s, and this is important in discussions about the causation of the 1890s housebuilding boom. It has been postulated that the building boom of the 1890s was due mainly to excess capital in the United Kingdom with no alternative outlets, or to supply factors.[91] Yet money was freely available in the 1880s, and building societies pleaded for people to use it, but this was not a sufficient impetus to building activity. It follows that similar financial conditions in the 1890s were not sufficient impetus either, and that other factors, more probably those affecting demand, were at least equally important.

Secondly, the relative stability of interest rates in building societies which, by the later nineteenth century, were not insignificant parts of the British financial system, has important implications for the working of the world international payments pattern. The Gold Standard operated by the movement of gold into or out of a country to finance a surplus or deficit in international trade. The price of gold was fixed (in the UK at £3 17s.9d./£3 17s.10½d. per ounce – £3.88/£3.89) and the supply of money severely limited unless backed by gold. Consequently, if gold flowed into the UK the money supply would increase and there would be inflationary pressure – only if the gold were sterilized could this be avoided. More significantly, gold movements out of the UK would have the effect of increasing the value of money and causing capital shortage. It was this process which curtailed both the home and overseas construction phases in Professor Brinley Thomas's long cycle model,[92] when money became scarce, causing finance difficulties in the UK and remedial action by the Bank of England which raised interest rates. Thomas's model required general rates to rise to end UK investment in the USA and to end the home construction boom in the UK. Consols show hesitations in rate reductions at the end of the 1870s home construction and at the end of the foreign investment boom around 1890, and rates positively rose after the home construction boom of the 1890s. Bank rate was more volatile and therefore less clear, though there were high rates in 1878, 1889–90 and 1899–1900. The serious omission is that building societies, important institutions in the financing of the building industry and in the United Kingdom's financial structure, were completely unaffected. It appears, therefore, that the building industry in the UK had its level of activity little affected by the international payments situation.

Despite the 1874 Act, which made it illegal for building societies to own property other than their offices (which, by the by, still causes societies to own large blocks so that they can rent out most of them to other people and keep within the law by using a small part of the blocks themselves), many societies found themselves holding quite large amounts of property at times. Much of this came into their hands when property was repossessed on the failure of loan repayments. Usually, societies followed the spirit of the law, and disposed of the property to recoup any outstanding debt, any surplus being given to the member in default. Even if property values had fallen since the advance had been made, societies were normally able to make good any loans that had been advanced. Maiwald's index showed a fall in house prices from 63 in 1873 to 46.3 in 1896, but most of this drop was in the years up to 1880. From then until 1914 there was no fundamental fall in values.[93] In any case, the deposit required by all societies, usually to a level of something like 25 per cent, provided a hedge against any deflation. This was its main function (not that of giving borrowers a financial interest in the property they were buying as is often thought). If a loan was given on a house worth £200 and the borrower then defaulted, and if house prices had fallen (say) 20 per cent, the building society had two safeguards. Firstly, enough of the loan may already have been paid back, though this was unlikely because in early years there was a lot of interest to pay and repayment of principal was very slow. If this was so, then the society could probably recoup enough to make good its losses because the borrower had outstanding debts of less than £160, the current value of the house. But of course, an advance on a house worth £200 would not have been to the full value. The most likely figure in this example would have been something in the region of £150. Consequently, even if the member defaulted right at the start of his repayments, and even if house prices had fallen through the floor immediately after the advance, the society could still recover its money by selling at the new market value of £160 because the actual advance had been £10 below that figure. There must have been odd occasions, with some properties, when land values, perhaps because of some local feature, fell heavily, and it was in these cases that building societies were tempted to hang on to repossessed property longer than was really allowed for under the law. While the property was in possession it was obviously sensible to let it, and the income from such letting was an obvious inducement to extend the period during which it was received. The movement into rentier activities was an easy one which some societies could not resist.

One such society was the Wakefield. It owned property for renting for many years, expressly against the regulations of the 1874 Act. There were many references to 'tenants' in society property in Sharleston where the Wakefield appears to have possessed property being purchased by the Sharleston Colliery Company. The mining company deducted rent from wages and paid it directly to the society.[94] The society appears to have suffered considerable trouble with its property in possession. Storms damaged their houses in Sharleston and Streethouse in November 1884, and there were complaints about the costs of repairs.[95] Later some land was put up for sale to a man wishing to build a chapel in Sharleston.[96] Towards the end of the year houses belonging to the society in Normanton Common were found to be emptying sewage into Choke Churl Beck, which was used as a water supply by the local flour mill, and this obviously upset the nineteenth-century ecologists.[97] In September 1886, 24 society houses in Fairburn were let to the Frystone Coal Company for 12 months, and the Sharleston property required reslating. In November, details of property for sale were given.[98] Streethouse property was not sold because no bids were received above the reserve price, but that in Snydale seems to have been put forward successfully. The various lots are given in detail, and they help to show the extent of the Wakefield Society's transgressions.

Lot 1. Ten cottages with annual total rent of £76. These were Nos 6–10 in both Lindley Terrace and Torre Street, and were probably back-to-backs.
Lot 2. Five through houses having frontages in both streets (Nos 1–5?).
Lot 3. Ten cottages as in Lot 1, with a total annual rental of £65. Nos 11–15, Lindley Terrace and Torre Street.
Lot 4. Eight houses, 25–8 Torre Street and 1–4 Eleanor Street, and a shop fronting into Whinney Lane (into which the streets and the terrace ran). Gross rental was £76 14s. (£76.70).
Lot 5. Six houses in Alpha Street and Whinney Lane near the Lancashire and Yorkshire Railway.

Real efforts to reduce this 'property in hand' were not made until 1894. It is not known if many other societies held this much property, but it was certainly a major problem to which the Chief Registrar turned his attention in 1894. The Halifax Permanent held property in possession to the value of £169,334 in November 1893, against total mortgage assets of just under 1 million pounds.[99] Brabrook insisted that each society entered in its annual report the extent of any property in hand, so that the covert rentier activities had to cease. There were obviously enough building societies emulating the Wakefield for the Registrar to consider taking such preventive action. It was an economic activity which societies dabbled in too readily.

In Bradford and Leeds figures are available which make it possible to construct graphs so that we may compare building activity rates as indicated by building plan submissions with building society advances and building society nett receipts (figs. 8 and 9). Plan submission figures were published by Parry Lewis,[100] and advance and receipt figures can be obtained from the Leeds Permanent, the Leeds Provincial and the Bradford Second and Third Equitables.[101] When making a comparison it should be remembered that plan figures reflect a straight intention to build, while advances and receipts of societies will have taken place on a rising trend, as the scale of business of the organizations increased. It could therefore be expected that the early rises in advances of the societies would exhibit a more gradual rise than that of building plan submissions, as shown in figures 8a and b. With this reservation in mind, the similarity between building plan activity and society advances is striking in both Bradford and Leeds, and with both societies in each town. The Provincial, which suffered a severe financial crisis in 1892–3, appears to have a different pattern of activity, but following the crisis its business was about half its former level. With this in mind, the pattern of activity is similar.

The nett receipts of the societies were calculated by adding investments and deposits, and subtracting withdrawals and repayments. Sometimes the figures include subscriptions from borrowers (repaying advanced mortgages); at other times these are not included. Mortgage repayments were a contractual obligation and reflected a level of previous business rather than a current intention to invest in building or make money available to finance the building industry, so that they may be considered a poor indication of investment intentions. Nevertheless, as the receipts of the Provincial show in the 1890s, mortgage repayments were an important source of liquidity. Nett receipts without borrowers' subscription fell after that society's crisis of confidence to a deficit of about £190,000.[102] Mortgage repayments kept the society solvent, and allowed it to continue its business, albeit at a lower level. It would seem justifiable, therefore, if we wish to look at the amount of finance available to the building industry, to include mortgage repayments where possible.

Comparison of society advances and nett receipts unarguably shows a close similarity. The obvious conclusion is that if societies had money they loaned it to house purchasers. This is not to say that they advanced as much money as was available, or we have already discussed the problems faced by societies with excess funds being offered to them.[103] There is ample evidence that receipts were, in most cases, controlled to match demand for advances, and that they reflected the demand for house purchase finance as indicated by advance requests.

The important relationship is therefore that between plan submission and advances, and as has already been stated, these showed a marked similarity as well. It seems likely that housing demand rose and building plan submissions were made. Builders, and subsequently house purchasers, then made application for advances which reflected the realized level of building activity rather than ex-ante activity indicated by plans (though the accuracy of the latter is in fact confirmed by the former). Societies then took steps to acquire the money necessary to fund the advances required, a task usually made easy by the eagerness of investors, particularly among the lower-middle and upper-working classes, to put their savings into building society accounts of one form or another.

If this analysis is correct, then the role played by building societies in the level of building activity was an enabling one, and they did not exert a positive influence in exciting or encouraging house-building activity.

5 Building societies and the quality of housing provision

While societies paid a good deal of attention to the moral attitudes of their members and to the social position of those who borrowed money for the purchase of property, little or no attention was given to the styles or types of property used as security. All available evidence in the West Riding suggests that societies did not enable the poorer working class to buy their own houses, but many of the houses bought with society advances would have been suitable for the poorer workers to live in. There were mortgages given on cellar dwellings, undoubtedly far greater evils than back-to-backs, and with over half of the housing in Leeds and Bradford in the form of back-to-backs societies in the area had little choice but to finance them. Indeed, one Bradford society only ceased to give mortgages on back-to-backs in the mid 1960s. This is yet another indication of the fact that much of the business

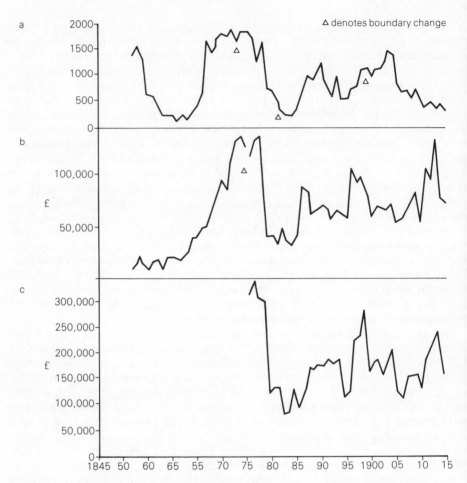

Figure 8a. House plan applications in Bradford, 1850–1915. (Source: J. Parry Lewis, *Building Cycles and Britain's Growth*, 1965, 323–5.)
b. Advances of the Bradford Second Equitable Building Society, 1850–1915. To 1875 figures are annually to July, but after this they are annual to December. The figures for July–December 1875 have been omitted to maintain annual sequence, marked by an arrow. Advances were low in the second half of 1875; inflated to annual figures they totalled only £102,504. (Source: F. E. Lumb, *Second Thoughts*, 1951, 22, 32, 41.)
c. Advances of the Bradford Third Equitable Building Society, 1870–1915 (from society reports).

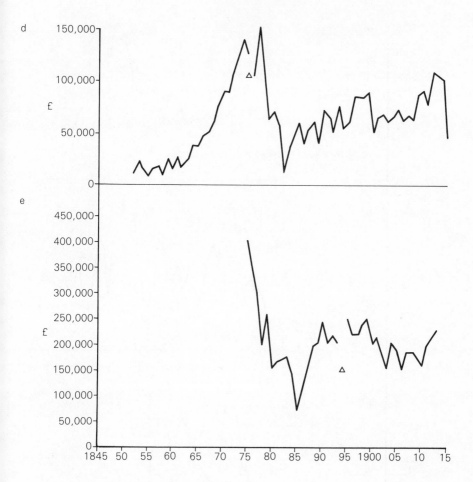

d. Bradford Second Equitable Building Society nett receipts, 1850–1915. Five months in 1875 omitted because of change in date of issue of the society annual report.
e. Bradford Third Equitable Building Society nett receipts, 1870–1915. Figures for 1895 are missing.

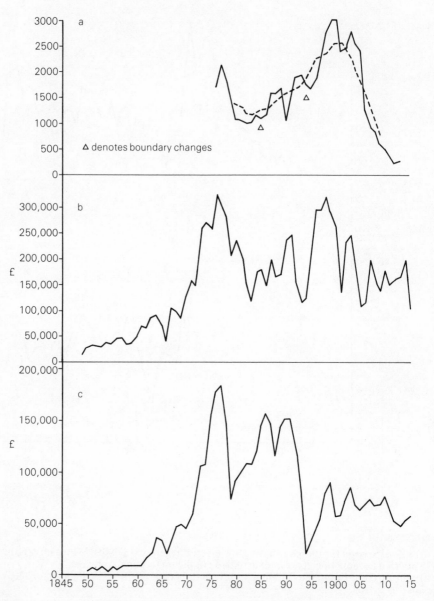

Figure 9a.   Leeds building figures and 9-year moving average, 1870–1915. (Source: J. Parry Lewis, *Building Cycles and Britain's Growth*, 1965, 309.)
b. Advances of the Leeds Permanent Building Society, 1845–1915.
c. Advances of the Provincial Building Society, Leeds, 1845–1915.

94

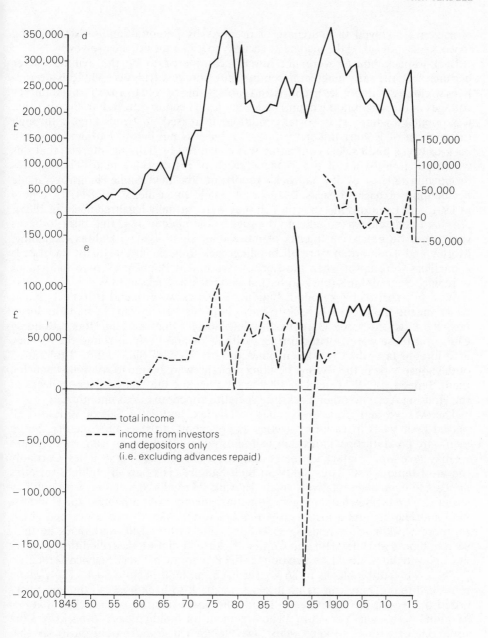

d. Leeds Permanent Building Society, nett receipts, 1845–1915.
e. Provincial Building Society, nett receipts, 1845–1915.

of societies involved the purchase of property by potential landlords for letting to workers who lacked the income or security to join a society themselves.

Back-to-back houses were not initially considered to be the evil they later became.[104] In the early nineteenth century they were relatively acceptable as alternatives to closely built houses in courts and yards within the old town or farm labourers' cottages in the surrounding countryside, but as the century moved on they became less popular as interest in social conditions increased, in Leeds largely through the concern of Robert Baker.[105] In 1840 a bill was put before Parliament to ban back-to-backs but a select committee was convinced by building interests that this would put houses out of the financial reach of the working man. The bill was dropped in 1842 to await Chadwick's report, but the 1848 Public Health Act made no mention of back-to-backs. Manchester made them illegal in 1844, Liverpool in 1861, and Bradford in 1860 (though they were virtually legalized again in 1865). All that Leeds did was to take up the suggestion made in 1842 that back-to-backs should not be erected in blocks of more than eight. Leeds, Halifax, Keighley, Morley and Todmorden were all building back-to-backs in the 1880s, and Leeds councillors were upset when the Local Government Board prevented their plans to replace cleared slums (back-to-backs) with back-to-backs in 1898.

With this sort of background, building societies were bound to reflect similar ideas. Indeed the very early back-to-backs in Leeds were erected by building societies, the Crackenthorpe Gardens Building Society and the Hill House Building Club. But these were isolated terraces with fields and fresh air round them. They deteriorated fast when Leeds surrounded them.[106] With the continued toleration of the house-type in the Riding, building societies were bound to continue financing them. Indeed, the Provincial in 1909 argued against the ban on back-to-backs in the Housing Act, and other Yorkshire societies appear to have sympathized.

The Akroyd and Crossley families of Halifax, and Titus Salt of Bradford all played their parts in various societies as presidents, trustees or directors. These men were philanthropic industrialists interested in improving housing, so that here we may have some contact between social reformers and building societies. Certainly the most famous was Titus Salt who built Saltaire. His part in building societies appears to have been relatively small. Edward Akroyd's connections with building societies were somewhat stronger. Sometime member of parliament for Huddersfield and Halifax and a local textile manufacturer, Akroyd was concerned about the poor working-class housing in Halifax, and in the 1840s and 1850s he built several blocks at Haley Hill and Copley.[107] Akroyd himself described the property at Copley to the National Association for the Promotion of Social Science in 1862.[108]

There were three blocks of 36 houses each, all built back-to-back. *The Builder* remarked that 'There can be no apology for back-to-back houses', though it conceded that those at Copley were 'by far the best examples of that class that can be found perhaps in Yorkshire'. The argument for building back-to-backs was the usual one of wishing to keep rents low, though *The Builder* went on to say that while rents were generally not reduced, the builder's initial outlay was, this form of house being cheaper to erect, and using less room, required smaller parcels of land and could produce greater total rent from a given area.[109] Akroyd obviously felt that his returns were too low on the investment (and he argued that no philanthropist could be expected to give without some return), because the second and third blocks were inferior to the first. Block One Houses consisted of one fairly large living room and a small scullery downstairs, with two bedrooms upstairs.

Each house cost about £120 and the average rent was £5 15s. a year (£5.75). The later blocks cost only £90 to £100 a house and rented out at £4 to £4 5s. (£4.25) a year, but had only one room upstairs. Akroyd's total expenditure on Copley amounted to about £11,500.

This experiment set Akroyd thinking about how one could build improved houses without much capital, and his interest returned to a building society formed in 1845 called the Halifax Union Building Society or the Go-Ahead Building Club'. It was an ordinary terminating society in which each share was a house,[110] suggesting that this society erected its own (though this would be a very late example of a self-building society). Akroyd and one of the Crossley brothers had become trustees. From this came the plan for Akroydon. Sixty thousand square yards of land were purchased in 1855. Akroyd then approached the Halifax Permanent. The scheme involved working men purchasing houses through the Halifax with Akroyd's assistance. By agreement with the society, if any man could not afford a 25 per cent deposit, the repayment period was extended from about 12 to 15 years, and Akroyd himself acted as guarantor for the deposit. Akroyd employed Sir Gilbert Scott to design the property, and had a uniform system of drains and services laid. Building began in 1861, and the Halifax provided £15,000.[111] The scheme was never completed.[112] Early blocks of 18 through-houses consisting of one living room and two quite large bedrooms as well as a scullery and kitchen, and with an ashpit in the back yard, were expensive and Akroyd made a loss because tenants or purchasers could not be found. The costs of later blocks were reduced from over £400 to £136.[113] Presumably standards also fell. The main distinction between Akroydon and other schemes such as Saltaire or Copley was that this was unconnected with any industrial undertaking, and was not built as a suburb for factory workers.

In 1862 John Crossley began a similar scheme in Halifax which became known as West Hill Park. Manchester architects designed the properties. The scheme was very much planned for outward appearance, with a better class of house with three bedrooms on the main street, and poorer housing hidden in back streets. When completed the better houses were to house 'artisans' but it was found that 'inhabitants of a higher class' eventually purchased them.[114] 'Architectural effect is reserved for the houses facing the main thoroughfares, which will be for a superior class of occupants.'[115] J.D. Taylor, secretary of the Halifax Permanent, was on Crossley's committee, and the Halifax advanced £45,000, £5,000 of it on the security of the committee itself.[116]

These were the main projects, though the records of the Halifax Permanent also show what may have been two similar projects. £2,044 was advanced to the Clay Pits Estate in 1869, and almost £4,000 was advanced to the Thornton Model Cottages scheme between 1870 and 1872.[117] Akroyd argued the advantages of such schemes as being that the working classes would be assisted to help themselves, and would not be simply receiving charity with the bad moral effects that entailed, and that any philanthropist's financial efforts would be multiplied by four. With the contribution of the workers themselves, any philanthropic donations, such as financed the Peabody Trust in London, could be put to much greater effect, merely paying for roads, drainage and design, and guaranteeing deposits.[118]

This appears to be one of the few practical moves by a building society into the realms of bettering housing conditions, and even here, the building society did little more than carry out its normal business of giving advances on property.

In fact, there was little more that they could do financially. The money they used was not their own, and their only criterion for its investment was safety, and profit for the investors. Where building societies could have had an influence was in refusing to mortgage certain types of property, and this they were unwilling to do.[119]

There was one other way in which societies could work, and this was by publicity and recommendation to their members. In its first report in 1849, the Leeds Permanent attempted just this. At the end of the 1840s in which Chadwick had been so much to the fore, the society surveyors reported that building societies could definitely help the working classes in the question of housing.[120] They pointed out that some people were living in cottages without a cellar, pantry or closet, that most had only one bedroom, often with a loom in it. Rooms were usually not provided with a ceiling so that there was a clear view up to the joists or roof slates. Caution was advised in giving advances to property of this description on the grounds that better property would then be erected and the value of these old cottages would fall. It was suggested that plans for houses should be offered to members, and five proposals were made. The first three required more than one house to be erected at one time, either for one person to let, or for one person per house to join together in a group.

1. A block of six cottages, probably back-to-backs, with living rooms 14 ft square, and two bedrooms, one 14 ft by 8 ft, and one 14 ft by 6 ft. Pantries, wash-houses and WCs were to be provided separately for each cottage. Cost per dwelling, £75.
2. Ten cottages in a row, with a living room downstairs 17½ ft square, and a bedroom upstairs of the same size. A larder and coal place were to be in a cellar. This was apparently suitable for a weaver, and each cottage cost £70.
3. Two back-to-back cottages for a clerk or overlooker with a wife and four to six children. There was a living room 15 ft square, a parlour 14 ft by 10 ft, a WC and other conveniences in the basement, and three bedrooms, two of them quite large, 15 ft by 12 ft and 15 ft by 11 ft. The third was 8 ft by 7 ft. The cost per dwelling was £150.
4. One house, with a living room 15 ft by 13 ft, a kitchen 7 ft by 5 ft 6 ins, and three bedrooms, two 15 ft by 13 ft and one 7 ft by 6 ft. The cost was £155.
5. One house, with a 15 ft square living room, a kitchen 15 ft by 10 ft, a bedroom 15 ft by 10 ft, and two 10 ft by 7 ft 6 ins, with a WC. These cost £125.

There is no evidence that any of these plans were ever extensively used, nor that the Leeds Permanent restricted its advances in the manner suggested. Similar model designs were produced by the Halifax and, in London, the Co-operative Permanent in the 1890s, but with their 'emphasis solely on the financial security of individual properties ... they were concerned simply with the construction of single units, and the designs remained restricted by the conventions of the traditional terraced house.'[121]

6 Conclusions

Society development in the woollen district of the West Riding grew out of the proliferation of self-help and philanthropic organizations found in the late eighteenth century, and saw the stages of the small terminating society which actually constructed dwellings, the early terminating society which advanced money but remained relatively small, and the larger, more sophisticated terminating society which charged interest to borrowers and gave interest to investors. There were then the interim types, those which produced terminating societies in series or which had permanent existence but ran terminating memberships, and finally there was the adoption of full permanent status.

While it was not possible to quantify the contribution of building society finance to West Riding house-building it was obviously considerable. Any sources of credit obtained by builders ultimately had to be paid, and much of the money available to the building industry came to it from purchasers who could freely borrow from societies more readily than from other institutions such as banks, especially in times when societies had excess funds for lending, for example in the 1880s.

Membership of societies was heavily weighted towards the upper working and middle classes, and evidence of the types of property on which loans were advanced and the size of advances leaves little doubt that while the working classes may have used building societies as their banks, it was the middle classes who borrowed money to finance house purchase, often multiple house purchase for renting. This was certainly true of the later permanents, but it may also have been true of some of the earlier terminating societies wuch as the Tradesman's Society in Skipton in 1823. It appears, therefore, that a pattern emerges of working men investing savings in building societies and either buying themselves a modest house to live in or perhaps even becoming a small rentier, or then living in rented property often purchased by middle-class rentiers using their money from the building society.

Quantitative evidence at the end of the nineteenth century shows that between a quarter and a third of all mortgages were for sums in excess of £500, which was already sufficient for the purchase of as many as ten houses around Leeds, Bradford or Halifax on the figures for advances in the late 1840s and early 1850s. House prices did not vary enough during the century to invalidate these figures. Moreover, mortgages in excess of £500 took between two-thirds and three-quarters of available finance. Building societies were thus an important vehicle of middle-class ethos and financial advance.

NOTES

1 For the purposes of this work the area involved is that defined by Heaton as the woollen and worsted region of West Yorkshire, H. Heaton, *The Yorkshire Woollen and Worsted Industry* (1920), 284. It is bounded by a line running north of Keighley and the Leeds out-townships, east of Leeds and Wakefield, and south of Wakefield, Huddersfield and Dewsbury. It has been extended west to include Skipton, and is similar to the post-1974 county of West Yorkshire.
2 J. Parry Lewis, *Building Cycles and Britain's Growth* (1965), 323–5.
3 *ibid.*, 309.
4 C.H. Bellman, *The Thrifty Three Million* (1935), 21.
5 This, however, must not be overstressed. Many savings clubs and loan societies only advanced sums of between 5s. (25p.) and £15, at least per share. More than one share may have been advanced at one time.
6 O.R. Hobson, *A Hundred Years of the Halifax* (1953), 17.

7 S.J. Price, *Building Societies, their origin and history* (1958), 16–31.
8 *Ibid.*
9 M.W. Beresford, 'The back-to-back house in Leeds, 1787–1937' in *The History of Working Class Housing*, ed. S.D. Chapman (1971).
10 *Ibid.*
11 Price, *op. cit.*, 59.
12 Beresford, *op. cit.*, 123.
13 M.W. Beresford and G.R.J. Jones (eds), *Leeds and its Region* (1967), 191.
14 Beresford, *loc. cit.*
15 E. Naylor, *Bradford Building Societies from 1823* (1908), 17–21.
16 E. Baines, *History, Directory and Gazeteer of the County of York*, I (1822, reprinted 1969), 149–56.
17 Price, *op. cit.*, 70.
18 E.J. Cleary, *The Building Society Movement* (1965), 16.
19 Mirfield Building Society, *Articles of a Society for Building, &c, formed at Mirfield, on the Tenth Day of September, 1806* (1807); Price, *op. cit.*, 63–4.
20 Naylor, *op. cit.*, 14, 61–5.
21 *Ibid.*, 62.
22 There are various advertisements for building society houses in the *Leeds Intelligencer*, see for example Price, *op. cit.*, 50 and 64.
23 Balloting presumably refers to a vote by all the members about who should get the next advance. It could be open to bribery and abuse. Later 'ballot and sale' societies balloted advances and winners then sold them to other members at a premium.
24 Conveyance indentures held by the Skipton Building Society.
25 S. Smiles, 'What is doing for the people of Leeds?', *The People's Journal*, I (1846), 136–8.
26 G.H.F. Nelson, 'Holbeck to Holbeck House, a short history of the Leeds and Holbeck Building Society', *The Beehive*, XVII (1963). In five parts.
27 See Sir E.W. Brabrook, *Building Societies* (1906), 59, and Cleary, *op. cit.*, 47.
28 Price, *op. cit.*, 89.
29 Stated rather vaguely, this provision was ignored by some societies. See below, 89–90.
30 This ensured that societies complied with the provisions concerning the ownership of property.
31 *First Report of the Royal Commission on Friendly and Benefit Building Societies*, PP, 1871, 177.
32 H.J. Dyos, *Victorian Suburb* (1961), 115.
33 H.J. Dyos, 'The speculative builders and developers of Victorian London', *Victorian Studies* (1968), 661.
34 *Ibid.*, 665.
35 *Ibid.*, 668.
36 *Ibid.*, 669.
37 *Ibid.*, 671.
38 E.H. Phelps-Brown and S.V. Hopkins, 'Seven centuries of building wages', in *Essays in Economic History*, ed. E.M. Carus-Wilson (1962), 178.
39 *Ibid.*
40 Bellman, *op. cit.*, 35, quoting the 1872 report.
41 Which is not the same as 'working class'.
42 *R.C. on . . . Building Societies*, 129, Q.5123.
43 See both Price, *op. cit.*, 207, and Bellman, *loc. cit.*
44 K. Maiwald, 'An index of building costs in the United Kingdom, 1845–1938', *EcHR*, 2nd ser., VII (1954).
45 A £400 advance represented the cost of the property minus a deposit of about 25 per cent.
46 Bellman, *loc. cit.*

47 Halifax Building Society, *Eighty Years of Home Building – the Halifax Plan* (1937), 7.
48 Bellman, *loc. cit.*
49 *R.C. on ... Building Societies*, 90.
50 Quoted in Bellman, *loc. cit.*
51 Bingley, Morton and Shipley Permanent Building Benefit Society, 3rd Annual Report, 1854. The use of the word 'confess' is interesting.
52 Bingley, Morton and Shipley Permanent Benefit Building Society, 4th Annual Report, 1855.
53 Leeds Permanent Building Society, 12th Annual Report, 1860. Not 'assist *in* elevating' – one wonders, then, who was assisted?
54 Leeds Building and Investment Society, Minutes. An advertisement dated 1847.
55 Held by the Leeds Permanent Building Society.
56 M.H. Yeadell, 'Building fluctuations and building societies in the West Riding of Yorkshire, 1785–1914' (M.Phil. thesis, University of Hull, 1981). For full details of membership in tabular form, see *ibid.*, 224–7.
57 Bingley, Morton and Shipley Permanent Benefit Building Society, 1st, 3rd, 4th and 6th Annual Reports, 1852, 1854–5, 1857. Yeadell, *op. cit.*, 228–31.
58 Bingley Building and Investment Society, 7th and 10th Annual Reports, 1853 and 1856.
59 The Skipton Tradesman's Building Society.
60 Leeds Permanent Building Society, 1st and 5th Annual Reports, 1849 and 53, Yeadell, *op. cit.*, 232–6.
61 Halifax Permanent Benefit Building and Investment Society, 1st and 2nd Annual Reports, 1854–5, Yeadell, *op. cit.*, 237–9.
62 *Ibid.* For details of these and for a history of the Leeds Provincial Building Society, see Yeadell, *op. cit.*, 407–71. On 29 August 1893, besides a mortgage of £4,030 over 40 years which was large in itself, £27,040 was advanced over 40 years to two officers of the society.
63 Provincial Building Society, 46th Annual Report, 1895.
64 Provincial Building Society, Annual Reports, 1896–1914.
65 Leeds Permanent Building Society, 45th Annual Report, 1893.
66 Leeds Permanent Building Society, Annual Reports, 1894–1914.
67 J.W. Alderson and A.E. Ogden, *The Halifax Equitable Benefit Building Society* (1921), 38, taken from the 1896 Annual Report.
68 Bradford Third Equitable Building Society, Annual Reports, 1896–1914.
69 Alderson and Ogden, *op. cit.*, 41.
70 Lund was an officer of the Bradford Third giving evidence to the Royal Commission in 1871, *R.C. on ... Building Societies*, 174, Q.6679.
71 S.D. Chapman and J.N. Bartlett, 'The contribution of building clubs and freehold land societies to working class housing in Birmingham', in *The History of Working Class Housing*, ed. S.D. Chapman (1971), 221–46.
72 *Ibid.*, 236–7.
73 *Ibid.*, 237.
74 *Ibid.*, 238.
75 *R.C. on ... Building Societies*, 64.
76 *Ibid.*, Q.4121.
77 *Ibid.*, Q.4126.
78 In theory. In practice, under the 1874 Act this would have been illegal as it would, obviously, have exceeded the annual subscriptions.
79 *R.C. on ... Building Societies*, 71, Q.4224.
80 Though Bowkett said members could withdraw without loss, *ibid.*, 66, Q.4163.
81 Bradford Freehold Land Society, *Tables* (no date).
82 Registry of Friendly Societies. A file on this society.
83 Skipton Building Society, 3rd Annual Report, 1856.

84 Haworth, Lees, Cullingworth and Keighley Building and Investment Association, *Rules and Regulations for the . . .* (1846).

85 Leeds Permanent Building Society, 5th Annual Report, 1853.

86 Yeadell, *op. cit.*, Graph 6, 268.

87 F.E. Lumb, *Second Thoughts* (1951), 32.

88 Provincial Building Society, 37th and 38th Annual Reports, 1886 and 1887.

89 For more detailed information on the actual movements of rates of interest and closure of departments to avoid the receipt of money see Yeadell, *op. cit.*, 270–3.

90 See encouragements to invest there rather than in the Bradford Third, Bradford Third Equitable Building Society, Annual Reports 1886 and 1894.

91 E.M. Sigsworth and J.M. Blackman, 'The home boom of the 1890s', *Yorkshire Bull. Economic and Social Research,* XVII (1965), 81.

92 B. Thomas, *Migration and Urban Development* (1972), or see Yeadell, *op. cit.*, 62–4.

93 Maiwald, *op. cit.*

94 Wakefield Building Society, Minutes, 1883 and 1884.

95 *Ibid.*, 3 Nov. 1884.

96 *Ibid.*, 18 Feb. 1885.

97 *Ibid.*, Sept. 1885.

98 *Ibid.*, Sept. 1886.

99 Hobson, *op. cit.*, 51.

100 Parry Lewis, *op. cit.*, 309, 323–5.

101 Lumb, *op. cit.*, 22, 32 and 41 for details of the Second Equitable. Figures of other societies from annual reports.

102 See fig. 9e.

103 See above, pp. 87–8.

104 For a full discussion see Beresford, *op. cit.*

105 Leeds Board of Health, *Report of the . . .* (1833); Statistical Committee of the Leeds Town Council, 'Report upon the Condition of the Town of Leeds and its Inhabitants', *J. Statistical Soc.* II (1839), 397–424; R. Baker, 'Report on the State and Condition of the Town of Leeds', *Reports from the Inquiry into the Sanitary Conditions of the Labouring Population*, PP, 1842, 342–409; R. Baker, 'On the Industrial and Sanitary Economy of the Borough of Leeds in 1858', *J. Statistical Soc.,* XXI (1858), 427–43.

106 Several other early Leeds societies built their own back-to-backs, see section 3 above. Nor was this restricted to Leeds, see Price, *op. cit.*, ch. 3 on the Longridge Building Society near Preston.

107 S. Smiles, *Thrift* (1875), 197.

108 E. Akroyd, 'On Improved Dwellings for Workpeople, with a plan for building them in connexion with Benefit Building Societies', *Trans. National Association for the Promotion of Social Sciences, 1862* (1863), 805–7.

109 J. Hole, *The Homes of the Working Classes with suggestions for their Improvement* (1866), 70.

110 Alderson and Ogden, *op. cit.*, 6.

111 Separate entries in the Halifax reports show only £5,765, but this was probably because subsequent payments were not listed separately from normal business, see Halifax Permanent Benefit Building and Investment Society, 9th to 19th Annual Reports, 1862–72.

112 Hobson, *op. cit.*, 34.

113 Hole, *op. cit.*, 74–5.

114 *Ibid.*, 77.

115 *Ibid.*

116 This figure was supposed to have been advanced in three years, see B. Dale, *The History of the Halifax Permanent Benefit Building Society* (1903), 84, but this is unlikely. Record can be found of £42,644 being advanced between 1864 and 1872, Halifax

Permanent Benefit Building and Investment Society, 11th to 19th Annual Reports, 1864–72.
117 Halifax Permanent Benefit Building and Investment Society, 16th to 19th Annual Reports, 1869–72.
118 Hole, *op. cit.*, 74. There was discussion of Akroyd's idea at Burlington House in June 1862 after he had read his paper. The general opinion was that his houses were remarkable 'both for the convenience of the houses and their picturesque appearance.' A Reverend Mr Molesworth thought Parliament had already done too much for the working classes, and a Dr Strachan believed that the working classes could easily build their own houses if they wanted to do so. Akroyd, *op. cit.*, 807.
119 In strict contradiction to their policy during the 1860s of not advancing on industrially produced housing, a very satisfactory and far more efficient mode of building than the usual.
120 Leeds Permanent Building Society, 1st Annual Report, 1849.
121 S.M. Gaskell, 'The suburb salubrious: town planning in practice' in *British Town Planning: the formative years*, ed. A. Sutcliffe (1981), 30.

The Welsh influence on the building industry in Victorian Liverpool

THOMAS A. ROBERTS

The Welsh influence on the building industry in Victorian Liverpool

THOMAS A. ROBERTS

1 Introduction

Researchers and commentators on the residential growth of Victorian towns have shown how manufacturers, whole industries, independent firms and the activities of like-minded individuals stimulated urban development, and in some instances contributed directly towards it. Such activity was generally confined to single aspects of that process – land speculation, the decision to build, or construction. The urban development of Victorian Liverpool was different and unique in the sense that it was undertaken in the main by Welsh migrants and their families.

By the early nineteenth century Liverpool, with its rows of warehouses eight or nine storeys high, stretching half a mile along the waterfront, was the first outport of the country. The structure and organization of trade and commerce which developed in the years of the slave trade adapted and expanded to meet the demands placed upon them by northern manufacture. With the increase in the volume of trade, both in raw materials and finished goods, came a corresponding increase in the labouring population, and thus in the number of working-class houses in the town.

The 100,000 houses constructed in the Liverpool area during the nineteenth century were built mainly because of Welsh initiative and enterprise using materials imported from North Wales. The Welsh presence in the town increased numerically because of continual migration and commercially because of the influence the Welsh exerted over the building trades and the supply of building materials. The strength of the Welsh community lay in the cohesive influence of chapel life and the persistence of the Welsh language and culture. It is therefore a remarkable testimony to the merits of a migrant community which experienced, in the Liverpool setting, problems of language and culture, that they should emerge as the dominant force in the process of development, achieving the command of most trades and occupations associated with it. This is what has made the urbanization of Victorian Liverpool such a unique event.

Figure 10.   Sherwood's plan of the Town and Township of Liverpool, 1821. (Courtesy Merseyside County Museums.)

The Welsh who came to live permanently in Liverpool brought with them skills associated with building. Many were conversant with the techniques and materials of the building trades. They were better educated and more responsible than other migrant groups, especially the Irish, who came destitute and unable to contribute in any way beyond that of unskilled labour.

The Welsh were to find steady employment in most aspects of building. Those who came to Liverpool from the 1830s onwards were readily absorbed into established Welsh firms. If not, they found employment in positions of trust outside the community, as managers, administrators, foremen and clerks with employers who displayed a marked preference for their diligence, thrift and reliability. Those who came in the early decades of the nineteenth century grew up with the town and shared in its prosperity, rising to positions of influence within their respective chapels. The Welsh chapel in the Liverpool setting, especially those of the Calvinistic Methodists, made an important contribution both to the Welsh community and to the urban development of the town, and this essay examines the interrelationship between building and chapel life.

As North Wales was a rich source of building materials, enterprise and labour, the linkage between Liverpool and the North Wales region consolidated into one business and a single enterprise. Such activity did much to bring this part of the United Kingdom more into line with national economic activity, so that it quickly shed the backwardness it exhibited in the eighteenth century.

The following chapter deals with the Welsh influence in the building industry in Victorian Liverpool. It draws upon the author's working experience of the Liverpool housing market and an earlier research paper submitted to the Department of Economics and Related Studies, University of York, 1977. In addition, recognition is given to the observations of other writers who have examined and commented upon single aspects of development and it pulls the relevant strands together to demonstrate the influence of the Welsh in house-building and its associated trades and industries.

2 The Welsh background

This sales advice appeared in the Liverpool Welsh Paper *Y Cymro* on 3 May 1894.

> The Liverpool Land Company Limited
>
> To Builders & Co – to be sold
> Freehold and 999 years Leasehold in
> lots to suit purchasers in Garston,
> Kirkdale, Walton, Bootle and Seaforth.
> Liberal advances will be made to builders.
> Property letting well in all the locations.
>
> Apply to E Owen, Secretary
> Liverpool Land Company
> 22 Lord Street.

There is nothing unusual in the content of the advertisement except that in earlier years Welsh newspapers, which enjoyed a wide circulation in the Liverpool District, would have carried similar notices in Welsh. However, the example above tells us quite a lot about the evolution of the Liverpool Welsh as a community. It indicates, like the advertisements which accompany it, that employment in the building trades was a prominent feature of Welsh life; that for many in the Welsh community Welsh was no longer the language of business as it had previously been; and that the assimilation of the Welsh into Liverpool society had to a large extent taken place by this date. Yet for almost 100 years Welsh had remained a dominant force and the common medium of communication of a powerful and industrious sector of Liverpool life, a community at the very centre of residential building at its most prolific.

The Welsh language persisted because of the continual flow of North Welsh to the town throughout the whole of the nineteenth century, and the central role of the chapel in the life of that community. Understandably, others in the town's population found difficulty in responding to, indeed, in participating in an industry which for the most part was the domain of migrant Welsh and their families. This situation was particularly true of the Irish who were effectively barred, especially in the early decades, from participating in house-building at a level above that of the common labourer.

Wherever British finance and ingenuity built, the materials and people of North Wales were conspiciously in evidence as important factors in the building process. Few materials, for instance, can claim such universal acceptance as slate, whose insulating properties protected as much against the cold of North America as the heat of the tropics.

Correspondingly, wherever the Welsh migrated they took with them not simply an awareness of such materials but the knowledge and skills associated with their use. In consequence, the contribution of the Welsh to building activity both at the national level and in Liverpool in particular has been substantial, widespread and distinctive. To appreciate the diversity of such a complex activity reference must first be made to the social and economic composition of North Wales in the third quarter of the eighteenth century.

In regard to the geographic location of building materials, the higher areas of Caernarvon, Denbighshire and Merioneth contain large deposits of slate and granite, while in Flint, especially in the region close to the Cheshire Plain, sandstone and lime predominate. Anglesey is somewhat different because of the bands of gneiss (crystalline rock consisting of quartz and feldspar), granite, slate and limestone which run south-west to north-east across the island.

Generally North Wales, with the exception of the high mountain regions which are drift-free, is overlaid with superficial deposits of boulder clay, alluvium and glacial gravel.

Commercially, initial interest centred upon the extraction of zinc, lead and notably copper of which Parys mountain in Anglesey is the most lasting example. By the closing years of the eighteenth century this enterprise controlled the world price of copper, a position not competitively challenged until the early nineteenth century by the Rio Tinto-Zinc Company.[1] Taken together with slate, gravel and brick clays, which made up the bulk of the trade in the Victorian age, there is no doubt that the area, whether mined or quarried, represented a vast resource of essential building supplies and materials needed in the construction industry.

Each commodity in turn began to assume commercial significance when systematically worked in response to outside stimuli, especially in the third quarter of the eighteenth century. By 1760 slate-quarrying was a flourishing and expanding feature of the region's industry and a significant factor of Caernarvon trade. A.H. Dodd's reference to the Meyrick Papers[2] suggests that by the last quarter of the eighteenth century the slate industry was highly organized and its product standardized. The systematic working of slate on the Penrhyn Estate (Caernarvonshire) and the successful reopening in 1764 of Parys Mountain (Anglesey) were examples where reorganization of the labour force was the crucial factor in meeting rising demand. Initially therefore, by remaining labour-intensive, owners and managers avoided the high capital charges incurred whenever new technology and equipment was introduced.

Such action undoubtedly eased the acceptance of Welsh building materials on to a wider market by enabling them to compete favourably, in terms of price and quality, with the traditional materials of other regions. Once these barriers had been effectively breached, and the initial problems of bulk transportation resolved, a firm footing was established at the crucial point prior to the period of most rapid growth within the building supplies industry. Welsh materials and Welsh enterprise were first in line to take advantage of the sustained upward movement in demand which came in response to signals from new and expanding centres of commerce and industry for regular and uniform supplies.

The labour-intensive nature of such enterprises accomplished three things. Taken collectively, it gave a much needed boost to the region's economy in terms of trade and the mobilization of resources; it concentrated what had previously been an agrarian society into relatively large communities; and it meant that the population began moving towards a way of life dependent upon the course of trade and enterprise rather than the weather. Each in turn exposed the population to the important step of migration, later to become the central theme of life on the Celtic fringe.

If social ties dissolved through outward migration, the opposite was true of trade and investment. English landlords, recognizing the potential of what was under their Welsh estates rather than what was on them, became actively involved with mining or quarrying, either personally or by leasing their mineral rights. For instance, Midlands brass manufacturers were by the 1790s heavily committed in Flintshire, while the Liverpool firm of Messrs Worthington & Co. were by 1803 firmly established as the sole concessionaries for the transportation of Penrhyn slate.[3] At this time the Ffestiniog quarries were leased to the Lancashire partnership of William Turner and the Casson Brothers,[4] while the Tan-y-bwlch estate had leased the Rhiw quarry to Samuel Holland.[5] In addition to slate, this enterprise was producing manganese for glass-making and powdered chert for the pottery industry. The opportunity presented by mining and quarrying in terms of investment eventually attracted, although not until 1825, the speculative talents of the eminent banker Nathan Meyer Rothschild. The investment vehicle took the form of the 'Welsh Slate, Copper and Lead Mining Company' – a title which left little to chance.[6]

In volume terms by this date, 345,000 tons of slate (equal to 500 cargoes) were annually being cleared from the purpose-built Port Penrhyn.[7] Like the Pennants at Port Penrhyn, the Assheton Smiths reconstructed Felin Helli (Port Dinorwic) through which they distributed the products of the Llanberis quarries.[8] The harbour facilities at Caernarvon were subsequently enlarged to take the increased draft of slate ships and facilitate the effective handling of a greater volume of traffic.[9]

The duration of the Napoleonic Wars changed the economy of Wales by improving the outlook both for mining and agriculture. In terms of organization and labour it brought the region more in line with the English agrarian experience, where enclosure consolidated the movement off the land. However, delayed and abandoned building projects led to a reduction in demand for products of the quarrying industry. Consequently, for the suppliers of building materials and the building trades as a whole, these were lean and depressing years.[10] The problems were further compounded by the duty imposed by government on brick and slate.[11]

In the depression following the Napoleonic Wars the relationship between quarrying and agriculture reversed as marginal land became uneconomic and demand for building materials improved. The previous heavy reliance upon agriculture decreased, resulting in a constant and sustained drift away from the land. The movement was to the new and expanding mining and quarrying districts or out of North Wales altogether; the latter in response to a backlog of building resulting from the war itself, and the opportunities created by the new growth centres of manufacture and commerce. For example, to maintain the commercial importance of Liverpool as the first outport of the nation required the construction of new deep-water berths and improvements to the existing network of docks and wharves. Quite apart from which, a ready market existed for the skilled and enterprising to build houses or contract for public works and ecclesiastical building.

A new social order emerged in North Wales which was directly related to migration. It was especially influential where the change of economic emphasis had been disruptive and prolonged. The roots of the movement, which cast doubt on the existing social structure, were given expression through the religious revivals of the time. Here community bonding and cohesion were increasingly represented by Nonconformity, whose influence brought stability to family life. The ascendancy, however, of the chapel as a central element of North Wales life, unlike the experience in the south, was long in taking hold in the region. Not until the Bala settlement of 1784 did Nonconformity become synonymous with the new mining districts.[12]

The strength of the religious revival was expressed by attendance at the existing chapels, the extent of new chapel building, and the place each occupied as a 'living centre' within the community in terms of religion, education and Welsh culture. In the wake of the religious awakening many old customs and traditions disappeared. In their place were entrenched the virtues of sobriety, thrift and deference to authority, and these became the social criteria of the new society. On reflection, it could hardly have been otherwise, especially in closed communities where the pulpit inveighed from the outset against excessive drinking and extolled the virtues of a well-ordered family life. For many, the chapel provided facilities for social intercourse, debate, education and religion within an atmosphere of mutual benefit and self-help.

The cultural background of the Welsh enabled those who emigrated to perform a productive and responsive role wherever they settled. J. Glyn Davies suggests[13] that this was because in the Liverpool experience there existed as far back as the end of the eighteenth century 'a non-coincidence of culture and economic strata' between the Welsh and English. This was in direct reference to the Welsh being poor but generally well-educated while their educated English counterparts were materially much better off. In effect, the Welsh associated intellectually with a comparatively high social order, but belonged financially to the lowest. In addition many appear to have experienced problems of language and this factor comes out clearly in the 1847 report on Welsh education.[14] While drawing attention to the deplorable state of the system, the report identified two major obstacles preventing the success of the labouring classes in acquiring a sound knowledge of English. Firstly, Nonconformist parents were reluctant to send their children to schools of the National Society where the emphasis was distinctly Anglican. Correspondingly, the non-denominational British Society which the Welsh favoured found extreme difficulty in persuading English landlords of Welsh estates to provide finance and ground on which to build. Landlords who were committed to the cause of Anglicization remained reluctant to give the British Society widespread support. Secondly, a general consensus placed the blame directly on the twin features of Welsh life: the persistence of the Welsh language and the influence of Nonconformist dissent.

The problems of education and language were largely overcome by Nonconformist Methodists, who placed great emphasis upon the concept of the English Sunday School. This was given a Welsh image by admitting adult pupils and so attracting the systematic teaching of the Welsh language as a basis for scripture, the introduction of rudimentary mathematics, and eventually the inclusion of English as part of the curriculum.

The characteristics, therefore, of the Welsh migrant resulted from his connection with the Adult School education system, the discipline of the chapel, and an ordered environment to which he was expected both to respond and contribute. Consequently, he arrived on the Liverpool scene with perhaps materially little more then enough for a few days but well equipped to take employment in a variety of trades. Compared with his Irish immigrant counterpart, his chances of finding gainful employment were high. Apart from the influential network of the Welsh community, non-Welsh employers considered the Welsh dependable, respectable and cheap to employ. In consequence, many rose to positions of responsibility and influence within non-Welsh firms.

a. The Welsh in Liverpool

The habitat of the Liverpool Welsh mirrored the communities of North Wales. They displayed in the course of events a remarkable insular attitude which was further entrenched by the persistence of the Welsh language in these areas. Yet they could readily engage without reservation in the task of building and constructing the very fabric of the town's residential form. Welsh factors were present from the very beginning when residential building, and for that matter construction in general, took off in the 1830s and 1840s. The sustained upward movement persisted long enough to establish members of the Welsh community in all trades and occupations associated with construction, especially the house-building sector. More often than not they aspired to positions of influence within individual trades where their standing was further entrenched by the use of Welsh as the common medium of business communication.

In part it may have been a deliberate attempt by some to keep the business within the community and thus prosper the Welsh cause in the town, but in all probability it was a matter of convenience. There was in fact a genuine difficulty experienced by early migrants in being understood. This was not the case later in the century when English was taught in Welsh schools. Glyn Davies recounts that 'pauper' was always pronounced 'paper' and 'lazy' as 'lessy' with the Welsh idiom being reflected in English sayings such as, 'I never laugh so many since I don't care when'.[15] For all this the Welsh intonation was a distinct feature of Liverpool life and remained unaffected by the accent of the town's dockland – the now familiar

Liverpool 'scouse'. Many sought employment amongst Welsh-speaking colleagues but whatever their occupation Welsh remained the language of the home.[16] Succeeding generations, however, took as a matter of course to the social habits of the English of comparable financial background. Generally speaking, the Welsh who settled in Liverpool between 1820 and 1880 would be closely associated with the period of the town's most rapid physical development; in consequence many would share in its rising prosperity. Furthermore, the second-generation Liverpool Welsh prospered by building on the foundations of their émigré parents. It was little wonder that Liverpool was claimed to be the 'Capital of Wales'.

In Liverpool the role of the chapel was significant. The diverse composition of individual congregations, which included self-employed craftsmen, proprietors of small businesses and trusted employees of others, was in marked contrast to the company villages of the mines and quarries with their heavy reliance upon one employer and the fortunes of a single enterprise.

The Welsh Chapel in Liverpool was not simply a dispenser of religious instruction, but a point of introduction and access to employment in numerous trades and businesses, the owners of which had struck out on their own. Many such associations were to flourish into long-term working agreements which would ultimately place them at the very centre of residential building. According to P.J. Waller, Anglesey men ran Liverpool's biggest building firms. Proprietors such as Owen Elias and David Hughes were cases in point. Both were members of the Calvinistic Methodist Chapel, a movement which ultimately came to exert a strong influence upon house-building in the town.[17]

Religious fervour in the Liverpool context was given political expression through chapel debating societies where the faithful restated an allegiance to return, as they had done in Wales, Liberal members of parliament, a following ultimately to be attracted to the socialist cause.[18] However, for those newly arrived the chapel was representative of the new order in life, the community provider and the single imperishable link with the homeland.

The rapid and sustained increase in Liverpool's population was occasioned by migration, of which the Welsh contingent was only a part; migration came from outside the region and not simply from the surrounding towns. According to the 1881 census return the joint population of Liverpool and Manchester numbered 1,070,000 and as Ravenstein points out,[19] rural Lancashire with only 1,315,000 inhabitants could hardly have been expected to provide a positive recruitment ground for labour, especially as numerous other large and growing towns existed in that part of England.

Increasingly in the nineteenth century Liverpool became a centre for those fleeing destitution, the result of the decline in the traditional rural way of life. For the Irish, who flooded into the town because of a succession of failed potato harvests and the total lack of alternative means of support, this simply meant emigrate or starve. The Welsh situation was less desperate and hence there was a marked contrast between the two groups. Migration for them was linked to the expectation and the prospect of a better life in which their individual skills would play an important role. Migration into Liverpool reached its peak in the 1840s. In the last quarter of 1846 some 9,000 utterly destitute Irish arrived, with the problem further exacerbated in the twelve months July 1847 to July 1848 when 300,000 more landed, to stretch the town's already limited resources.[20] Some, of course, were absorbed directly into the community, sufficient in number to establish a distinct Irish colony located along the tidewater area. But the majority dispersed to other regions or crossed the Atlantic as emigrants to North America.

The migratory flow was supplemented by the Welsh, who came in increasing numbers following the collapse of the iron industry in the 1820s and the demise of the traditional Welsh textile industry by mid century.[21] Of this steady and regular flow of North Welsh continually arriving in the port many took up permanent residence. In determining the distribution and composition of this migration Ravenstein records thirty years later:

> Proportionally to its population North Wales furnished a larger contingent to Liverpool than any other part of the United Kingdom, for out of every 100 natives of North Wales enumerated in other parts of England and Wales, as many as seventeen per cent resided in Liverpool in 1881, that was 18,297 of the total population of 552,500 were Welsh born and had migrated.[22]

In large measure this was consistent with the continued improvement in coastwise passenger transport. As early as 1821 a daily service was in operation in the summer to Bagillt.[23] The service was extended the following year to sailings once a week to Beaumaris, Bangor and Caernarvon. It was not long before three to four boats were plying daily between Liverpool and the Menai Straits. With the journey time to Liverpool considerably shortened, and regular summer and winter sailings maintained, practically all Welsh emigration to New York and Philadelphia went via Liverpool, in preference to Caernarvon. In addition, during the summer months there was a busy emigrant traffic on ships returning to Quebec in the Canadian timber trade.

Provided the necessary £3–£4 was available for the Atlantic crossing, in addition to provisions sufficient for the voyage, Welsh agents in Liverpool were on hand to arrange the passage and organize temporary accommodation. This traffic created a whole new set of business opportunities for the Welsh already established in the town.

Language was a standard form of recognition and the strict adherence to temperance a prominent feature of Welsh boarding house advertisements. For those who sought permanent residence such hospitality was often accompanied by the prospect of employment. Alan Conway notes that the network was not exclusive to Liverpool.[24] It was maintained through recommendation to similar establishments in the United States where the Welsh enjoyed a reputation for hard work and where their skills were much in demand. Conway writes:

> In the northern industrial centres, particularly in the mines and foundries, the Welsh remained for long the elite of the labour force. Most skilled (Welshmen) rose to managerial positions in charge of semi-skilled or unskilled Hungarians, Poles and Irish.[25]

The Welsh who settled in Liverpool found regular and continuous employment in house-building and construction.[26] The fluctuating natures of these two major employers were not necessarily consistent with one another. However, the workforce were sufficiently mobile to adapt their skills to movements in demand for their labours.

In the period 1827 to 1847 a simultaneous and sustained boom was experienced in both sectors which stretched the existing resources of manpower and materials. Firstly, as a result of a series of short but intense periods of building, there was an unprecedented increase in the number of cheap working-class dwellings. The first occurred roughly between 1827 and 1833 and the second between 1841 and 1844. This was partly in response to demand and higher rents but more especially, from the late 1830s, in anticipation of new legislation (finally introduced in 1842 and 1846) to regulate residential building in the town. Secondly, this coincided with a 50 per cent increase in dock facilities. In this instance demand was not simply for stonemasons who could carve stone as carpenters shaped wood; dock-building, like housing, required armies of labourers, bricklayers and joiners.

The Welsh, with their close association to both builders' materials and allied skills, were well placed to participate in the physical and commercial expansion of the town.

3 Liverpool. The context of the city

The heavy and continual stream of migrants, even before the crises of the 1840s, had identified the pauper accommodation abounding in the town, with all its attendant inadequacies. Legislative control was seen as a solution, with the first curative steps being taken with the reorganization, in 1835, of a corporate municipal structure which had been in existence for over 450 years. It abolished ancient privilege through an elected council with freedom to deal with the most pressing and immediate problems of inadequate sanitation resulting from a total disregard for planning, unsound building and unfit accommodation. The target districts were the increasing areas of slums around the docks where contagious disease was both endemic and pervasive. To determine the exact cause and extent of the problems and to facilitate a programme of action, a surveyor was appointed to mark the official start to clearing structurally unfit dwellings. The task was doubly difficult because of the vociferous objections of landlords and the lack of provision for those displaced by clearance. It merely served to transform marginal slum areas into even worse slums than those cleared, as displaced, problem and destitute families were squeezed into them. Public washhouses were provided and, to a degree, supervision was imposed to regulate new housing, but general complacency had ascendance over effective proposals to deal with the situation. The problems were not new but the scale and pace of events were such that trial and error loomed large in both legislation and practice. The experiences of Liverpool in the 1840s suggested that the point had long since passed when the problem would have demanded less stringent action.

The report on health and sanitation in 1840 observed at first hand the living conditions of the labouring poor and destitute. The conclusions jolted the prosperous sector of the community into considering positive action. Population density in some districts was then equal to 100,000 per square mile, the highest in the country. In these areas one in twenty-five suffered each year from contagious disease, which in most cases proved fatal.[27] The people worst affected were those living close to the docks, where gainful employment could be as little as two days in seven.[28] Low incomes resulted in undernourishment, overcrowding and poor sanitation, the very factors which produce a high incidence and frequency of disease. The dwellings provided in these districts were mainly the court or yard type of

Figure 11.   No. 7 Court, Hunter Street, in 1933; now the site of the Gerard Gardens flats. (Courtesy Merseyside County Museums.)

accommodation. The system evolved partly through infilling of the existing urban fabric, initially with single-storey lean-to buildings and later with planned schemes of tightly packed courts which stretched across the narrow field widths of the Liverpool Parish. Each court block contained from twelve to twenty units, and in general were grouped two courts deep with a connecting passageway. The dwellings measured approximately 12 ft × 12 ft, one room per floor, usually three storeys high and erected back-to-back with the dwellings in the adjoining court. Low rents were a feature of such 'Salt Box' housing, the principal type of accommodation for the working classes prior to the bye-law regulations of the 1840s. The heaviest concentration of such housing was to be found in Vauxhall Ward. As Treble notes, by the 1840s the proportion of houses letting at under £12 per annum in this district was as high as 71 per cent while in Scotland and Toxteth wards it was around 60 per cent.[29] In 1801 rents of £12 per annum and less applied to 7,677 of the 11,466 dwellings in the town. By 1841 the figure had increased to 11,880 but in a population of houses three times greater. B.D. White records that only 36 per cent of Liverpool's new housing stock in that year was built for rent at under £12 per annum.[30] Twelve years later rentals in this category accounted for less than 6 per cent of all new houses built. It was to remain in low percentage figures through to 1914.

116

According to the *Liverpool Mercury* the movement towards higher rents was well under way by the late 1830s. On 14 September 1838 it reported

> that the Liverpool building trade was preoccupied with constructed houses for the middle classes at rents above £25 per annum . . . the fact that most houses were taken up in most neighbourhoods as fast as they were habitable indicated that at least in the short term such a trend was likely to continue.[31]

This significant and sustained upward shift in the proportion of new houses at higher rentals was partly related to the increased cost of building, but more especially it was in response to higher investment returns achieved with larger properties. A large proportion of the 64 per cent of new housing erected in 1841 at rents above £12 per annum were located on green-field sites within the 1835 boundary extension. This reluctance, or inability, on the part of the building industry to keep pace with the quantity of new houses at rents which the labouring classes could afford was well illustrated by the number of people per dwelling. As early as 1790 the figure was already on the increase; a situation which persisted almost uninterrupted through to the 1850s. Set against this background the reality of what was taking place can be judged by reference to table 13.

Table 13   Population and housing returns for Liverpool Parish, 1801–51

census year	inhabited houses	population	no. of persons per inhabited house	numbers per family	no. of persons/ inhabited house England & Wales
1801	11,446	77,653	6.8	4.6	5.6
1811	15,589	94,376	6.0	4.6	5.7
1821	19,007	118,972	6.2	5.5	5.7
1831	25,732	165,175	6.4	5.4	5.6
1841	32,079	223,003	7.0	5.6	5.4
1851	35,293	258,236	7.3	5.3	5.5

Source: 1801–51 *Census Extract for England and Wales*; B.D. White, *History of the Corporation of Liverpool 1835–1914* (1951).

According to White,[32] 18,000 houses were built in Liverpool between 1841 and 1851, only a small number of which were constructed within the boundary of the Liverpool Parish. Consequently, those who could not afford the higher rents in the newer districts (and these included many migrant families), crowded tighter into the insanitary environment prevailing in that area. This is further emphasized when a comparison is made between family size and the numbers accounted for in each dwelling. While the average number per family rose from 4.6 in 1801 to 5.3 by mid century the numbers per dwelling rose to almost the equivalent of three families to every two houses.

In 1832 the parliamentary boundary was extended and in 1835 a municipal adjustment was made to coincide with it. The new districts were equal to twice the old Liverpool. The complexities of further urban growth and the projection of the existing experience compelled action. The causes of the recurrence of cholera and typhus were fivefold – overcrowding, inadequate accommodation, a lack of waste disposal facilities, inadequate water supply, and general poverty occasioned by the persistent low level of subsistence.

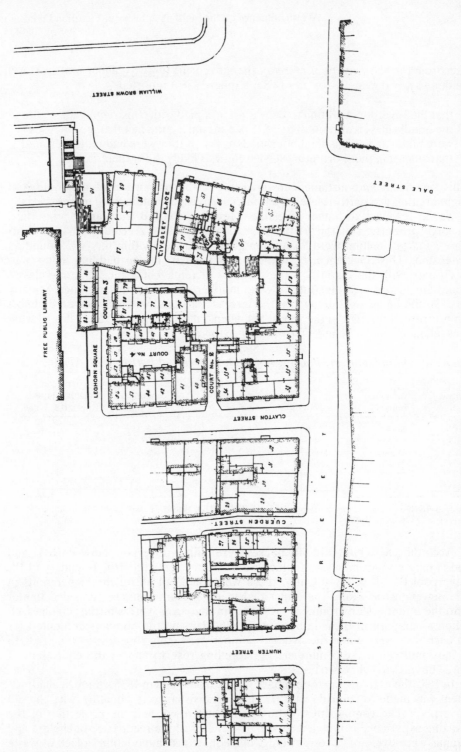

Figure 12.   Infill court dwellings, Byrom Street, in 1877, from a lithograph by Thos. W. Riby, Liverpool Improvement Plan, 1877–8. (Courtesy Merseyside County Museums.)

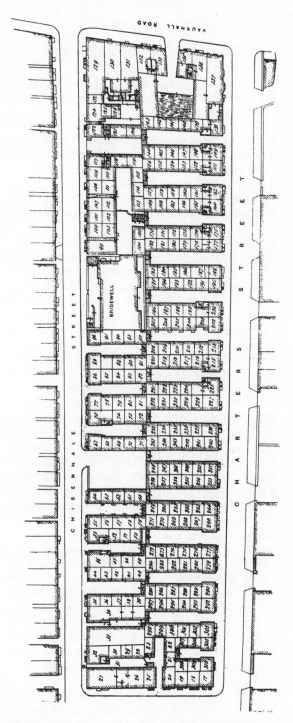

Figure 13.   Planned scheme of court dwellings, Vauxhall Ward, erected c. 1830, from a lithograph by Thos. W. Riby, Liverpool Improvement Plan, 1877–8. (Courtesy Merseyside County Museums.)

Cholera and typhus between them for the five years 1839 to 1844 accounted for 35 deaths per thousand compared with the national average of 23 from all causes. Typhus was directly attributable to poverty, overcrowding and bad hygiene, the worst examples of which could be found in the numerous courts and cellar dwellings in the town.[33]

The Corporation Surveyor's Report of 1842 computes the extent of the housing problem. There were 1,982 courts or yards containing 10,692 dwellings, about one-third of all dwellings. In regard to the much criticized cellar dwellings 20,000 people inhabited 6,000 cellars, although only 10 per cent of these were in courts.[34] Consequently if courts in general were bad other sectors of the housing market where the remaining 90 per cent of cellars were situated must have been much worse. This suggests that at least 50 per cent of the town's housing stock was defective.

a. Municipal reform

W.H. Duncan, medical practitioner, and Samuel Holmes, a local builder, drew upon their professional experiences to become two of the most vociferous advocates of reform. In 1843, when reporting to the commissioners enquiring into the conditions prevailing in large towns, they placed sanitation as the first priority. The private bill promoted in parliament in 1842 enabled the municipal corporation henceforth to legislate appropriate action. The key was to be the control of new residential building and the imposition of higher standards on the worst of the existing stock. Cellar dwellings and courts were particularly objectionable. These were the first steps towards better living conditions in urban areas, sharply criticized by builders and landlords and viewed with some scepticism by the general public. What was happening was a declaration of future minimum standards, which inevitably came to represent the maximum standard which the investing public and their working-class tenants would consider equitable.

The most significant contribution to urban renewal in the 1840s was that of the Liverpool Sanitary Act 1846 which remedied weaknesses in the 1842 Liverpool Health of the Town Act.[35] More stringent regulations were introduced: new streets were to be at least 30 ft wide instead of 24 ft and all cellars, a continual aggravation of an insanitary environment, were henceforth to have their ceiling height at least 3 ft above the level of the pavement. Furthermore, landlords could now be compelled to connect court drains with the main sewer. To ensure compliance, an inspector of nuisances and a borough engineer were appointed to identify and eliminate potential sources of disease in the town.

The 1840s were indeed to prove the watershed which changed the course of future development in Liverpool. Samuel Holmes, in his evidence to the committee on sanitary conditions of the labouring population of England (1843) stated that: 'Liverpool already possesses a Building Act which is strictly enforced and a different and improved mode of building has resulted from its salutory provisions.'[36] He also pointed out that the officers appointed to enforce the Act were sometimes deceived. Two examples are worth mentioning.[37] In a yard of six houses he could recall that 2 tons of lime were used in construction whereas at least 12 tons was the norm, and it was not unknown for loam with a sprinkling of lime in it to be substituted for mortar. The second was in reference to the statutory 9 inch thickness of party walls where it was frequently the practice to build two $4\frac{1}{2}$ inch brick breadths separately, i.e. not bound together, one being built with sand and loam. Following certification by the building inspector that the house complied

vith the building regulations, one brick breadth was taken down and the materials
used elsewhere.

Henceforth yards and courts would never enjoy the confidence of the municipal
authority, which contended that they were synonymous with the ills of the town.
Although they continued to be built they were not actively encouraged.[38] Initially
they decreased as a percentage of the stock as alternative new forms of housing
entered the market, and later numerically because they were located in areas
required for industry and new dock facilities. Throughout the remainder of the
nineteenth century they were to remain target housing for clearance.

. Housing types: the Welsh influence in design

Out of imposed functional order through legislation and resultant building regulation evolved a design of house which would herald the demise of the court system.
Such a design satisfied two central issues. On the one hand were the standards
implied and demanded by legislation, designed to be partly curative as well as
preventive, and therefore unregulated by market forces. On the other, new housing
would be built, not because of any increase in the population, but only if the
balance between rents and incomes was equitable. Rents therefore had to be at
a level which tenants could afford, yet provide a return on investment sufficient
to warrant the speculation.

From the 1840s a belt of gridiron streets of terraced housing was erected between
the outlying suburbs and the overcrowded courts of the inner urban centre. The
terraced cottage was a distinctly working-class housing type which evolved as a
direct response by private landlords and builders to imposed building regulations
and the market.

Welsh enterprise, an established feature of Liverpool house-building by the 1840s,
recognized the significance for the industry of legislation which rendered the court
and yard system obsolete overnight. Welsh initiative produced a house plan which
complied with the provisions of the new legislation in terms of the distribution
of internal space and measurement (room size and ceiling height), the size and
location of windows, as well as building regulations.

The four-roomed, two-storey accommodation contained within a simple building
envelope was the initial response for a house design which matched the criteria
upon which the first mass market for cheap housing could be supplied. In terms
of cost, Samuel Holmes computed that the new building regulations, excluding
the land charge, did not add above 10 per cent to the cost of building such working-
class cottages.[39] In terms of street plan it marked a decisive break with traditional
back dwellings and airless courts. For the working class, not at the bottom of
the social and economic ladder, it provided the opportunity to emulate the better
off and be housed in terraces which fronted on to open-ended streets where the
width between parallel rows could be three times that of the courts. Such small
box-like houses were basic and functional, cheaply produced, but sound in construction with few decorative or distinguishing features. In these compact dwellings,
where the total floor space could be less than 400 square feet, the living room
was used as a work-space with the area under the stairs utilized for storage; brick
or tile paving was used over the whole of the ground floor.

A six-roomed cottage (three bedrooms), although not so prominent at first,
merged in the 1850s to dominate the market henceforth for new working-class
housing. Here the parlour was distinct from the kitchen and this provided separate

Figure 14.   Gridiron terraced housing, West Derby Road, looking west. (Courtesy Merseyside County Museums.)

Figure 15.   Non-forecourted terraced cottages, Beacon Lane area, Everton. (Courtesy Merseyside County Museums.)

Figure 16.   Six-roomed terraced cottage, Gwydis Street, Toxteth. (Courtesy Robert Hook.)

Figure 17.   Six-roomed terraced housing with chequered brickwork, Arundel Street, Toxteth. (Courtesy Robert Hook.)

living and working areas as well as the opportunity for more elaborate furnishings. The parlour was the best room and as a consequence had higher quality specifications which were often extended to include the hallway. Usual features were decorative cornices, ceiling roses and bosses at the base of the relieving arch in the hall, deep skirting, wider architraves than the rest of the house, a good fireplace and alcove cupboards. The parlour and hall tended to be the only ground-floor areas where a suspended floor was used; joinery and brickwork were generally of good quality.[40]

Doors to the main rooms were of heavy pine, and usually comprised four panels with moulded surrounds. The large rear room was the kitchen, generally plain and functional in design, containing the cooking range and built with a solid red or black quarry-tiled floor. An alcove beside the range had a floor-to-ceiling cupboard. These larger cottages had a rear scullery extension, containing the only tap in the house, and a shallow sink. Windows were of small panes, usually sash without weights. Staircases were steep, which helped to make the cottages more compact, and usually, though not always, they were without windows. Later versions had a copper for laundry, some outbuildings such as a cold store, a privy and other enclosures built to one side of a rear walled yard. A significant feature of the design of these cottages, especially those erected by the Welsh, was the shallow pitch of the slate roof and the inclusion of a blind window over adjacent front doors.

These dwellings have been variously described as Welsh or Welsh cottage.[41] Any similarities between the design of the North Wales cottage and the houses in urbanized Everton, Kirkdale and Toxteth were purely coincidental. However, this is not an unwarranted association when account is taken of the attitude of the Welsh peasant to his housing.[42] Here the fundamental issues were clear. Social, climatic and geographic considerations combined to produce functional architecture. In practice the Welsh peasant knew what he wanted and he built as simply as possible, deriving practical rather than aesthetic value through the use of locally available materials.

It was much the same in the Liverpool setting where new initiatives in housing and the mobilization of resources owed much to the ingenuity of the resident Welsh community. Furthermore, the basic materials used in the construction of these houses had their origins in the Welsh mountains.

Through the addition of a bay window, and by increasing the overall floor area, builders transformed the basic design of the six-roomed terrace cottage into that of a house. The external appearance of these dwellings to the 1880s was distinguished by the use of stone for cornices, gutters and bay windows. The increased angle of the pitch of the roof compared to that of the cottage was also a notable feature. The extensive use of buff (white) brick in the last quarter of the century enabled a variety of colours to be intricately arranged in a single elevation, either as patterned brickwork or brick banding. These houses represent some of the most elaborately decorated working-class terraced property built in England in the last century. The average value of property of this type in the 1850s ranged between £140–£160 rising to £180–£220 by the 1870s.[43]

Derivatives of these basic styles became synonymous with accommodation for the working class not only in Liverpool but in many industrial towns. Although it would be difficult to claim that all such designs originated in Liverpool, it would be true to say that Liverpool builders were amongst the earliest exponents of their

Figure 18.   Six-roomed terraced housing, Chirkdale Street, Kirkdale, with ground plan and house plan. (Photograph courtesy Robert Hook.)

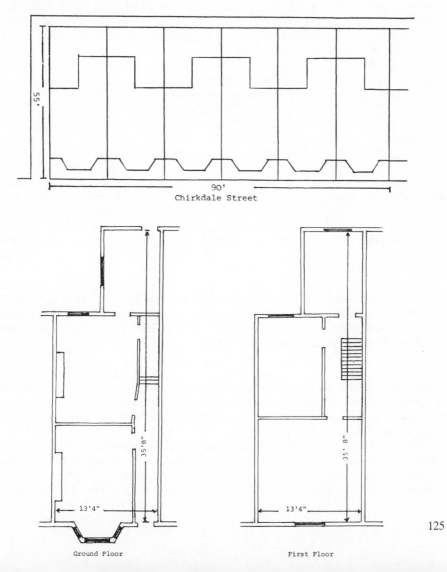

55'

90'

Chirkdale Street

35'8"

13'4"

Ground Floor

35'8"

13'4"

First Floor

merits. Welsh enterprise and initiative took advantage of the opportunities presented by the urban expansion of the town. Sir Giles Scott stated in 1944 that '90 per cent of contemporary Liverpool had been built in the last 100 years, and that the Welsh had played a large part in that period'.[44]

4 The Welsh and the building industry

The publishers of the 1821 Liverpool Town Map felt that four townships then outside the Liverpool Parish Boundary warranted recognition – Kirkdale and Everton to the north and north-east, West Derby in the east and Toxteth in the south. Each was expanding in response to the demands of speculative development. Even by this early date the white stuccoed villas of merchants and traders, on their elevated positions along Everton Brow, were under threat from working-class housing already in command of the lower slopes. By the late 1830s they had lost their uninterrupted views over the Mersey estuary to the Welsh hills under the constant onslaught of urban development. Parliamentary and subsequent municipal boundary extensions in the 1830s consolidated a movement then being experienced in most districts adjacent to the old town.

Table 14   Houses and population within the Liverpool Parish Boundary and the townships of Kirkdale, Everton, West Derby and Toxteth, 1841–91

	Liverpool Parish inhabited houses	population	persons per house	townships inhabited houses	population	persons per house
1841	32,079	223,003	6.9	12,182	71,648	5.9
1851	35,293	258,236	7.3	21,099	129,713	6.1
1861	37,041	269,742	7.3	28,740	174,196	6.1
1871	34,293	238,411	6.9	44,110	254,994	5.8
1881	31,634	210,164	6.6	60,673	342,344	5.6
1891	25,293	156,981	6.2	65,941	360,999	5.5

The 1835 boundary lasted until 1895 when Walton, Wavertree, rural West Derby and Toxteth were incorporated.
Source: *Census extracts*, 1841–91.

The extent of Welsh residential building, the place of the Welsh in house-building, and the characteristics and distinctiveness of their contribution, can be judged by reviewing house-building over the period 1831 to 1891 in the four townships of Kirkdale, Everton, West Derby and Toxteth.

a. Urban development
In the Kirkdale district the extent and composition of building was well illustrated by the detailed 1848 Ordnance Survey. The concentration of cramped courts and narrow lanes, a product of pre-bye-law housing provision, mingled uneasily with factories and workshops, especially at the point where the Leeds–Liverpool canal connects with the deep-water basin at Stanley Dock. The commercial and industrial emphasis of these sites would change many times over in response to new initiatives in manufacture and the increased demand for warehousing.

Manufacturers, especially those who relied heavily upon the transportation of bulk raw materials, sited their works along the canal, often well into the countryside, or wedged themselves between it and the docks. Such would include kilns for firing tiles and bricks, processing works for soap, dyes and chemicals, foundries, small ship-repair and fitting-out yards, as well as warehouses and bonded stores. Textiles were represented by Kirkman's Union Cotton Mill, referred to for many years as the Welsh factory on account of the origins of its workforce.

Beside all this new development traditional industry still flourished; for instance there were the sandstone quarries at Bankhall, worked extensively by Welsh quarry-men in response to local demand for stone sills and lintels. A number of quarries sited on the higher ground off Netherfield Road supplied facing stone for public buildings. Close by were the Georgian villas of Northumberland Terrace, Church Street and San Domingo Lane where the houses and their commanding positions were greatly admired. Many were demolished and the ground divided into building plots; those which remained were quickly hemmed in with rows of houses and small tenements.[45] Once Victorian house-building gathered momentum, rural villages and the green environment between were bridged systematically in response to the ever-increasing demand for building land. Roscommon Street, for example, had by 1835 already connected Great Howard Street with Netherfield Road South. Here Robert Evans was erecting houses on infill sites as late as the 1850s and building further east as Boundary Street acquired residential significance as a major urban artery. The urbanization of Kirkdale was closely associated with the north-ward extension to the system of docks and warehouses. Because of the dualistic nature of development up to the 1860s the district did not experience the volume of house-building recorded by other areas. This was to come into its own in the 1870s and 1880s when residential development spread inland towards the north and north-east. The nett addition to the housing stock in Kirkdale in these decades was about 6,000 dwellings. The true extent of house-building, however, was much greater because a large number of the 8,000 dwellings demolished in Liverpool between 1872 and 1891 had been situated in Kirkdale.[46]

The adjacent town of Bootle, to the north, had extended by the last quarter of the nineteenth century to meet and eventually mingle with Kirkdale in one continuous, uninterrupted band of housing and industry. The largely residential areas of Seaforth, Waterloo and Crosby further north would become the focus for speculative house-building undertaken by the sons and grandsons of these early Welsh builders.

Some 60 per cent of Everton's housing stock was constructed in the 1850s and 1860s. Liverpool town maps and associated street names clearly indicate that residential development was conceived as a series of individual interlinked estates. An interesting social phenomenon which accompanied this urbanization was the number of Welsh households which congregated in Everton. Gore's directories record the extent of the Welsh presence in individual streets which enforces the claim that Everton in the nineteenth century was the Goshen of the Cambrian race.[47] Previously, Welsh families herded with the Irish along the tidewater areas, hemmed in by the cramped courts and narrow alleyways of an age before building control brought some semblance of order to the expansion of the town.

The Welsh, with their strong Nonconformist principles, wished to distance themselves from the strange tinker ways of the Irish.[48] It was the Irish addiction to the beer shop and the public house which was so alien and in marked contrast.[49] Such establishments occupied the corner sites at most major street intersections

Table 15   Housing and population returns

	Kirkdale district, 1831–91 inhabited houses	population	no. of persons per inhabited house	Everton district, 1831–91 inhabited houses	population	no. of persons per inhabited house
1831	364	2,562	7.0	737	4,511	6.1
1841	690	4,268	6.2	1,680	9,221	5.5
1851	1,440	9,893	6.9	4,267	25,513	6.0
1861	2,542	16,135	6.3	9,288	54,848	5.9
1871	5,220	32,978	6.3	16,339	90,937	5.6
1881	9,793	58,145	5.9	19,133	109,812	5.7
1891	11,368	66,131	5.8	19,981	110,556	5.5

	West Derby district, 1831–91 inhabited houses	population	no. of persons per inhabited house	Toxteth district, 1831–91 inhabited houses	population	no. of persons per inhabited house
1831				3,814	24,067	6.3
1841	2,898	16,864	5.8	6,914	41,295	5.9
1851	5,652	32,973	5.8	9,740	61,334	6.3
1861	6,378	36,527	5.7	10,532	66,686	6.3
1871	9,177	50,687	5.5	13,374	80,392	6.0
1881	12,752	67,727	5.3	18,995	106,660	5.6
1891	15,231	76,971	5.0	19,361	107,341	5.5

Source: *Census Extract* 1841–91; *Gore's Directory* 1841.

in Vauxhall Ward; especially along Scotland Road, Stanley Road and the streets running parallel and adjacent to the docks. Here local publicans were in strict competition with one another as the social centre of the local community.

Public houses, although never an endangered species even in Nonconformist districts, were almost outnumbered by the frequency of Welsh Chapels.[50] Owen Elias, a prominent builder, held strong reservations about including public houses on residential estates.[51] He believed that they exerted a detrimental effect upon residents and consequently upon the neighbourhood. As a business man, however, he could simply have been catering to a particular market.

The construction of working-class houses in Everton enabled Welsh families to congregate in a more pleasant environment. The rents were appreciably higher than the £12 per annum for accommodation within the old town boundary or close to the docks. Nevertheless the Welsh were both able and willing to meet the higher charges. It was no wonder that the building trades in the 1840s were kept fully extended in order to satisfy a market for houses in excess of £12 per annum.

Higher rents achieved for the new property had a resounding impact upon the local housing market and eased the introduction of a new housing layout based upon uniform housing contained in open-ended streets instead of courts and yards or multi-occupied premises. Similarly the improved level of rent absorbed the increase in cost required to build houses in compliance with the new bye-laws. The Welsh families were sufficiently numerous to sustain that demand in Everton and encourage the movement towards better housing to the point of general acceptance by the rest of the population of Liverpool..

This shift towards higher rents was observed by Treble who comments: 'In 1846 out of 3,460 houses completed that year only 710 were for letting at rents under £12 per annum, while 2,328 were erected for letting between £12 and £25 per annum.'[52] House-building was heavily concentrated in the Everton district in 1846.[53] Clearly this scale of rentable values applies here. Although Everton house rents in the main would only have been marginally higher, probably in the range of £12–£16 per annum,[54] it was nevertheless a margin sufficient to attract investment.

David Hughes, originally a journeyman joiner, and a close associate and supplier of bricks and clay products to Elias, had his own brickworks on the north side of the town in competition with another Welshman, David Jenkins of Great Homer Street. They set up their enterprises to take advantage of the abundant quantity of brick clays to be found between Great Homer Street and the Mersey. In general, however, Liverpool bricks were of lower standard than those produced around Ruabon.[55] To improve the quality Liverpool manufacturers, and they could have included Hughes and Jenkins, imported brick clays from North Wales for firing in Liverpool stacks.[56]

Owen Elias had extensive interests in house-building. In consequence, quite apart from the claim that he was a champion of the Welsh cause in the town, he has been variously described as a land speculator, builders' financier and house-builder. Arriving in Liverpool in the 1830s, he was to be involved with one form of residential speculation or another until his death in 1880. He was assisted by numerous business associates during a career that spanned some 50 years but none were more notable than with his son William. This firm was most productive in the Walton area where their model houses on the three estates in the vicinity of County Road are so titled that the first letter of each street taken together spell the names of members of the firm.[57] Such activity was not confined solely to the principals of the firm, for two clerks employed by Owen Elias and Partners were also building on their own account in the Edge Hill district and on Nursery Fields, Walton.[58] Similarly Edward Williams, 325–327 Westminster Road,[59] and Rowland Williams, 244 Westminster Road, were building close by their yards in the Everton and Walton districts, while Henry Roberts, 9 Tegid Street, Everton, built six-roomed houses in this street and adjoining Aubrey Street.[60]

From the 1840s cellar dwellings, like courts and yards, although in the main discouraged by legislation, continued to be built.[61] In these new districts market forces were sufficient to ensure their continuance as a source of cheap affordable accommodation for the labouring classes. The versatile Welsh, like Thomas Jones, complied with the new building regulations in 1849 and erected four-roomed cellared houses in Henry Street, Everton.

However, it would be untrue to suppose that all new house developments were without their critics. Residential building was so concentrated in the Everton township by 1900 that the population density was then the equivalent of 160,000 per square mile, twice that of any other district of the town. Even as early as 1860 the continuous rows of brick houses gave cause for concern environmentally. By the end of the century many neighbourhoods in Liverpool had scarcely a parallel in the country for overcrowding and squalor.[62] Thousands of these early regulation houses, mainly of the four-roomed type, lacked the basic amenities of mains water, main sewerage and gas, and had to share a communal WC. Even when gas and electricity were commonplace in other districts, such housing lingered on without the benefit of either until demolished after the Second World War.

In adjacent West Derby and Kensington it was much the same. Land speculation resulted in large block developments of terraced rows, constructed and laid out with an almost total disregard for individual or communal open space.

Even though the density of housing was similar to other districts there was a marked contrast in the numbers per dwelling and this remained a constant feature of the residential development of this district. It was due almost entirely to each new phase of house-building being sited further and further away from the docks. In consequence areas like Kensington were less affected by the constant inflow of emigrants and the wide fluctuations in employment associated with the docks and the river. Instead, regular employment could be found in a wide range of industry and manufacture which included confectionery and tobacco, or within the town itself. The slump in house-building in the late 1840s and 1850s was particularly severe in this area. However, building was again under way in the 1860s as Everton builders increasingly turned their attention further afield. The form and style of residential estate development, which was to be repeated time and time again, was not dissimilar to that experienced in Everton. Names such as Evans, Jones, Owen and Parry predominated in the lists of builders and allied tradesmen.[63] There was a high degree of geographical mobility within the industry with builders' premises generally located close to where they were erecting houses. By the 1890s most of these early builders, in Kensington as elsewhere, had either moved to other locations as the line of building extended from the centre of the town or had gone out of business. Some, of course, remained where they continued to build, mainly on infill sites.[64] Welsh surnames were no less conspicuous both as tenants and landlords of such properties.

William Jones, a native of Carrig-y-Druidion, was an early Welsh builder and developer who came to Liverpool sometime towards the end of the Napoleonic Wars. He commenced building shortly after, concentrating his activities in the centre and south side of the town. Initially he built on vacant land then well within the old town boundary, especially in the Duke Street area. Later he extended his activities to include Upper Duke Street, where he erected substantial town houses for merchants and their families. Generally they doubled as residential and commercial premises. His attention was diverted from house-building for a time in the late 1820s when he contracted to R.L. Stephenson for station-building on the Liverpool–Manchester railway. From the 1830s onwards he was again heavily committed to house-building, in Parliament and Upper Parliament Street and along Catherine Street (named after his mother). The layout out of these streets and the house-building which followed eventually encroached upon Faulkner Square, which in the eighteenth century had been an urban outpost and commercially a white elephant. R. Saunders Jones, recalling Edward Faulkner, the High Sheriff in 1788 who laid out the area, states:

> After Faulkner Square had been commenced it stood so long in a skeleton state, and was considered so far out of town, that it was called Faulkner's Folley.[65]

Yet once nineteenth-century development was under way it stood out as one of the few green areas in the town. Between 1820 and 1850 Myrtle, Parliament and Hope Streets towards Lodge Lane and all the area within, were built up almost entirely with good-quality housing.

In marked contrast was this reference to Cleveland Square (Park Lane) in 1828 which draws attention to the plight of the older parts of the south side of Liverpool:

A tremendous change has taken place in the district (Toxteth) since 1750. The extension of the docks has caused every available plot of land to be built upon and as there was no superintending authority, nor building bye-law, the houses have been built without any regard for air, space and elementary sanitation.[66]

While lamenting the passing of better times, the writer goes on to refer to the form and style of residential building then currently under construction.

The gardens of a generation back are now converted into courts with tucked up houses whose bedroom windows overlook reeking earth closets. The builders appear to have grudged to make any spaces except as passages. As a result of all this building, the district which reaches to Parliament Street to the south and Great Georges Street to the east numbers 28,000 inhabitants.[67]

The surrounding and adjacent areas were little better, having become thickly dotted with inns, taverns, and beer houses some no bigger than cottages. Following the enforcement of regulations governing house construction in the 1840s there was a distinct change of emphasis. Toxteth from this date began to exhibit a similar pattern of urban development to that of Everton and Kirkdale, as builders recognized the distinct possibilities of the four-roomed terraced cottage as housing for dock workers, a major employer in the area. They proved popular both as accommodation and as an investment. In consequence more four-roomed cottages were built in the 1840s and 1850s in this district than any other type. The six-roomed model was popularized in the 1860s and dominated the market for new housing, especially in the Toxteth building boom of the 1870s when on average 500–600 houses were being erected each year.

D. Daniel was a speculative builder who purchased building plots in this area on which he erected four-roomed non-forecourted terraced houses. He would also build in Warwick Street in the 1860s,[68] before progressing to Princes Road, Upper Parliament Street, Amberley and Upper Warwick Streets. Periodically he contracted to erect six-roomed houses such as those in Churchill Street.

Until the second half of the nineteenth century, Lodge Lane had been a semi-rural road bordered by large houses and extensive gardens. From the 1850s the extension of the town led to its gradual urbanization. One by one the big houses were pulled down, their gardens divided and sold as building sites and streets cut through them. By 1870 retail shop-building was a major feature of this street and by the end of that decade the whole of the west side had been built upon. One of the older properties which survived for a time was Windsor House, where today Moss Grove intersects with Lodge Lane. The Methodist congregation had conducted services in the house but were forced to vacate the premises when the site was redeveloped by William Edwards, a speculative builder who would also take credit for parts of Munro Street and Peel Street.[69]

William Bannister Bar, a builders' merchant, was erecting a shop and warehouse nearby on the corner of Tagus Street. He offered to build a meeting room over the shop premises and this venue became part of the Wesleyan circuit. Eventually a chapel was built to a design by the Liverpool architects C.O. Ellison & Son.[70]

Parallel to house-building in the Lodge Lane area was the systematic urbanization of Warwick and Parliament Fields.[71] Kingsley, Granby, Mulgrave and Selbourne Streets cut through from Upper Parliament Street to form a series of intersecting streets. The subdivision of the areas contained within these blocks was quickly infilled with numerous rows of labourers' and artisans' cottages.

While the development of these streets was under way little difficulty would have been experienced in recognizing the gutteral intonations of the Cambrian dialect and the extent to which Welsh tradesmen were committed to building in the district.[72] For instance Hugh Jones of Jones Bros. (Registered Builders), 10 Kimberley Street,[73] and William Williams who arrived in Liverpool from Anglesey in 1869, built continuously in this area.

Observations of the style and frequency of building line which occurs between individual building projects suggest that a single builder was often responsible for the construction of one side of a street, or even both sides for part of its length. However, the undertaking could be considerably less if the work was speculative and on a thin market. Monoah Evans, for example, erected rows of houses in Mulgrave Street and on one side of Beaconsfield.[74] Evan Morgan, with a yard at 189 Edge Lane,[75] eventually built shops in Granby Street alongside those of William Williams to serve residents of houses Williams had recently built in Roseberry and Dalkeith Streets. The list is long,[76] especially when note is taken of jobbing bricklayers and joiners who built from time to time on their own account, although the number of properties they would decide to build at any one time was usually small.

Occasionally, due to the conjunction of two separate developments, awkward street configurations broke up the uniformity of the gridiron plan. Hugh Jones was involved in such a site around the Thackeray and Arnold Street area in the 1870s. Two streets to the west, along Upper Warwick Street, he was also working in Tennyson Street before erecting the majoirty of the 300 cottage-type houses which comprised the Moss Bank Estate (Lodge Lane–Alt Street).

In the 1870s Wilson J. Williams was erecting small terraced houses in nearby Elaine Street. A long career in the building trade would eventually take him to the Laurel Mount Estate where he concentrated his work base in St Michael's and Belgrave Road. Here Richard Owens, the architect and surveyor to the Cambrian and Clarence Building Societies, built extensively on his own account in the 1880s.[77] It was possible, therefore, from the 1880s to leave the gates of Toxteth cemetery and walk due west to Brunswick Dock along Welsh named streets built by teams of Welsh-speaking tradesmen and labourers and all achieved through the mobilization of Welsh materials, organization and manpower. Streets of gridiron-terraced houses with names like Rhiwlas and Powis, Madryn and Dovey, Gwendoline and Geraint could be nothing other than the manifestation of Cambrian enterprise.

The tightness of the urban plan around Windsor and Mill Streets, and especially the back dwellings close to Herculaneum dock, was not so pronounced a feature of later development. When Harlow Street was laid out it cut through Princes Road and opened up the area beyond for new housing. The distance from the town centre and the presence of special factors produced a greater social mix in these newer areas. For example, the laying out of Princes Park was an influential factor in attracting upper middle-class pockets of housing with their ornate facades and terraced landscaped gardens. Belvedere Road, Sunnyside and Wellesley Terrace were a direct response to the demands of the middle class to be housed in a pleasant environment convenient to the town centre.

b. *The Welsh influence in the building trades*

Whatever the occupation or location of the Welsh tradesman, subcontractor or speculative builder, Friday was always settlement day. Builders and tradesmen settled accounts with suppliers, ordered materials, paid off short-term loans and arranged further credit, negotiated the purchase of building plots and discussed with others in order to determine the current trends and movement within the housing market. To a large extent, then, the market for new houses was continually under short-term review by those with a practical knowledge and working experience of the industry. Saturday was like any other day where the hours, like the work, were determined by light and the weather. Sunday, as one would expect, was reserved almost exclusively by the Welsh for the Chapel.

Extracts from Gore's directories taken at 10-year intervals provide data on a

Figure 19.   Mawdsley's map of Liverpool and suburbs, 1895 (Courtesy Merseyside County Museums,)

whole range of trades and industries associated with building on Merseyside.[78] The distinctiveness of the Welsh surname enables the extent of the Welsh presence to be determined from the lists of firms recorded for individual trades.

Building firms were an important sector of the building industry by the 1840s, previous to which building, especially house-building, had been associated more with individuals or particular trades such as joinery. The origins of many building firms, therefore, can be found in the ranks of the building trades themselves, where the volume and continuity of house-building tended to establish many as recognized builders, rather than individual craftsmen. Best suited to make the transition on a permanent basis were the joiners, where a grasp of mathematics gave them a distinct business advantage.

From a peak of 600 joinery firms recorded for the late 1870s[79] the numbers continued to fluctuate downwards to the end of the century. The movement coincided with a corresponding decrease, which had commenced 10 years earlier, in the number of recorded joinery firms who in addition were house-builders. In the 1860s 63 per cent (355 firms) of all registered joinery firms were house-builders; some 40 years later the figure had dwindled to less than 18 per cent (77 firms). A similar situation was experienced in bricklaying where in the late 1860s 75 per cent (51 firms) of recorded bricklaying firms were recognized builders, but by 1901 there were only six.[80] Few slaters or plumbers became house-builders, preferring instead to subcontract their labour. As one would expect, most slaters were Welsh either by birth or extraction.

What was the extent of the Welsh presence within the building trades, and in house-building in particular? The numbers of Welsh joinery and bricklaying firms for the period 1850 to 1890 imply a consistent presence somewhere in the region of 30 per cent, while for building firms it was about 10 per cent higher. This overview of Welsh involvement tends to disguise the actual extent of Welsh house-building. Residential building for the most part was carried on by numerous small firms. These one-man businesses showed an independence of mind and a marked reluctance to work for others. Nevertheless, individual tradesmen did combine their respective skills on a 'blood for blood' basis in order to undertake a contract.[81] Whether such associations were temporary or longer term, individual tradesmen cultivated a reputation in their respective skills to which they could return in periods of business depression. But for all this, residential building came to be dominated by a few large firms which rose from their ranks.

An outstanding example was Owen Elias with a yard at 286 Scotland Road in the 1850s; the premises were extended over the years to take in numbers 288 and 290. By 1891, the firm had yards and premises sited in districts where house-building was most active: 195 Beckfield Road (Everton), 211 Rimrose Road (Bootle) and 2 Arnot Street, County Road (Walton).[82] J.R. Jones attributes the building of hundreds of houses in the Everton and Kirkdale districts to this firm alone.[83] Indeed, the extended Scotland Road premises were ideally placed to serve both these districts. In addition J.A. Picton points out that the development of Everton,

is almost entirely the work of Welsh builders, several of whom . . . have succeeded in amassing considerable property by their exertions. A large part of the population is from the principality.[84]

Indeed, the total number of houses constructed in Everton between 1841 and 1891 accounts for approximately 35 per cent of all houses built within the Liverpool boundary extension of 1835.[85] Another substantial Welsh house-builder was David Hughes, a long-time associate of Elias. By 1880 he was building whole streets of four-bedroomed houses with a chamber floor, in the Walton district.[86] Each building project involved upwards of 30 houses. In November 1881 he was offering 66 terraced houses for sale in two streets in Walton: 35 in Wylva Street valued at £8,925 on a ground rent of £77 per annum and 31 in Arkles Lane valued at £8,170 on a leasehold of 99 years at £56 per annum.[87]

Taking into account the size of these Welsh building firms in terms of the extent of their business premises and the size of many of their housing schemes, then the extent of Welsh involvement was considerably in excess of the figures suggested simply by the number of Welsh building firms.

An important feature of the housing industry has been the service sector; the architects, surveyors, estate and land agents. To the architect in the urban setting the terraced house was the bread and butter of his practice. Many firms concentrated their activities on designing a series of small house types which catered to the volume end of the market. Here house plans could be used many times over as an estate developed, or adapted to fit a different set of criteria in another. Speculative builders and investors, noting the style and type of dwelling which proved both popular and easy to let, either negotiated to buy the plans, commissioned an architect or simply copied a design which was selling well and submitted for building approval their own house plan based on observation and measurement.

Of course, some architects were retained by expanding building firms to design the house style for individual estates.[88] On the other hand, large and established firms like Owen and William Elias were in a position to design for themselves a model terraced cottage which appeared throughout Kirkdale, Everton and Walton. A good example of this design can be found in the streets between County Road and City Road in Walton.[89]

Similarly Samuel Holmes, of Samuel and James Holmes, the advocate of housing reform whose evidence before the 1842 Select Committee was so damning of inner urban housing, was not only a builder and joiner but a recognized architect and surveyor,[90] while Richard Owens was, from the early 1860s, consultant surveyor and architect to the 'Cambrian' and the 'Clarence' (Street) building societies. His specification and letter books from 1864 note his strong preference for Welsh firms and tradesmen to undertake building work. He frequently praised the workmanship of Welsh builders who erected many of the properties he was asked to appraise and value.[91]

R.T. Roberts, with offices in South Street, Everton, and later in Scotland Road, produced a basic terraced house plan which, determined by the mood of the client or the market, could be adapted to include both refinement and ornamentation. The addition of a rear scullery and decorative brick banding were cases in point, and internally the quality and extent of fittings could be scaled to the demands of individual clients or geared to a specific price range within the market. In the 1860s Hugh Grey, an architect of Welsh extraction, was designing four-roomed houses to be erected in Amos Street, Everton, and simultaneously a six-roomed version for Welsh clients to the south in the Lodge Lane district. Hugh Grey's offices were in North John Street; this central position, like that of Richard Owens in Crosshall Street, enabled these firms and practices like them to take advantage of building in all sectors of the town.[92]

The variations in house plan and style which emerged from the 1850s were, however, derivatives of the basic four- and six-roomed terraced cottage. According to J.R. Jones these models were quickly copied by English builders.[93] Resultant competition, far from reducing the quality of the houses, actually increased the amenities. Welsh speculative builders went one better than their English counterparts by providing a bathroom to every new house constructed. Bathrooms became a notable feature of the six-roomed Welsh house from the 1880s.[94]

The list of Welsh surnames in the building professions generally and architecture in particular was impressive.[95] Their involvement, at least in the Liverpool experience, suggests that the role of the architect at the design and planning stages of Victorian working-class housing estates was far more influential than previously determined.[96]

5 The broader Welsh influence

Crucial to the building industry was the availability of raw materials and a constant and uniform supply of finished products. The linkage between North Wales and Liverpool, already well established by the 1830s through migration, was consolidated by a flourishing and expanding trade in essential materials such as slate, stone, brick and clay products. North America was the primary source of timber imported through Liverpool for use in house-building and construction. In each instance Welsh factors were well represented as local agents and regional distributors of these supplies.

a. Building materials
By 1850 seventy timber merchants were established in the town, many of whom were Welsh. Almost all had established international trading links, especially with New Brunswick and Nova Scotia. The role of the Liverpool timber trade in the process of house-building can be determined by reference to table 16. Imported sawn timber planks, as against logs, were generally better seasoned and more readily available to the building trades.

Table 16   Liverpool timber imports, 1838–52 (000s cubic ft)

		1838	1842	1846	1848	1850	1852
North	Yellow, red pine	5,816	5,869	4,735	5,175	6,392	6,024
America	Quebec oak	370	378	384	468	525	472
	Elm, Ash hardwood	293	300	330	326	319	371
	New Brunswick (planks)	7,492	12,940	14,500	16,584	21,913	34,152
		13,971	19,487	19,949	22,553	29,149	41,019
Northern	Danzig	343	571	684	903	304	1,008
Europe	Deck planks	6	4	3	2	4	3
West	Mahogany	10	11	17	19	27	19
Indies	Cedar	16	21	24	26	17	18
Logs	Rosewood				5	5	3
	Pitch pine	94	111	122	145	351	150
	Teak	79	48	49	49	88	140
Total		14,519	20,253	20,848	23,702	29,945	42,360

Source: W. Heaton Wakefield, *History of Joseph Gardner & Son 1748–1948* (1948).

Braithwaite Poole describes Liverpool, Hull and London during this period as collectively receiving over 30 per cent of the total imports of timber.[97] The 1852 tonnage exceeded any previous year with 80 per cent of Liverpool timber, in that year, being either absorbed locally or sold forward within a radius of 100 miles. American and Baltic firs were the woods chiefly used by the building trades.[98] Liverpool merchants account for a major part of the North American business. Baltic firs, on the other hand, which accounted for only a small part of the Liverpool trade, were transacted through Hull.

The constant supply of yellow pine entering Liverpool was almost all sold to the London merchants, being greatly favoured by London builders.[99] Northern builders preferred Canadian timber planking from the saw mills of New Brunswick. The phenomenal increase of imported New Brunswick planking from 7.5 million cubic feet in 1838 to 34 million by 1852, cannot be accounted for by building in Liverpool alone. The late 1840s and early 1850s were years of depression for the Liverpool house-building industry as the town digested the rash of speculative building which peaked in 1846, and considered the implications of the new building regulations.

By the middle of the nineteenth century Liverpool was supplying builder timber to all towns eastward as far as Bradford, Huddersfield and Leeds.[100] To serve northern industrial interests the firm of Joseph Gardner kept an agent permanently in Turkey to negotiate the purchase of Caucasian boxwood, which was turned into shuttles for the textile industry, supplying mills in Lancashire and Yorkshire.[101]

Unlike timber planking the quality woods did not exhibit, in volume terms, a corresponding growth pattern. They were used mainly in the production of furniture where the demand, although increasing, was for cheap furniture in which veneers go a long way.

Liverpool of Today, published in 1887, makes reference to some of the principal Welsh timber firms, many of whom had set up in business in the 1840s. They established in response to the trading opportunity presented by the boom in house-building and the prospects offered by a wider regional market. The upswing in the importation of building timber around 1850 was due in part to the formation of these new companies.

Of the new timber firms, Farnsworth & Jardine, managed by Peter Owen,[102] built extensive sheds in the north docks for the importation of mahogany and fancy (furniture) woods, while Joseph Owen & Sons (St Anne Street), Walker & Roberts and David Roberts & Son, all established around 1850, consolidated the Welsh influence on the trade.[103]

Because of the ever-increasing volume of business the centre of the international trade gradually moved to new docks at the north end of the town, and when Canada Chambers was built to coincide with the opening of this new complex in 1858 it was occupied solely by timber traders.[104] Following the continued increase in demand for timber and wood products in the 1860s other Welsh-named companies were established, such as John Hughes & Co. and Isaac Evans & Co.

The saw mills and wood yards of Liverpool timber merchants, which include many Welsh surnames in addition to the above,[105] were regional suppliers and distributors of timber to a variety of trades. However, in the Liverpool setting the connection with house-building could amount to a direct involvement. R.H. Roberts, for example, a partner in Roberts & Williams, Boundary Street, built on his own account in the Edge Hill district. J.R. Jones recalls that Roberts was one of four Welsh directors of the Liverpool & Birkenhead House Investment Company.[106] Therefore the relationship between the timber trade and house-building was not always that of a supplier.

With the exception of English landowners owning Welsh estates, slate was almost entirely the business of the Welsh. The early standardization of this product, which ranged in size from Duchesses at 2 ft by 1 ft through Countesses and Ladies down to Doubles, which were approximately half the size, was a recognized feature of production as early as the 1760s. However, because of its weight, slate did not come into its own as a roofing material outside North Wales until problems of organization and transport had been overcome. This was largely resolved by improving internal communication (ultimately with railroads), the bulk-handling facilities at Caernarvon and the creation of new ports at Dinorwic and Penrhyn by the leading quarrying companies.

Liverpool merchants employed their own agents in Wales to ensure continuity of supply and quality of product, as well as actively pursuing a profitable export trade to North America and Ireland from their base in Caernarvon. Slate bound for Flanders and the West Indies went via Liverpool.[107] Of course, the practice of having agents on the spot was not solely confined to Liverpool merchants. Merchants in other towns either had their own agents or invested directly in quarrying. Even York, a town associated more with pantiles than slate, had a merchant partner in the Cilgwyn Cefn du Slate Company of Hafodlas.[108]

During Pitt's administration the taxation already levied on bricks and tiles was extended to include other building materials. In consequence slate and stone, carried as coastwise traffic, were forced to pay an *ad valorem* duty of 20 per cent at the port of delivery (equal to one-third of the prime cost), but this did not greatly affect the Irish or international business which flourished in response to the relative cheapness and availability of the material.[109] The whole business expanded rapidly once the rhythm of building was established after the Napoleonic Wars; later with the abolition of duty, and more importantly the self-sustaining momentum of residential building generally from the 1830s, it never looked back. Associated products such as writing slates, blackboards, powdered chert and manganese extended the range of products and consolidated the profitability of the enterprise.

Slate may have been the most distinctly Welsh of builders' materials, but of crucial significance was a continuous supply of good-quality brick and lime. Both of these products were in abundant supply around Denbigh and Flint. Welsh builders in Liverpool either preferred brick fired in North Wales, mainly in the Ruabon area, or bricks manufactured in Liverpool from Welsh clay. In the early years they were hand-moulded and fired by the method associated with clamp bricks. Imported bricks were considered more durable than those produced from Liverpool clay. Quality control of Welsh products, whether stacked or kiln-fired, was more exact because it involved classification according to the degree of hardness and the depth of colour. The former depended on the position of the bricks in the kiln while the latter resulted from the combined action of heat and the percentage of salt in the mixture. This type of brick was preferred by Welsh builders because of its durability and variety of colour.

Stone was used extensively in housing, for load-bearing over doors and windows as well as for decoration. In the first half of the nineteenth century the Liverpool stone quarries at Toxteth Park, Park Road, Everton, Knowsley, Ince Blundell, Woolton and St James Mount proved adequate for local needs. With the increase in demand for stone in the second half of the century, a string of quarries stretching from Abergele to the great Orme combined with those of Anglesey to supply Liverpool with mortar and building stone.[110] Of singular importance here was the extensive Cefn Mawr stone quarry in Denbigh which, with the Trevor in Caernarvon, was a major supplier of road setts. In 1861 there were 500 employed in the industry – some 10 years later it had risen to 2,000, in response to the demands for better road surfaces in urban areas.[111] For a short period during the Napoleonic Wars Anglesey marble (Mona Marble), whose potential was recognized by a Liverpool Welshman, replaced Italian marble for use in chimney pieces.[112]

b. Financial considerations

Speculative builders frequently experienced difficulty in maintaining the supply of short-term credit. To meet the increasing demand and regulate the flow of new money, building societies were established which broke the traditional monopoly enjoyed by the organized network of solicitors and attorneys. The problem was especially acute in the boom years of the 1840s and late 1850s when the number of dwellings in the town doubled to 66,000 and difficulties were experienced in generating an ever-increasing volume of finance on a regular and sustained basis. The problems were further compounded by the severe competition then experienced in the capital market from railway and industrial investment.

To increase the flow and maintain continuity of supply, groups within individual Calvinistic Methodist Chapels began to tap the element of thrift and mobilize the savings within their respective congregations. They took the form of building societies with titles such as 'The Clarence' (Street), 'The Chatham' (Street), taking their lead from the earliest of these societies 'The Crown' (Street).[113] In addition there were The Working Men's Calvinistic Methodist Trust and the Cambrian Permanent Building Society.[114] All were established in the early 1860s to supply the financial needs of the local house-building market.

Indices of owner-occupation in Liverpool correlate with those at the national level, accounting by 1914 for some 10 per cent of all houses. However, given that so much local money was being channelled into residential building, one would expect some of the money to have filtered through to owner-occupation. Of course some did, but it was an age of landlord and tenant, with the population expressing a marked reluctance towards owning their own homes. Such institutions were therefore solely for the benefit of builders borrowing on short-term renewable loans and the investing landlord, that is, the tradespeople and the shopocracy of the town. A further rash of societies was established in the early 1880s when demand spawned the Liverpool and Birkenhead Building Society in 1880 and the City of Liverpool Permanent in 1881.[115] These societies, although founded and administered by members of the Welsh community, had titles which were more anglicized and which catered more to the general population of the city.[116] The Llewelyn Friendly Tontine Society founded in 1874 was somewhat different, servicing for short-term loans and savings repayable on agreed dates.

Prominent members of the Calvinistic Methodist movement were more often than not at the helm of these fund-gathering organizations. In the Chatham Street congregation for instance, Thomas Williams, one of the early builders in Everton and Walton (Nursery Fields) was a founder member of the Chatham Building Society, along with Morris Owen (President), a joiner and builder responsible for much of the housing off Smithdown Road and many of the blocks of shops along it. A later deacon at Chatham Street, in the 1890s, was William Jones, who had built extensively in Everton and was then concentrating his activities in the Woolton area, while Samuel Evans, another director, constructed many of the houses in Harrow, Finchley, Hornsea, and Willmer Roads, Anfield.[117] It could well be argued that such organizations were set up for the exclusive use of a small group of individuals and their associates. This may be true in large measure, but in doing so they generated a volume of business activity which was to benefit most sectors of their respective congregations in one way or another.

D.P. Davies, Director of the Clarence Building Society and head of the timber firm of Davies Williams and Co., joined the Stanley Street Calvinistic Methodist Chapel where another William Jones, a contractor building churches and meeting houses in Bootle and Kirkdale, was also a member. Like Edward Owen, a close associate, many of the Calvinistic Methodists were either of Anglesey or Caernarvonshire extraction and skilled in the joinery trade.

The Princes Road Calvinists in the Parliament Fields district could count large numbers of builders and allied tradespeople amongst the congregation. The Princes Park Permanent Benefits Building Society, established 1860, was a direct response to the extensive opportunity which the district presented for residential building of all kinds.[118] Some builders spent their entire lives employed in and around the Princes Park district and were life-time supporters of the Princes Road Chapel. Similarly, the head of the building firm of David Roberts and Son, which was instrumental in laying out part of the land for housing, was for a time a member there.[119] Although this firm is best known for estate development for the Liverpool Corporation in the 1920s and 1930s, its roots were firmly established in this nineteenth-century residential area. Hugh Jones was also a member who frequently purchased land from Roberts, where the scale of enterprise varied from a single building plot to a 10-acre site on which he built upwards of 300 houses at a density approaching 32 houses to the acre.

Calvinistic Methodism remained attractive because of its purist approach. It encouraged and sustained the use of good Welsh, preserved the best of the culture and provided a sense of purpose and belonging. Conflict did not arise as to whether Welsh or English Methodism was best; this was never a point of argument, one remained steadfast and resolute in belief or sought religious solace elsewhere.

Unlike the terminating building societies, the early permanent societies, such as those already referred to, were mainly collecting agencies for the investment of individual savings rather than encouraging the industrious and thrifty to buy their own homes. The management of these societies was, after 1872, increasingly taken over by the educated bourgeoisie and shaken loose from the movement's working-class origins. The Liverpool experience mirrored this pattern of events, especially in the last quarter of the nineteenth century. To appeal to a wider public the building societies established in this period took more general-sounding titles and occupied town-centre offices. As notices and advertisements in the *Liverpool Mercury* reveal, they were Welsh-initiated and remained essentially under Welsh management. In this way wealthy second-generation Welsh supporters of the movement aspired to positions of influence in Liverpool society generally.

Once established and prosperous, many Welsh families moved to the rural environment of Calderstones and Childwall in the south, and 'down the line', as it became known, to the coastal villages between Waterloo and Southport, to take advantage of the bracing air. For those, the disuse of Welsh was recognized as the prerequisite to acceptance into polite English society. A few families who bridged the gap and attained a firm footing in English society dropped their Welsh connections entirely. But for most, the geographic move to a better locality did not herald total absorption by their new surroundings. Families preferred instead to maintain strong links with chapel life, especially as financial standing carried a certain prestige in Welsh society. In addition, the near absence of class barriers within the chapel made it possible for the well-to-do to hold on to the Welsh traditions to which they felt inseparably attached.

The Calvinist Methodist, with no satisfactory English counterpart, did not suffer the dilution by desertion experienced by the Baptists and the Wesleyans. Calvinists therefore retained a strong, enduring and influential presence within the community.[120]

Since many were connected in commercial enterprise, and not a few with building, there were bound to be close working ties between individuals of the same trade attending the same place of worship. They interacted as a matter of course in a mutually beneficial way. Leaders and administrators of lending institutions had to place money somewhere, so why not with members of their own congregation, people whom they knew to be reliable and engaged in a business with which they were familiar?[121] So it was not solely for religious sustenance that members turned to the chapel, it also provided an excellent forum for business, an environment where a man's worth could be discreetly assessed and where individuals could themselves test the market in terms of information, new ideas and the general drift of business enterprise.

It was essential, therefore, that newcomers should quickly seek an introduction to the chapel network, and indeed in most cases it was automatic since the chapel was a focal point and agency of aid in the uncertain period of transition following migration. However, this was not merely out of tradition and a certain nostalgia for things Welsh. It was invarably an economic necessity, a place where property and the pulpit went hand in hand; a situation which encapsulated the very essence of the Protestant ethic.

6 Welsh social cohesion

Although large numbers of the Welsh became established as heads of important businesses, unlike the Anglicans they did not automatically seek or aspire to great prominence in Liverpool society. R.W. Jones postulated a number of reasons for this which emphasized the lack of mastery of the English language as the prime cause.[122] He noted in particular the absence of suitable words to express thoughts freely on business and social matters, lack of fluency in the use of phrases and in expressing opinions and thoughts. Continuously, therefore, for first-generation Liverpool Welsh, accent and language placed them apart.

The extent of the problem can be gauged from the first-hand observations of John Hughes, MD, in the dispute over the direction of service at St David's Church, Princes Drive. Based on the fact that by 1842 more than 30,000 Welsh could be positively identified as living in Liverpool, he states:

> that a considerable portion of this number were almost wholly unacquainted
> with the English language – that thousands of them were members of the

Established church; – nevertheless, that their ignorance of the Saxon tongue rendered it impossible for them to derive advantage from ministerial teaching in that tongue – that in this dilemma they were driven to the alternative either of neglecting Divine Worship altogether, or of turning aside into the paths of dissent, and attending some one or other of the Welsh chapels of the town.[123]

The situation was less acute in later decades as the teaching of English in Welsh schools became a common practice.

Those who chose to work in the Liverpool building trades experienced little difficulty in communication, because the Welsh command of building generally, and their numerical strength within the industry, enabled them to conduct business in their native tongue. This was a major factor in sustaining such a large Welsh presence within the industry. This obviously worked to their advantage by excluding those not so well-versed in its use. On the other hand, as the Reverend Hughes points out, language may have provoked prejudices among some sections of the Anglican community to the extent that many Welsh were barred from admittance into conformist society.

Wherever the Welsh chose to settle they took with them a common culture and language, each sustaining the other in an environment more often than not indifferent to the needs of the newcomer. The contrasts were perhaps most striking for the Welsh in the environment of an international seaport such as Liverpool. The two major social problems with which they had to contend were the totally alien customs of the Irish and the difficult-to-comprehend ways of the English. The first presented problems of association while the latter proved difficult to master.

a. The living centre
The pivotal element of the social fabric remained the chapel, the strength of which was reflected in the weakness of the Episcopalian church in terms of the number of Welsh attending English services, and the unflinching belief that it could never match, let alone challenge, the reforming influence and social cohesiveness of chapel life. This is what made the problems at St David's in the 1840s so contentious, because the Welsh congregation had steadfastly rejected any attempt to assimilate them into English ways. For the Welsh, the chapel engendered a feeling of belonging, encouraged affability and a leaning towards communal pursuits, especially outdoor activities, and participation in chapel debating societies. These were features which the Welsh contended were not to be found in an Anglican congregation.

By 1900, 26 Nonconformist chapels and one Anglican church catered to the spiritual needs of the Liverpool Welsh.[124] Thousands of homes were Welsh-speaking, especially in the Everton district, while the numbers in the total Liverpool population who were Welsh-born and had migrated was never less than 9 per cent.[125] Taking into account second- and third-generation Welsh, the number would have been substantially greater.

The problem of estimating numbers is compounded by the continued absorption of the Welsh into English ways. Assimilation did of course lessen individual family associations with chapel life but the strength of most established congregations and the creation of new ones were sustained by a steady stream of newcomers. Glyn Davies recalls that 'the numerical strength of the Welsh chapel was kept up by the migration alone.'[126] Although there is some substance to the claim it is not entirely true. However, the observation does highlight the continuity, the strength of purpose, and the central role of such organizations. For those Welsh families who settled in Liverpool, before anything else they were assimilated into the ways of Liverpool's Welsh community.

How well equipped were these émigré families to master the realities of the urban environment? By all acounts they experienced few problems, for in the main they were part of the process which determined that environment. However, the trade and commercial fortunes of a seaport were prone to wide fluctuation. Those who arrived in periods of economic depression took the same course of action as John Pritchard and others like him. They emigrated to North America for three to five years, returning when there was the prospect of an upturn in their particular trades.[127] Whatever the state of the local economy the Welsh appear to have enjoyed preference over other migrant groups. Although the building trades were their strong point they were by no means confined solely to them. Administrative and organizational abilities plus a smattering of arithmetic carried one a long way in those days and the Welsh made ideal managers, bookkeepers and clerks. Because of their diligence and reliability most tally clerks and scribers on the docks, as well as the warehousemen of the town, were from Welsh families. The importance to the community of the building trades, like the warehousemen, was that both were the established domain of the Welsh who automatically gave preference to their own. Several of those connected with the town's physical development, there-fore, amassed considerable wealth, and in the process acquired prestige within individual communities. In consequence, the offspring of well-to-do migrants acquired the social habits of the English of similar financial background. Their parents, however, held to their chapels and the domestic use of Welsh. In so doing they had provided their children with a good grounding in the language and a sound introduction to business. They were ably equipped, therefore, to participate in the building trades but rarely to converse in Welsh at the intellectual level of their parents. How could they? They had little first-hand knowledge of Welsh mat-ters and knew nothing of mean, dirty neighbourhoods and deprivation. Except therefore for attendance at chapel on Sunday, they were English.

For the wealthy the eventual disuse of Welsh was recognized as inevitable and was frequently expressed in the transition to the English chapels of the Baptists, Wesleyans and Congregationalists. For one group, however, there was no English counterpart – the Calvinistic Methodists, for whom the chapel remained the 'living centre' of the community.[128]

It is principally within this branch of Methodism that we can detect the conscien-tious champion of the Welsh cause, underpinned by a strong Liberal purpose. The Calvinistic Methodist meeting houses in Princes Road, Chatham Street, Pall Mall, Holt Road and Ashfield Road included in their congregations large numbers of builders, builders' merchants and suppliers, while Park Road, Stanley Road, Belmont and Bedford Streets had many jobbing and speculative builders.[129] Within each persisted a strong element of self-help and mutual benefit. This was given expression by Welsh mutual benefit societies, savings clubs and sickness benefit funds, represented by such organizations as The Cambrian, Ancient Britons and The Druids which acted as both lender and insurer for individual tradesmen and their families.

The chapel and the Welsh language represented the cohesiveness of the Welsh culture and helped retain the values within the community. They also set the com-munity apart, giving it identity and exclusiveness. As the town grew, the Welsh community grew with it, and as residential building was their business, the language and the chapel tended to work to their advantage. Chapel for many become synonymous with business, with prominent leaders in particular fields favouring members of their own congregation with business and access to continuity of employment.

7 Conclusion

Studies of urban development have demonstrated how individual manufacturers, whole industries and independent firms stimulated the growth of Victorian towns. For the most part, their activities were confined to single aspects of that process – land speculation, the decision to build, or construction. It is therefore remarkable testimony to the merits of a migrant community, which experienced problems of culture and language, that they should emerge as the dominant force in the process of development, achieving the command of most trades and agencies associated with it.

The history of the Welsh in Victorian Liverpool has demonstrated that, as a community, they were a crucial factor in the town's physical growth. Their influence was so firmly established when the big drive came in the 1830s that they expanded on a broad front and in consequence became involved in a wide spectrum of building activity. The Welsh were the most able, well-equipped and best connected to provide the necessary resources in the quantities demanded and ensure continuity of supply, whether in terms of manpower, materials or finance. And provide they did, in increasing volume and numbers.

The pervasive nature of Welsh enterprise suggests that the distinctive influences noted in Liverpool house-building may not have been an isolated occurrence. This experience may well have been repeated in other towns, especially in the Midlands where strong commercial links with the principality were in evidence as far back as the eighteenth century. The extension of this argument could well provide fertile ground for future research.

NOTES

1 R. West, *River of Tears: The Rise of the Rio Tinto-Zinc Corporation Ltd* (1972), 16.
2 A.H. Dodd, *The Industrial Revolution in North Wales* (1971), 205.
3 *Ibid.*, 211.
4 Michael Burn, *The Age of Slate* (1976), 12. Turner purchased the Diffwys quarry for £1,000. He and the brothers Casson raised the capital locally to work the quarry. They eventually sold out for £12,000. During the Napoleonic Wars Turner contracted to roof the military barracks on the south coast of Ireland.
5 *Ibid.*, 12. Samuel Holland sold the lease of the Rhiwbryfdir quarry to Nathan Rothschild's Welsh Slate Company in 1825; Lord Palmerston was the Chairman.
6 Dodd, *op. cit.*, 211.
7 *Ibid.*, 211.
8 For 21 years prior to 1809 the Dinorwic estate was exploited by two Caernarvon lawyers, after which it was worked by the Assheton Smiths, the estate's owners.
9 Caernarvon was the outport for the Nantile group of quarries in the Nantile valley. By 1850 the joint tonnage of slate cleared from Caernarvon, Penrhyn and Dinorwic was approaching 200,000 tons annually.

10 A.H. Dodd, *Life in Wales* (1972), 121, notes that the Napoleonic Wars brought a temporary halt to the fortunes of the North Wales slate industry. However, by 1820 it had fully recovered with employment in the industry having risen tenfold, output twentyfold, and profits eightyfold.

11 1831 saw the repeal of the duty on the coastwise trade in slate. This inaugurated 50 years of rising and continuous prosperity.

12 Dodd, *Life in Wales, op. cit.*, 132. Thomas Charles settled in Bala in 1784 and made the town the centre of North Wales Methodism. Field preachers carried Methodism to the new quarrying areas of Snowdonia in a succession of revivals.

13 J. Glyn Davies, *Nationalism as a Social Phenomenon* (1965), 23.

14 Dodd, *Life in Wales, op. cit.*, 144.

15 Davies, *op. cit.*, 24.

16 *Ibid.*, 25. The old folk, especially the Welsh-born, steadfastly stuck to their chapels, never doubting their religious tradition and the intellectual calibre of the pulpit.

17 P.J. Waller, *Democracy and Sectarianism; A Political and Social History of Liverpool 1868–1939* (1980), 9.

18 D. Ben Rees, *Chapels in the Valley: A Study in the Sociology of Welsh Nonconformity* (1975), 209.

19 E.W. Ravenstein, *The Law of Migration. Second Paper* (1885), published in the Bobbs–Merrill Reprint Series in the Social Sciences, 481–510.

20 Ramsey Muir, *The Victoria History of the Counties of England,* Vol. 4: Lancashire (1966), 38.

21 D. Jenkin Williams, *The Welsh Church and Welsh People of Liverpool* (1927), 17. Welsh textile workers came to work in the large cotton factory 'Union Mill', Vauxhall Road, owned by Messrs Kirkman & Co.; its popular name was the 'Welsh Factory'.

22 Ravenstein, *op. cit.*, 481–510.

23 Dodd, *Ind. Rev. in North Wales*, 129.

24 A. Conway, 'Welsh emigration in the 19th century', in *Wales through the Ages, from 1485 to the beginning of the 20th Century*, ed. A. J. Roderick (2 vols, 1961), 156.

25 *Ibid.*, 159.

26 Waller, *op. cit.*, 9.

27 Evidence of W.H. Duncan MD, *First Report of the Commissioners for Inquiring into the State of Large Towns and Populous Districts* (1844), 19.

28 R. Lawton, 'Population of Liverpool in the mid-nineteenth century', in *Trans. Hist. Soc. Lancashire and Cheshire*, cvii (1956), 99.

29 J. H. Treble, 'Liverpool working class housing 1801–1851', in *The History of Working Class Housing*, ed. S.D. Chapman (1971), 179.

30 B.D. White, *A History of the Corporation of Liverpool 1835–1914* (1951), 204.

31 *Liverpool Mercury*, quoting the *Liverpool Albion*.

32 White, *op. cit.*, 204.

33 See Evidence of Samuel Holmes. *Second Report of the Commissioners for Inquiring into the State of Large Towns and Populous Districts* (1845).

34 Recorded in Evidence of W.H. Duncan, *State of Large Towns*, 14.

35 *Health of the Town Bill*, 1 Nov. 1842, the clause governing inhabited cellars in the old houses did not take effect until July 1844.

36 Evidence of Samuel Holmes, *State of Large Towns*, 191.

37 Holmes, *op. cit.*, 193.

38 St Katherine's College, Liverpool, Search Papers 18, *Black Spot on the Mersey: Victorian Terraced Housing in Liverpool* (1979), 12. In 1864 there were 3,073 courts containing 17,800 dwellings, by 1903 1,000 survived. The last Liverpool courts were finally demolished in the 1960s Clearance Programme. Also *Reports* of the City Building Surveyor for Liverpool 1896–1914.

39 Holmes, *op. cit.*, 194. 'A cottage built in a court costs, exclusive of land, £95–£105 according to its internal finish; out of this sum the duty on bricks is £5.18.0.

40 Archives of H.A. Noel Woodall (successor to Richard Owens & Sons), RIBA. Specification books 1868–1935, Main Letter books 1864–1937, Special Letter books 1865–1901.

41 Waller, *op. cit.*, 9.

42 J.A. Picton, *Memorials of Liverpool, Historical and Topographical* (1903), 353, 407.

43 Noel Woodall Archives, Valuation/Survey books 1881–1900, Specification books 1868–1935.

44 Sir Giles Scott, architect of the Anglican Cathedral in Liverpool, recorded in J.R. Jones, *The Welsh Builder on Merseyside: annals and lives* (1946), 163.

45 *Annual Report* of the Great Homer Street Methodist Mission (1933) describes Everton in 1830 as 'a hill studded with beautiful villas and mansions of wealthy merchants, with scarcely a rival in the country.'

46 See Weber in *Building Cycles and Britain's Growth*, ed. J. Parry Lewis (1965), Appendix 8, 335. The houses demolished were not all in a state of disrepair – many were cleared because the land was required for purposes other than housing.

47 Picton, *op. cit.*, 353: 'The Redevelopment of Everton is almost entirely the work of the Welsh builders. . . . Placards in the Welsh language may be seen on the walls and Welsh newspapers in the shop windows.'

48 *Ibid.*, 59: 'The Irish are principally to be found clustered in the Scotland and Vauxhall Yards where the Roman Catholic Churches abound and Tipperary brogue may be heard.'

49 Holmes, *op. cit.*, 29: 'there appears to be, amongst the lowest of Irish, such an innate indifference to filth, such a low standard of comfort, and such a gregariousness, as lead them, even when not driven by necessity, into the unhealthy localities where they are found to congregate, and which they render still more unhealthy by their recklessness, and their peculiar habits.'

50 *Mawdsley's town map of Liverpool and suburbs* (1891), provides a clear picture of temperance in some districts. In Everton and Toxteth (south of Upper Parliament and east of Park Lane) few public houses were built in relation to the size of area and the number of houses. It suggests both a strong Welsh residential presence and building influence in these districts.

51 See 'Owen Elias, 1806–1880', in Jones, *op. cit.*

52 Treble, *op. cit.*, 170.

53 *Black Spot on the Mersey, op. cit.*, 8.

54 Samuel Holmes, *op. cit.*, 194.

55 Following the repeal in 1849 of the *ad valorum* duty on bricks transported coastwise, increasing quantities of Ruabon bricks entered the Liverpool market to become a feature of Welsh house-building enterprise.

56 Clamp bricks were produced by taking hand-moulded, soft clay bricks, stacking them loosely, packing them with turf before firing at a steady heat for about seven days, after which they were graded according to hardness and colour.

57 This system produced between: City Road and Goodison Road – E.A.L.F.R.E.D. Goodison Road and County Road – O.W.E.N.A.N.D.W.I.L.L.I.A. County Road and Bedford Road – M.O.W.E.N.

58 Jones, *op. cit.*, 29.

59 *Gore's Directory 1891*.

60 Noel Woodall Archives, Miscellaneous, Book 1, 87.

61 Jones, *op. cit.* Owen Elias built court houses in Earl Street, Everton in 1849 according to plans approved by the Health Committee of the Liverpool Corporation.

62 F.W. Grimshaw, *North Zion Independent Methodist Church, Tetlow Street, Liverpool 4* (1959), 7, records 'that the rural area along Everton Hill started to disappear rapidly by the middle of the nineteenth century. Poverty and disease were rampant and the expectation of life was less than 20 years. The first register of North Zion revealed that nearly all the members died before the age of 50 years. Few lived beyond that age.'

63 *Gore's Trade Directories 1871*, 788–90.
64 William Parry, 51 Coleridge Street, Kensington, *Gore's Directory 1891*, 624.
65 R. Saunders Jones, *Liverpool in the Last Quarter of the Eighteenth Century* (1926), 7.
66 *Centenary Handbook 1815–1915*, St Michael's-in-the-Hamlet, Liverpool (1915), 5.
67 *Ibid.*, 5.
68 Jones, *op. cit.*, 15.
69 M. Corey Dixon, *Half a Century of Methodism at Lodge Lane, Liverpool 1884–1934* (1934), 1.
70 *Ibid.*, 1.
71 W. Heaton Wakefield, *History of Joseph Gardner & Sons Ltd., Timber Merchants, Liverpool 1748–1948* (1948), 27.
72 Jenkin Williams, *op. cit.*, 59.
73 *Gore's Trade Directory 1891*, 429.
74 Noel Woodall Archives, Miscellaneous, 33.
75 *Gore's, 1891*, 573.
76 See *Gore's Trade Directories'* list of joiners, addresses and geographic location of Welsh-named firms of bricklayers, builders, plasterers and slaters.
77 Noel Woodall Archives, Miscellaneous.
78 *Gore's Liverpool Street Directories 1841–91*.
79 *Ibid.*, 1871.
80 *Ibid.*, 1901.
81 The 'blood for blood' system of building was different to subcontracting in that a joiner who built on his own account would undertake to do the woodwork for, say, a bricklayer, if that party agreed in exchange to undertake the other's brickwork.
82 *Gore's 1891*.
83 J.R. Jones, *op. cit.*, bibliography.
84 Picton, *op. cit.*, 353.
85 The number of dwellings and inhabitants within the Liverpool parish reached a peak in the 1850s. The 1861 Census records 37,041 dwellings and 269,742 inhabitants. By 1891 the figures were 25,293 and 156,981 respectively.
86 Noel Woodall Archives, Miscellaneous Plans, 33, 34.
87 *Ibid.*
88 A large number of these nineteenth-century housing estates can still be seen in Liverpool where the individual features of both the houses and the estates remain largely intact.
89 Waller, *op. cit.*, 509.
90 *Gore's Trade Directory 1839*.
91 Noel Woodall Archives, Miscellaneous Volumes, Book 1.
92 There was a tendency amongst the Welsh who had been successful in business to move to more centrally located office premises. Observed changes of address of individual firms, over time, suggests that the movement to the town centre was undertaken in stages.
93 Jones, *op. cit.*, 19.
94 Noel Woodall Archives, Miscellaneous Book 1, 202. Dacy Street, Everton.
95 *Gore's 1839, 1841, 1851, 1862, 1871, 1881, 1891, 1900*.
96 F. Trowell, 'Nineteenth-century speculative housing in Leeds, with special reference to the suburb of Headingly, 1888–1914', unpublished D.Phil. thesis, York (1982).
97 Braithwaite Poole references in F.A. Latham, *Timber Town* (1967), 5.
98 Latham, *ibid.*, 16.
99 In 1848 the London and North-Western railway line out of Liverpool's south dock carried 10,000 tons of timber for the London market. 1829–46 were years of prosperity for Liverpool's timber merchants as many hospitals, churches and public buildings as well as residential houses for all classes of the populace were built. Major building

works were the North and South Dispensaries, the Sessions House and Bridewell (Chapel Street), St Andrew's (Rodney Street), St Martin's in the Field, St David's (Brownlow Hill), St Augustine's (Shaw Street), St Mary's (Edge Hill), and the Amphitheatre (Queen's Square site of the present Royal Court Theatre).

100 Latham, *op. cit.*, 16.
101 Heaton Wakefield, *op. cit.*, 13. Gardner's had an extensive saw mill and joinery workshop in Clyde Street, Kirkdale, in the 1840s.
102 Peter Owen was originally a clerk with E. Chaloner & Co., English Timber Merchants.
103 Latham, *op. cit.*, 18–19.
104 *Minutes of Evidence taken before the Timber Inquiry Committee, Liverpool 1850.* The purpose of the inquiry was the siting of a new timber dock: 255,000 sq. yds of dock timber space was then in use in Brunswick dock area. The new facilities at Canada, 1858, and Brocklebank Docks, 1862, doubled the available quayside storage.
105 See *Gore's Street Directories.*
106 Jones, *op. cit.*, 46. The principal business of the 'Liverpool & Birkenhead' was advancing short-term funds for house-building and arranging finance for housing investment.
107 The Liverpool slate yards were located in Waterloo Road, close to Prince's Dock Basin. Welsh quarries, like the Assheton Smith's of Velinhelli, employed Liverpool agents such as Horley & Marsden, 21 Waterloo Road.
108 Dodd, *Ind. Rev. in North Wales*, 311.
109 *Ibid.*, 205.
110 *Ibid.*, 223.
111 *Ibid.*
112 *Ibid.*
113 John Lloyd Jones, Secretary to the Chatham, and Morris Owen, its President, also acted in this capacity to the Third Canning Permanent Building Society. Morris Owen was a prominent joiner and builder. The Chatham Building Society, Fenwick Street, Liverpool, remains to this day under Welsh management.
114 *Liverpool Mercury*, Jan. 1871, records that the Cambrian was established in 1863. Trustees were Owen Roberts, R.O. Evans, Thos. Hughes, John Jones, Councillor William Williams, Sec. John Parry. Meetings were held in Netherfield Road Welsh Independent Chapel.
115 *Gore's 1891.*
116 The firm of D.B. Jones & Elsworth were agents and secretaries to the Islington, Enterprise, Constitutional, Woolton, Wavertree, Equitable and Second Equitable Building Societies.
117 Noel Woodall Archives, Miscellaneous, Book 1.
118 *Liverpool Mercury*, Jan. 1865.
119 David Roberts & Son was founded by John Jones Jnr in the 1820s and produced two men who gave outstanding service to the Liverpool Welsh community. John Roberts, a large donor to higher education in Wales and his son, John Herbert Roberts, later Lord Clwyd, who aided the Welsh population in Liverpool.
120 Davies, *op. cit.*, 27. Calvinistic Methodists actively supported and subscribed for a new college to be established at Aberystwyth because they saw it as a training base for their preachers.
121 The North & South Wales Bank 'y North and Sowth' founded in Liverpool in 1836 and incorporated with the Midland, 1908. A large number of its directors, managers and staff were Welsh. The bank funded many Welsh builders who had no other skills except industry, good character and a trade. Such were known personally by the officers of the bank, many of whom were office-bearers in the same church where shrewd opinions were formed as to character.
122 R.W. Jones, *Welshmen in Liverpool in the Nineteenth Century and Earlier* (1921), 6.
123 John Hughes MD, *Statement of the Case of the Welsh Church of St. David, Liverpool*

(1842), 2.

124 Davies, *op. cit.*, 23.

125 Numbers of Welsh-born calculated by the Welsh Charity in St David's Brownlow Hill, Minute Books 1840. See also Thomas Bains, *History of Commerce and the Town of Liverpool* (1852), 624.

126 Davies, *op. cit.*, 23.

127 J.R. Jones, *op. cit.*, recalls that John Pritchard arrived in Liverpool during the depression in house-building in 1850. He spent three years in America, returning in 1853. He built houses and shops in Smithdown Lane, Chatsworth Street and Longfellow Street, built Welsh Baptist Church, Edge Lane.

128 Davies, *op. cit.*, 21.

129 See *Chapel Anniversary Booklets, Annual Reports* of Nonconformist Churches and Missions of Liverpool, Reference Section, William Brown Library, Liverpool.

The Victorian building industry and the housing of the Scottish working class

RICHARD RODGER

The Victorian building industry and the housing of the Scottish working class

RICHARD RODGER

1 Introduction

In 1842 the 'brilliant aristocratic quarter ... contrast[ed] strongly with the foul wretchedness of the poor of the Old Town'[1] in Edinburgh. The Glasgow working class, estimated at 78 per cent of the population of the city in 1841, inhabited areas 'which exceed in wretchedness and squalor the lowest nooks of St Giles and Whitechapel, the Liberties of Dublin, the Wynds of Edinburgh'.[2] These 'ill-venti-lated, high-piled, waterless, and dilapidated houses' led one early Victorian commentator to remark that he had

> seen wretchedness in some of its worse phases both here (in Britain) and upon the Continent, but until I visited the wynds of Glasgow I did not believe that so much crime, misery and disease could exist in any civilised country

and another contemporary observer noted that 'the poor in Scotland, especially in Edinburgh and Glasgow, are worse off than in any other region of the three kingdoms, and that the poorest are not Irish, but Scotch.'[3]

Seventy years on, a Royal Commission report was no less blunt. Rural housing – 'badly constructed, incurably damp' – and mining towns – 'monotonous miners' rows flung down without a vestige of town-plan' – were not exempt from severe criticism.[4] But utter despair surrounded the accounts of urban housing conditions in which the majority of the Scottish population lived. It was the 'clotted masses of slums' and 'groups of lightless and unventilated houses', 'old houses converted without necessary sanitary appliances' and 'streets of new tenements ... developed with the minimum of regard for amenity' which produced to the 'amazement' of the Commission the 'gigantic' proportions of the housing deficiency, quantitative and qualitative, in Scotland on the eve of the Great War.[5] The Census of 1911 revealed that 8.4 per cent of Scots lived in one-roomed houses and 39.3 per cent lived in two-roomed houses; in England the figures were respectively 1.3 and 5.8

per cent.[6] Even though Scottish rooms were approximately 20 per cent larger, 47.7 per cent lived in one- and two-roomed houses compared to 7.1 per cent of Englishmen. Had the English Registrar-General's criterion of overcrowding – more than two persons per room – been applied to Scottish burghs, then Wishaw, Coatbridge and Kilsyth with more than 70 per cent of their residents living more than two to a room would be ten times more overcrowded than Liverpool or Salford.[7] Residents in Clydebank, Cowdenbeath, Airdrie, Govan, Hamilton, Motherwell, Barrhead, Johnstone, Port Glasgow and Renfrew with 60–69 per cent living more than two per room were ten times more overcrowded than in Hull or Manchester.[8] In the cities – Glasgow, Dundee, Aberdeen and Edinburgh – the overcrowded percentages were, respectively, 55.7, 48.2, 37.8 and 32.6.[9] In Scotland overall 45.1 per cent lived at a density regarded as overcrowded south of the border where the figure was 9.1 per cent.[10] Even if the criterion was devalued to more than three to a room, more than one in five of Scots was housed in overcrowded conditions and in those burghs mentioned above it was still likely to be 30–40 per cent overcrowded. Not surprisingly then, the Royal Commission calculated the housing shortage of 1911 as 11.6 per cent, and if the existing standard was to be brought up to that of England, then 22.5 per cent more houses were immediately necessary.[11]

Evidently the building of the Scottish industrial city had been far from successful. Civil and social engineering had jointly failed, generating as a by-product conditions far more extreme than in the remainder of the United Kingdom. In a separate chapter the Royal Commission concluded that 'bad housing may fairly be regarded as a legitimate cause of social unrest.'[12] Rent strikes, workers' demonstrations and women's organizations were not then the upshot of wartime conditions or short-term blackmail by munitions workers on Clydeside.[13] Quite the reverse, they were the expression of deep-seated and long-standing grievances over wage and rent levels, experienced in a number of urban locations,[14] though the gradual politicization of the housing problem in the last two Victorian decades exploded in 1914–15 on Clydeside with the most extreme housing conditions in Britain.

2 Principal design features of tenement housing

The morphology of Scottish towns could not be blamed for such congested living conditions for this differed hardly at all from the physical circumstances of other British boroughs. Urban sites displayed as much variety as in England. And, as elsewhere, the legacy of fortified and ecclesiastical town foundations shared many common features on either side of the border. Certainly, there were a number of Scottish towns planted, even planned, as early as the twelfth century, though this determined little more than the location and direction of the principal thoroughfares in the Victorian age.[15] What was unique in urban Scotland was not how the streets were laid out but what was built on them. 'The tenement of three, four and in certain cases five or more storeys represents the final development of housing during the nineteenth century in the great majority of the larger Scots burghs.'[16] This was the architectural hallmark of Victorian Scotland, 'so different from the two-storey self-contained cottages which form the prevailing type in English towns.'[17] So distinctive was the Scottish urban form that not only was a different definition of overcrowding applied, as mentioned above, but British statutes proved inapplicable in urban Scotland; the census office until 1881 used 'tenement' and 'house' interchangeably though there could be 16, 20 or more separate flats or houses in one tenement, and many contemporary commentators, as now, remarked that the high-rise, high-density housing 'was very similar to the European pattern of a few, large undifferentiated rooms.'[18]

Such large, block dwellings were 'to be found from Dumfries in the South to Lerwick in the far North'; in 'small county burghs immediately surrounded by open fields', and 'from the county hamlet to the great cities'.[19] The external arrangement of tenement blocks generated several problems. Firstly, the 60 ft high four-storey tenements built on narrow streets often no more than 30 ft in width, denied light and air to the residents. So dark were the houses that many tenants had during daylight hours to burn gas to light their flats. At the cost of about 1s. per week, up to 5 per cent in 1900 of subsistence wages, this was no small burden and a considerable inconvenience. Supposing they were so inclined, residents found daytime reading difficult without gas light. Poor Law inspectors, sanitary and other officials admitted that they needed 'to strike a match' or 'carry an electric torch to see the names on the doors'.[20] The psychological impact of living perpetually in semi-darkness is difficult to imagine, an effect compounded by the smoke pollution which blackened the sandstone and even the granite facades of Scottish tenements in stark contrast to the almost cheerful red brick of English boroughs. This unrelieved greyness of Scottish building materials did nothing to counteract the gloom caused by high-rise construction.

Another feature, a 'further defect', reinforcing the lack of sufficient light and air, was 'the arrangement of tenements in hollow squares, with no opening or only a very narrow opening at the corners.'[21] Building to the rear of the plot effectively produced 'a box some 60 feet deep'.[22] One- and two-apartment houses in these 'back lands' were therefore denied even that limited light and ventilation available to street-front tenements, and though also influenced by other considerations, general death rates, infant mortality, pulmonary and zymotic disease rates were commonly 15–30 per cent, and not infrequently 50 per cent, higher in the back lands compared to those of the front tenements.[23] The scale and generality of the back lands in the burghs of central Scotland represented as acute a problem as the court and cellar dwellings of Liverpool where at worst three-storey brick houses arranged in groups of up to 10 houses were common.[24] This progressive in-filling allowed the development of the back lands to proceed throughout the nineteenth century and added to already considerable difficulties of access associated with narrow closes and wynds dating from the medieval period. In width they might be as little as 2 ft 6 ins, sufficient only for pedestrian access, though others were wide enough to allow entry to the nightsoil cart, and for vehicular access to workshops also located in the rear of the hollow square. Though often no more than rectangular gaps or entries in the tenement wall, for many residents closes epitomized darkness, morbidity and a subculture of crime and vice.

Characteristically, four-storey Scottish tenements were built in stone. Frontages of dressed stone and rear construction of rough courses of stone rubble were virtually universal. Brickwork was sparingly used, usually only for external stair towers, interior and gable walls, though after the withdrawal of the brick tax in 1850 and with the development of factory-produced bricks and increasing pressure on adjacent quarry resources, brickwork did assume a greater importance in the second half of Victoria's reign. But the solidity and durability of stone tenements created a uniquely Scottish urban townscape.[25] According to one architectural historian, it produced 'long vistas of anonymous stone frontages, stretching in apparently endless lines'.[26] If pre-industrial urban expansion modestly added buildings on an occasional basis, the rapidity of nineteenth-century urban growth generated a striking degree of architectural unanimity.[27] Taste, architectural fashion, maximizing the use of existing party walls and utilizing every inch of the building plot, and the Dean of Guild Court requirement to lodge – and thus provide the opportunity to copy – plans, produced a consensus regarding tenement housing design which assumed the status of stereotype.

This architectural convergence was expressed in a number of features. Classical inspiration affected mouldings, columns, window proportions, horizontal emphasis in elevations and brickwork courses, and many other finer details. Although there were variations reflecting differences in wealth and status, doorways, closes, lobbies, windows and stairs all conformed to general patterns and were part of the communal tenement living experience with shared access and amenities in stark contrast to the developing privatization of space in English boroughs as individual terraced houses increasingly enclosed and contained the plot, notably the backyard.[28] National building provisions outlined in the Public Health Act 1875 accelerated a trend previously adopted by some major English provincial cities by private legislation. Contrary to Daunton's view, Scottish tenements, by the very nature of their shared lobby and stair access, communal wash-houses and drying greens, toilet and refuse arrangements, physically could not achieve the introspection and insularity of the mid and late Victorian English terraced house.

Multi-storey living required access to the various levels. Two principal variants occurred.[29] In one, upper floors were entered from a projecting open stair at the rear (fig. 20a). A passage through the tenement gave access to the ground-floor flats and to the rear stair tower which replaced the more dangerous open stairs of the early nineteenth-century buildings. Circular or 'turnpike' stair towers rose four floors in an almost continuous spiral, with only small landings for access to each level. Although as much as half and sometimes two-thirds of the circular stair tower might be within the tenement block, to maximize rentals on a limited plot builders often placed the stair tower entirely outside the essentially rectangular box formed by the tenement. By about 1850 turnpike staircases lost popularity to a rectangular stair design in two parallel flights of about ten steps to each landing, and this became the standard design in the last quarter of the nineteenth century. The second staircase variant (fig. 20b) was entirely within the building. Indeed, it was located at the very centre of the tenement, and was circular, or elliptical, but later usually rectangular in design. The external staircase had the benefit of natural lighting; the internal stair obtained only a limited amount of daylight from a small skylight in the roof. Minimum dimensions for such central stair wells and skylights were operational in many of the principal Scottish burghs by the 1890s, at which stage their advantages in economizing on available rental space was so slight as to give way to a more generous 'dog-leg' staircase and landing which became widely adopted in the quarter century before the First World War.

Architectural change was, nonetheless, perceptible in the Victorian tenement. Safety considerations led to enclosed staircases by the early years of the nineteenth century; by the 1860s fire precautions prevented continuous roof spaces, brick partitions being required; lighting problems encouraged wider central stair wells by the 1890s; from about 1880, especially in Dundee and Edinburgh tenements, front access from balconies was introduced; brick-built WC stacks were added from the

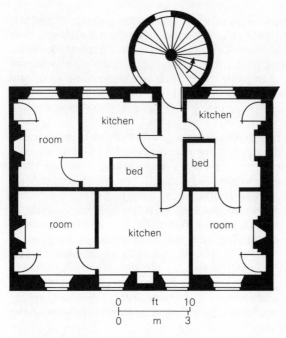

Figure 20a.   Upper floor plan of a typical working-class tenement (external stair).

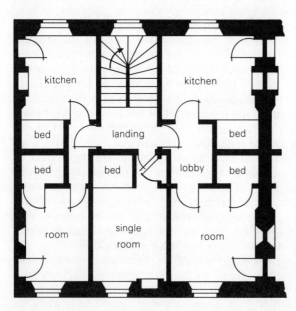

Figure 20b.   Floor plan of a typical working-class tenement (internal stair, no internal sanitation.)

1860s to the rear of the tenements to provide shared sanitary facilities on each landing, rather than basement or back court dry-closets or privies; windows were enlarged in the second half of the nineteenth century. All were variations upon a single theme, block buildings with communal access and facilities. The degree of sharing might alter according to changing minima acceptable to municipal sanitary officials or changing income and expectation levels amongst residents, but the basic residential format for the majority of Scottish urban dwellers was, until 1914 at least, immutable.

The mere existence of the tenement therefore created urban housing problems.

If a building of four or five storeys in height is to remain structurally sound and weatherproof for a reasonable time it must be built substantially, and the specification for all the main timber must be on generous lines.[30]

Walls were 2 ft thick. If these standards of construction had the dual advantage of discouraging jerry builders and encouraging Scottish investors, the solidity made adaptation to changing amenity levels expensive, and consequently delayed. Design impeded ventilation and lighting; extending windows by removing portions of 2 ft thick walls was both difficult and costly. Similarly, the addition of a water closet or wash-houses was problematical in such large, solid, and yet confined spaces. For example, the introduction of piped water supplies throughout the tenement, in contrast to the ground-floor supply to English terraced houses, presented technical problems of water engineering to supply the upper floors, as well as additions to cost resulting from additional piping, valves and storage. Furthermore, agreement to introduce new amenities, with the inevitable consequence of a few pence on weekly rentals, meant that landlords often undertook such improvements belatedly, and at the lowest common denominator acceptable.

3 Living conditions and behavioural patterns

If the external structure and layout proved unconducive to healthy living conditions, two central objections were also directed at the internal design of tenements.[31] Firstly sanitary arrangements, and secondly congested access through a central stair and landing, generated a degree of opprobrium unrivalled by other numerous defects attributed to Scottish housing.

Typical of many mid century Scottish tenements was 21 Middleton Place, Glasgow built c. 1850 (fig. 21). Entrance was in this case from the rear, which also served to reinforce the monotony of the street frontage, and the irregularity of buildings at the rear. Other typical designs permitted entry from the street in the centre of the block, using a central lobby and internal stair well. In both cases the key design feature was the 'T'-shaped passage which gave access to each one- or two-roomed flat, and at Middleton Place this 44 ft passage was entirely dark. Initially the only sanitary convenience for the entire block of 34 houses and a population of about 130 was one privy or dry-closet in the court. Only 2 ft 6 ins wide, the transverse 'T' passage would run left and right from the stair head; another design was 'L'-shaped, associated with tenements where the passage would run the entire central length of the tenement with the stair access at one end. Such passages, consistent with the maximization of rental space and the minimization of public and thus non-rentable space in these basically rectangular boxes, inclined the Glasgow Medical Officer of Health to the view that the tenement was 'the curse of Glasgow', 'an aggravated form of the back-to-back house' where 'right through this tenement longitudinally, you have a solid partition, which divides the back houses from the front houses'.[32] The Greenock MOH concurred. In fact both took the argument further, because 'as through ventilation was quite impossible'[33] and as building new back-to-back houses was, after 1909, illegal and therefore presumably unacceptable in standard and thus uninhabitable, then existing tenement houses of the back-to-back 'T' or 'L' passage variety were also uninhabitable.

Mid century housing arrangements did not remain entirely static, as fig. 21 of Middleton Place shows. Often initiated by the Sanitary Department, responses to typhus and other endemic infectious diseases produced modifications to existing tenements. For example, to enlarge living space and reduce congestion partition walls were removed. Often two 'single end' flats were thus enlarged on each floor, eight in a four-storey tenement, and other modifications to tenement design included additional entries and skylights to increase ventilation and light, and the replacement of privies by shared WCs on stair landings in most parts of urban Scotland from the 1880s. Such additions did not disturb the essentially back-to-back features of tenement construction which were faithfully reproduced until 1914. The density of occupation in high-rise Scottish tenements therefore remained at levels which had caused controls on block dwellings to be introduced in Liverpool in the 1840s, in Newcastle in 1866 and in Birmingham in 1876.[34] While mid Victorian English municipalities were somewhat hesitantly dealing with their courts and back-to-back dwellings which 'at worst were boxes open above to the free air', Scottish domestic architecture retained these essentially unchanged before 1914. The 'Scotch common stair (was) at best a longer, narrower box, fully open only at the lower end. . . . In their worst form the Scotch common stair (was) a . . . stark noisome tunnel buried in the centre of the tenement.'[35]

Exacerbating the problems of deficient space, light and ventilation was the 'made-down' house, the subdivision of large flats into smaller units, and a process 'as

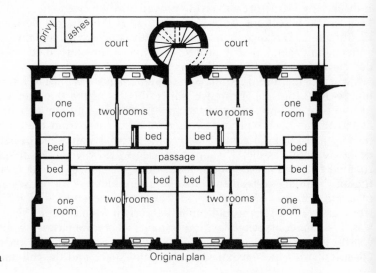

a   Original plan

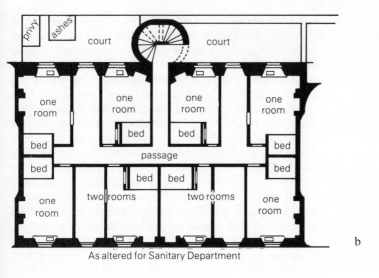

b

As altered for Sanitary Department

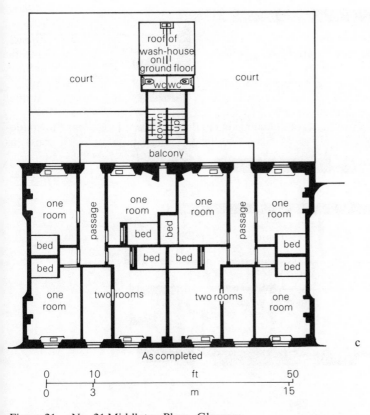

c

As completed

| 0 | 10 | ft | 50 |
| 0 | 3 | m | 15 |

Figure 21.   No. 21 Middleton Place, Glasgow.

necessary as a second-hand clothes market'.[36] An unexceptional example of the procedure involved the conversion of a Glasgow tenement of 6 houses, each of 4 apartments, into 21 one-roomed houses.[37] Annual rental increased from £78 to £134. Again in Glasgow, a tenement of 6 houses, each of 6 apartments, was 'made-down' into 12 units of three rooms each; the annual rental in this case rose from £175 to £222.[38] In Edinburgh two tenements, each originally comprising 7 houses and about 35 residents, were subdivided, one into 23 houses and 73 occupants and the other into 43 houses and 134 residents. In another Edinburgh case, 8 flats housing 40 people were subdivided into 34 houses with 114 occupants, while in Dumbarton many Dennystown room and kitchen houses of 1,800 cubic feet had been subdivided into 800 cubic feet 'single ends'.[39] Fig. 22 illustrates how a single large room was transformed into as many as three separate units. Continuing urban immigration and natural increase,[40] very limited conversion costs and minimal monitoring from the local authority, spectacularly attractive and ongoing increments to landlords' rentals, and the regular appearance of suitable houses vacated by the middle class in their accelerating flight to the suburbs, created perfect conditions for the 'made-down', second-hand house. To the tenant even such limited accommodation, with the evils of darkness, damp and disease associated with the lobby,

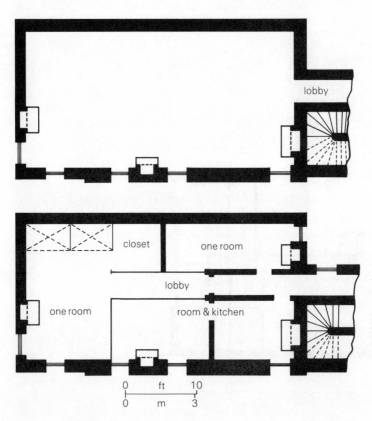

Figure 22.   'Making down' – the subdivision of one room into three.

the stair and the shared privy or closet, these 'single-ends' offered attractions –
a separate household, and an alternative to the common lodging house or the
transience of being a lodger in another family's flat.

Sanitary arrangements in Scottish houses drew especially vitriolic condemnation
due to the continuation well into the twentieth century of shared facilities. Clydebank, described in 1917 as 'the best example of an almost entirely modern and
tenement town',[41] had 40 per cent of houses with shared WC accommodation.

Table 17   Water closets in Clydebank, 1914

no. of apartments	houses of various sizes no.	%	% of houses provided with WC accommodation in the proportion of:			
			one for each family	one for two families	one for three families	one for four families
1	1,455	16.63	41	4	42	13
2	5,475	62.59	56	6	31	7
3	1,279	14.62	83	7.5	9	0.5
4	197	2.25	97	3	—	—
5+	342	3.91	99.5	0.5	—	—
Total	8,748	100.00	60	5	28	7

Source: PP, 1917–18, XIV, Royal Commission on the Housing of the Industrial Population of Scotland,
    Report, para. 373.

In fact 35 per cent of WCs were shared by three and four families, 18–20 people
sharing one WC (table 17). Greenock Housing Council showed Clydebank in a
favourable light when they reported a ratio between 22 and 43:1 WCs in their
tenement properties. The position in Clydebank, for all the claims of modernity,
was worse than in Edinburgh and Glasgow where, respectively, 29 and 35 per
cent of houses shared WCs.[42] In Port Glasgow, by contrast, 95 per cent of two-
roomed and even 50 per cent of three-roomed houses shared a WC, though even
this level of communal usage might seem attractive in Arbroath, described in 1905
as a 'dry-closet' town, or Galashiels where 'the pail system' was 'so insanitary and
objectionable' that in 1910 it produced a 'crusade' against it, or to the prevalence
of privy middens in Airdrie and Coatbridge.[43] Indeed in all burghs over 20,000
population a systematic link between privies and enteric fever was established
because the storage of sewage allowed for 'repeated reinfection of soil in the neighbourhood of dwelling houses, and the opportunity this gave for infection of food
by flies and other natural agencies'.[44] In Airdrie, for example, between 1894 and
1909, 87.5 per cent of cases of enteric fever occurred in houses with privies.[45]

Typical of prevailing living conditions and shared amenities in many mid Victorian
tenements were the Edinburgh properties described by Dr Henry Littlejohn, the
Edinburgh Medical Officer of Health in 1865. Gowanloch's Land in the High Street
and both Old and Middle the Mealmarket Stairs were very mean houses; 3 East
Richmond Street, 58 Blackfriars' Wynd, Elphinstone's Land and 341 Cowgate were
all 'comparatively modern structures' but had been extensively subdivided; Birtley
Buildings and Crombie's Land were further cases of landlords' rental avarice while
8 Cowgate housed a rather 'better' working-class element and 23 St James Street
was in the New Town. The pressure on WCs, sinks and general living space, and
the constraints on children, were not unusual in mid Victorian burghs under pressure

Table 18   (a) Water closets in Edinburgh, 1915

	size of tenement 1-room		2-rooms		3-rooms		4-rooms	
	no.	%	no.	%	no.	%	no.	%
shared WCs	6,661	93.4	8,267	35.9	1,364	7.7	202	2.0
separate WCs	445	6.3	15,199	64.3	14,507	92.3	10,040	98.0
houses	7,106	100.0	23,466	100.0	15,871	100.0	10,242	100.0

(b) Water closets in Glasgow, 1915

	size of tenement 1-room		2-rooms		3-rooms		4-rooms	
	no.	%	no.	%	no.	%	no.	%
shared WCs	38,407	92.9	68,938	61.9	5,097	11.4	353	2,4
separate WCs	2,947	7.1	42,513	38.1	39,694	88.6	14,274	97.6
houses	41,354	100.0	111,451	100.0	44,791	100.0	14,627	100.0

Source: PP, 1917–18, XIV, Royal Commission on the Housing of the Industrial Population of Scotland, Report, p. 77.

of population expansion and convey some impressions of the extent to which amenities were shared. In these eleven properties, typical of much of mid Victorian Edinburgh, 412 families were housed in 545 rooms. A total of almost 1,700 people, including 332 children under the age of five, shared 28 sinks and 11 WCs.[46]

The sanitation situation on the eve of the First World War, therefore, as represented in Edinburgh, Glasgow and Clydebank (tables 17 and 18) and elsewhere, was a substantial advance on conditions in mid Victorian Scotland. In relation to Paisley, the Sanitary Inspector stated a situation not dissimilar in a number of Scottish burghs, namely that since 1890 an active and progressive (sanitary and drainage) policy had been pursued by the corporation, with the result that 'the town has transformed the privy midden system of conveniences into the water carriage or water-closet system'.[47] As in other burghs, the objective of this sanitary campaign in Paisley had been based on the less than generous standard of 'one water closet for each flat, or one for every three houses'.[48]

Shared closets were only one aspect, albeit an important one, of shared facilities. In Edinburgh, in 1913, 43 per cent of one-roomed, 6 per cent of two-roomed houses, had communal sinks – 8.2 per cent of all houses in the capital.[49] Other burghs were in a similar position, though curiously the situation was much better in Glasgow. Another source of serious irritation was shared washing facilities. The back court or green – alternately muddy and dusty rather than green – was the common drying area for tenement dwellers, the washing itself being undertaken in the basement or in a separate wash-house on a rota basis. This inflexibility in washing times, friction over the responsibility for the wash-house key, drying poles and other essentials, offset much of the neighbourly spirit associated with tenement life. Barrow-in-Furness, hardly Utopia, might seem an inauspicious location for a commentary on the shared washing arrangements in Scottish tenements, but a survey of migrants there from Govan, Partick, Dundee, Dalmuir, Kilmarnock and Glasgow conveyed their vehement castigation of the wash-house system, the inconvenience of the rota and the fortnightly wash.[50]

Closets, sinks and wash-houses were shared on an occasional basis with other families. What was shared day and night was limited domestic floor space. Private Acts, obtained by some Scottish municipal authorities as early as the 1860s and standardized in 1903, set minimal cubic capacities for houses with different numbers of rooms, commonly 1,000, 1,600 and 2,400 cubic feet for one-, two- and three-roomed houses.[51] On the meanest assumptions of an 8 ft ceiling to allow for maximum floor space, this meant 125, 200 and 300 sq. ft, respectively; on average, 11 sq. ft for a one-roomed house, with the addition of 8.5 sq. ft for a second room and another 10 sq. ft for a third room. Though some houses below these minima remained – for example, in Glasgow one-roomed houses of 700 cubic feet, approximately 9 sq. ft, were well known – by the turn of the century new house-building frequently exceeded the statutory limit, one-, two- and three-roomed houses often having 1,400, 2,000 and 3,000 cubic feet of space. If this seemed generous by English standards it should be remembered that older, smaller properties – the vast majority – were the norm, that subdivision remained unregulated, and that while cubic capacity might be 50 per cent greater than in two- and three-roomed English terraced houses, once ceiling height was taken into account floor space per room might be only 20–25 per cent greater. Furthermore, English houses increasingly possessed a scullery – a rarity in Scotland[52] – and this additional room was not included in the English floor-space calculations. Finally, it was not just room size but the number of rooms available to a family which was crucial. As half the Scottish urban population lived in one- and two-roomed houses, specialized use of rooms – for cooking, eating, living, sleeping – was impossible in the manner available to an Englishman.

Limited floor space used in a multi-purpose way had an important consequence for daily household routines, and for work creation. In the commonest of Scottish housing types, the two-roomed flat or 'room and kitchen', the 'room' contained a bed closet: a double bed built into a large cupboard, hidden from view by doors and lacking direct lighting and ventilation.[53] In addition to the window sink, range, larder and coal bunker, and a few rudimentary shelves, the kitchen included a 'bed-recess' or 'box' bed, a low built-in bed with storage space below, often for a special children's bed which was wheeled out at night. The work created by these sleeping arrangements, not to mention the irritation which the congestion produced, was vividly communicated by Mrs Mary Laird of the Glasgow Women's Labour League. 'Where the family included boys and girls', she explained,

the mother in deference to feelings of womanly delicacy and, in the interests of her family's morality, tries to make up a separate bed for the boys and this bed has to be made down on chairs, etc., every night and packed up and tucked away with no chance of airing every morning.[54]

It goes without saying that for a family in a one-roomed house this situation was the norm, and thus 'the constant succession of lifting, folding and handing up' constituted 'a very great deal of extra labour on an already overdriven class'.[55]

Eventually, in the twentieth century, enclosed bed closets were banned, as were box-rooms such as those of less than 100 sq. ft used as sleeping quarters. Bed recesses drew less condemnation because of the recognition that there was some ventilation and light, and that in a one-roomed house it was difficult to contrive an alternative sleeping arrangement. Bed recesses in single-ends were, however, criticized for their location, farthest from the window, towards the centre of the building, and frequently separated from the communal WC by only a thin, and often porous, partition wall.[56]

Sickness, infirmity, childbirth and death pressurized sleeping space in one- and two-roomed houses. The Glasgow MOH, Dr J.B. Russell, captured the domestic stress for many Scottish city dwellers in his lecture *Life in One Room* in which he stated,

> When you die, you still have one room to yourself, where in decency you may be washed and dressed and laid out for burial. If that one room were your house what a ghastly intrusion you would be! The bed on which you lie is wanted for the accommodation of the living. The table at which your children ought to sit must bear your coffin.[57]

Another vivid account of domestic intrusion of the dead in the absence of municipal mortuaries was given by Mary Laird:

> The beloved dead is laid on the bed, and all the usual round of domestic duties, including the taking of meals, has to be done with ever that still, pale form before their view. Night comes on and the household must go to rest, so the sad burden is now transferred from the bed and laid on the table, or it may be the coal-bunker lid. In the morning, to admit of the table being used for breakfast, or to let coals be got for the fire, the body has to be lifted on to the bed again, and so on for the customary three days, the broken-hearted relatives feeling it to be a sacrilege thus to hustle about the mortal remains of a much loved one.[58]

At birth, too, the noise and stress associated with congestion and competition for floor space had an adverse effect on the delivery, maternal welfare, and the efficiency of medical and nursing services.[59]

Unanimously, the Royal Faculty of Physicians and Surgeons argued that,

> a very large number of tubercular cases are treated at home, and we hold that the houses for the poor at present existing in Glasgow are totally unsuitable, taking any room and kitchen house in Glasgow.[60]

They were not only 'unsuitable for home treatment', but had an adverse impact on the other family members. For example, in 250 cases of pulmonary tuberculosis in Glasgow in 1911 the need for the sick to occupy the bed forced other members of the family to sleep in chair beds or to share the sick bed.[61] Unsurprisingly, such sleeping arrangements were reflected in spectacular tubercular death rates in one- and two-apartment houses.[62] None of these problems of stress and congestion associated with birth and bereavement was lessened by the frequency of lodgers, whose presence ranged from 5 per cent in Aberdeen houses to 26 per cent in Bothwell.[63] Russell commented on this additional source of floor-space pressure by rhetorically presenting the implications to middle-class daughters who had

> no rude rabble of lodgers to sully the purity of your surroundings, how could you live and preserve 'the white flower of a blameless life' – in one room?[64]

The 'law of density' as formulated by the Registrar-General for England, Dr Farr, stated that '[T]he nearer people live to each other the shorter their lives are.'[65] This was based on empirical work which showed that 'the denser the city is, the more befouled is the earth with organic impurities.'[66] Scottish mortality rates bore ample testimony to the connection between density of living and the likelihood of dying. The inverse correlation of house size and death rates is particularly clear from table 19 and is valid in many burghs other than Glasgow. Nor can age and sex composition account for the variation as the corrected Glasgow figures for 1911 show (table 20).

Table 19   Glasgow mortality rates according to house size, 1901 (Death rate per 1,000)

size of houses	census popln.	all causes	zymotic	phthisis	respiratory disease (incl. croup)
1 room	104,128	32.7	7.4	2.4	7.7
2 rooms	348,731	21.3	4.5	1.8	4.6
3 rooms	151,754	13.7	1.9	1.2	2.4
4+ rooms	136,511	11.2	1.0	0.7	2.0
City*	761,712	20.6	3.8	1.8	4.3

* Including institutions and deaths not traced.
Source: A.K. Chalmers, 'The death-rate in one-apartment houses: an enquiry based on the Census returns of 1901', *Proceedings of the Royal Philosophical Society of Glasgow*, 34 (1902–3), 131.

Table 20   Glasgow mortality rates according to house size, 1911, corrected according to age and sex structure

	crude death-rate per 1000	corrected death-rate per 1000
1 room	25.9	20.1
2 rooms	16.5	16.8
3 rooms	11.5	12.6
4 rooms	10.8	10.3

Source: PP, 1917–18, XIV, Royal Commission
on the Housing of the Industrial Population
of Scotland, Report, para. 658.

Furthermore, if density as reflected by the frequency of one-roomed houses had declined sharply by 1911 – though still 1:12 of all Scottish houses compared to 1:77 of English houses – this had formerly been very much higher (table 21). Two out of three Scots lived in a 1- or 2-roomed house in 1861, and though the number of 'single-ends' diminished steadily over the next 50 years to that 1:12 ratio in 1911, the 2-roomed proportion invariably remained the abode for two out of five Scots families.

It was, however, the impact of these living conditions upon children which increasingly caused alarm. This concern took a number of forms: physical, mental and moral. As Dr Russell explained,

Place 126,000 human beings in one-roomed houses and 43,000 in houses of five

Table 21   Scottish housing, 1861–1911

	1-room houses %	2-room houses %	3+-room houses %
1861	26.2	38.6	35.2
1871	23.7	38.5	37.8
1881	18.0	39.5	42.5
1891	14.3	39.4	46.3
1901	11.0	39.5	49.5
1911	8.7	39.2	52.1

Source: PP, 1913, LXXX, Report of the Twelfth
        Census of Scotland, ci.

rooms and upwards and . . . you have at once determined for them much of both their moral and physical future.[67]

Brought up above ground level, '[T]he playground of most of the children of Glasgow below five years of age [was] the lobby and the stairhead'. So dark were the lobbies and stairs that it was 'a sorry thing to hear their voices, and to feel them, for often you cannot see them . . .'[68] Consequently children's games and exercise opportunities were constrained by the tenement system of building:

Pent up in common stairs and in back courts without a bit of space which they can call their own, their play inevitably becomes a great part of mischief.[69]

In the second half of the nineteenth century advancing social control by municipal agencies – local bye-laws, policing and enlarged civic responsibilities – affected street games, as did the advance of vehicular traffic. Alternatives to street play existed. From the 1860s municipal authorities consciously pursued a policy of land acquisition for the purposes of parks and playgrounds, though these were both few in number and distant from many housing concentrations.[70] Another alternative was the back court. Limited in area, 'grassless and altogether unsuitable for playgrounds', they also represented a health hazard, being close to dustbins, disused middens and dry-closets.[71] For slightly older children the stairs and lobbies offered some alternative to both the home and the street. Descriptive of play in many tenements, and of the moralizing associated with it, were the comments of the Rev. Dr Watson:

The children are forced out of doors to give the housewife room to work. This, to me, is the saddest result of wretched housing. In my evening visitation I find the children everywhere – sitting in the closes and on the stairs, trying to play, often half asleep, on bitter winter nights. Sometimes they play in the dark, evil-smelling courts, sometimes in the dimly-lit streets, and they learn no good. They see sights which demoralise, and hear language which corrupts.[72]

It was not such a great jump to see how idle chalk-writing on walls, climbing on roofs, removing bricks from dilapidated walls and congregations of adolescents in closes were seen as formative influences in juvenile delinquency, and informed opinion such as that of the Medical Officers of both Liverpool and Birmingham was particularly condemning about the effects of flatted accommodation of the Scottish type on child development.[73]

For very young children, play had to be entirely within the tenement flat because of the danger posed by steep and ill-lit stair wells. Annually between 60 and 70 accidental deaths to children under five were recorded in Glasgow alone by the Registrar-General, and it was 'wholly in these small houses that such deaths occur'.[74] Half were smothered by drunken parents; the remainder fell down stairs or from windows, were scalded or drowned in tubs of water. In a lecture on child health, Dr J.B. Russell noted that 'women [spend] three-fourths and children in their earliest and most susceptible years practically the whole of their lives within the house space'.[75] Another expert concluded that Paisley 'mothers cannot have proper supervision of their children of tender years while playing outside and these must therefore be kept indoors for the greater part of their time'.[76] Not unnaturally this had adverse effects on the efficiency with which household chores were discharged, on the learning experience and social skills of children themselves, and had a detrimental effect upon domestic demeanour due to cramped living and household working space.

Whether eating, sleeping or playing, environmental conditions in one- and two-roomed houses – the overwhelming majority for most of the nineteenth century – were strongly correlated with indicators of social deprivation. At one extreme, infant and child mortality rates confirmed the correlation. After half a century of sanitary reform in Edinburgh, infant mortality in 1910 for the city as a whole was 110 per 1,000; in those areas of larger 3- and 4-roomed houses, such as Merchiston, the rate was as low as 46 per 1,000, whereas in wards of predominantly 1- and 2-roomed houses the infant mortality rates climbed as high as 155 in St Giles, and 277 per 1,000 in the Cowgate ward.[77] The corresponding situation in Glasgow is shown in table 22. The physical effects of the peculiarly Scottish urban environment were, however, far more insidious. 'The child is physically, even more than morally, father of the man', remarked Dr Russell, because 'it may change morally, but it cannot get rid of ricketty bones, or impaired organs, or a tainted constitution.'[78] Thus uniquely Scottish environmental deficiencies connected with tenement life – 'foul air to breathe, impure water to drink ... cramped in space and cradled in dirt' – meant that children 'must grow up through sickly and unhappy adolescence into weak and stunted manhood.'[79]

Table 22   Infant and child mortality, Glasgow, 1910

size of houses	death rates per 1,000	
	under 1 year	aged 1–5
1 room	210.3	40.6
2 rooms	163.8	30.2
3 rooms	128.5	17.9
4 rooms	102.6	10.3

Source: Scottish Land Enquiry Committee,
    Scottish Land (1914), 371.

Although surveys were undertaken in Dundee and Edinburgh,[80] the most comprehensive study of physical development covered 72,857 Glasgow schoolchildren in 1905–6.[81] It conclusively showed that for boys and girls of all ages, Glasgow children

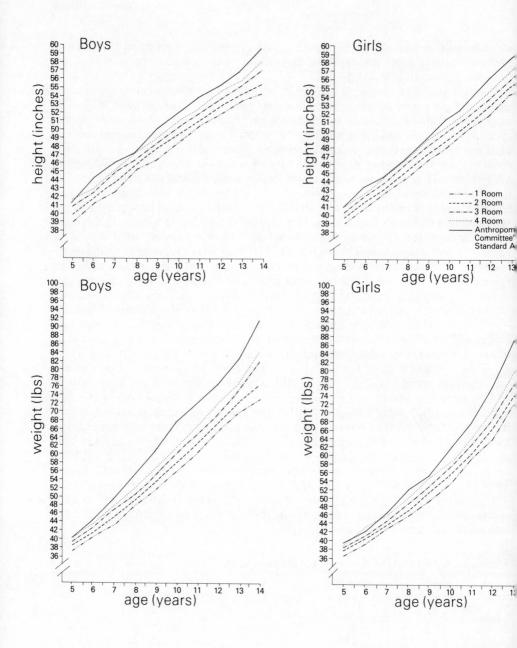

Figure 23.   Glasgow children compared to the national average, 1904: height and weight according to house size. (Source: Scotch Education Department, *Report on the Physical Condition of Children Attending the Public Schools of the School Board for Glasgow*, HMSO, 1907, tables VIII A, B, diagrams 3–6.)

were below the national standards for height and weight, and were progressively further below according to whether they lived in 4-, 3-, 2- or 1-roomed houses (see fig. 23). This was all the more significant given that Scotland was peopled by a race taller than that in England and Wales (table 23). There were, however, significant variations within Scotland and the small size of urban Scots in relation to all Scots and to the national anthropometric standards was reflected in the size of adult males recruited to the army (table 24). Though counties and cities were undifferentiated, it was normally the urban counties and notably the west central grouping of Lanarkshire, Renfrew and Ayrshire which recruited adult males up to 3 per cent smaller than those north of the Highland Line, findings which confirmed the general tendency noted in 1870 for urban dwellers in Edinburgh, Glasgow, Dundee and Fife burghs to be smaller than natives from rural parishes in Ayrshire and the Borders.

Table 23   Heights and weights of adult males in Britain, 1883

	mean stature (ins)	mean weight (lbs)	height ÷ weight
Scotland	68.71	165.3	0.416
Ireland	67.90	155.0	0.441
England	67.36	154.1	0.435
Wales	66.66	158.3	0.421

Source: British Association for the Advancement of Science, *Final Report*, (London, 1883), 4–7.

Table 24   Geographical variations in stature: Scottish adult males, 1914–18

recruiting area	mean stature (mm)	standard deviation (mm)
Lanarkshire, Renfrew, Ayr	1,699.17	58.75
Fife, Forfar, Clack., Perth, Kinross	1,706.26	55.15
Midlothian, Linlithgow, E. Lothian, & E, Borders	1,719.78	62.75
Aberdeen, Elgin, Banff, Kincardine	1,719.78	58.50
Stirling, Dumbarton, Argyll, Bute	1,720.66	54.00
Dumfries, Wigtown, Kirkcudbright	1,731.54	58.65
Orkney, Shetland, Caithness, Sutherland, Ross, Cromarty, Inverness, Nairn	1,746.09	59.65

Source: J.F. Tocher, *Anthropometric Observations on Samples of the Civil Population* (1924).

4 Intensification of tenement building and housing problems

a. Influence of incomes and tenure

The ledger of tenement living contained some credit entries. For the housewife, aged and infirm, rooms on one level were a convenience. A high proportion of urban Scots lived above ground-floor level, and arguably this reduced the susceptibility of their housing to dampness, though lack of ventilation and damp courses, and stone construction offset this to a degree. Shared facilities kept rentals down and high-density living allowed larger numbers of workers to live within a convenient distance of their workplace, a not unimportant consideration for the casually employed. Communal blocks contributed to a sense of security against burglary and fire. Against these advantages the most vigorous impeachment of the tenement system came from the Edinburgh City Engineer:

> the discomforts and inconveniences of the common stair, the greater risks of infection, the diminished floor space offered by the tenement system, the higher standard of rent required . . . the diminished light and air upon the lower floors, the absence of any piece of garden ground attached exclusively to each house, and all this absence means to the physique and morale of family life.[82]

Why, then, did tenement building gain such widespread currency in Scotland? If the disadvantages were as pernicious as maintained, why was the tenement tolerated by tenants and reproduced so faithfully by builders until council housing after 1919 smashed the mould?

Two fundamental characteristics set the framework of builders' responses. One was institutional, namely the legal code governing land tenure; the other, the structure of demand, determined the type and quantity of accommodation affordable. Builders, like other producers, neglected market conditions at their peril, and a pattern of weak and unstable urban incomes more pronounced than in England set Scottish builders a basic requirement – to produce cheap rented accommodation. The construction of block tenement dwellings with site development, common foundations and roofing, shared amenities and other costs split amongst a large number of residents was an obvious solution.

Weak and unstable demand for housing emanated from the very basis of the Scottish economy. As an industrial late developer compared to England, its access to international markets rested on dual advantages: cheaper raw material costs and lower manufacturing costs. Central to the latter were lower labour costs, and Scottish wages reflected this throughout the nineteenth century. In relation to United Kingdom wage levels in 1886, pay in all grades characterized Scotland as 'a low wage economy'.[83] In fact, the Scottish-UK differential was narrowing over time. In the 1830s and 1840s Scottish wages were often 20–25 per cent adrift of identical English trades; by the 1860s the differential had narrowed to 16–19 per cent; erosion during the last quarter of the nineteenth century meant that the gap was reduced to 9–13 per cent.[84] Even on the most generous assumptions Scottish wages in 1886 were no more than 94.8 per cent of those equivalent occupations in England.[85] In many cases they were substantially lower, and A.D. Campbell's conclusion, in relation to the interwar years when the narrowing of the gap had obviously run its full nineteenth-century course, that 'income per head has been lower in Scotland, fluctuating between 87 and 96% of the United Kingdom average'[86] was closer to Victorian reality. Moreover, Scottish industrial productivity, and presumably therefore entrepreneurs' ability to pay wages, remained below that of the United Kingdom as a whole, according to the Census of Production in 1907.[87] Lower Scottish productivity applied to a wide range of industrial activities, many of which were major branches of Scottish employment. In quarrying, iron and steel manufacture, chemicals, clothing trades, the expanding food and drink industry, carting, coopering, electricity, building and municipal employment, Scottish productivity compared unfavourably to the national average. Although there were, of course, some bright spots, too – mining, matting, oil, distilling, leatherwork, brush- and brick-making, scientific instruments – these areas of improving industrial productivity and performance were unable to offset the dragging effect of Scottish industrial productivity and other influences on Scottish wage levels generally.

More significantly, Scottish incomes were highly unstable.[88] Sizable elements of male and female employment were susceptible to broken time. Interruptions to already below-average wage levels affected between 1 in 4 and 1 in 5 of all Scottish male workers, and a slightly lower proportion of the female workforce, and this reduced the weekly sum which could be allocated to rent. Treble has identified 27.2 per cent of male Glaswegians as casually employed and the equivalent figures for Aberdeen, Edinburgh and Dundee were respectively 24.4, 24.2 and 20.0 per cent. Messengering, portering, building employees, gasworkers and other areas of casual employment were consequently heavily represented in Scottish industrial centres and this had important implications for the standard of affordable accommodation.[89] Seasonal, casual and other irregular employment therefore dampened the already weakened demand for housing accommodation, and in conjunction with the conventions governing the letting system,[90] the volume of housing space purchased was constrained to the minimal levels previously described.

Flour and bread, butter, tea, four cuts of pork and bacon and seven of beef, eggs and cheese were conspicuously more expensive in Edinburgh, Leith, Falkirk, Galashiels, Perth, Dundee, Aberdeen, Paisley, Greenock, Glasgow and Kilmarnock than they were in 70 English and Welsh boroughs.[91] Coal, oil, milk and mutton were on a par with prices paid by urban dwellers south of the Cheviots. Overall, taking 29 items constituting more than 60 per cent of weekly expenditure on food, Scottish urban prices were 2 per cent higher even than those of central London and 11 per cent above those of North of England boroughs and Midland towns in 1905. Even when fuel prices, which favoured the towns of the central belt of Scotland, were taken into account, the Scottish price index was on a par with central London and still about 9 per cent above the towns in the cheapest of the English regions, the Midlands (table 25).

Table 25   Real wage variations, 1905

| geographical group | number of towns | Mean Index Numbers rent and prices | | | wages (skilled)men | |
		rent	prices	rent and prices combined	building, engineering and printing trades	approximate relative level of 'real wages'
ENGLAND AND WALES						
London	—	100	100	100	100	100
Northern counties and Cleveland	9	62	97	90	86	96
Yorks. (– Cleveland)	10	56	94	87	84	97
Lancs. & Cheshire	17	54	92	84	87	104
Midlands	15	51	93	85	85	100
Eastern counties	7	50	98	88	76	86
Southern counties	10	61	102	93	80	86
Wales & Monmouth	4	60	96	89	86	97
SCOTLAND	10	69	102	95	83	87
IRELAND	6	50	97	87	84	97

Source: PP, 1908, CVIII, Report of an Enquiry by the Board of Trade into Working Class Rents, Housing and Retail Prices, xl.

In 1905, real wages in Scotland were 16 per cent below those in 17 boroughs in the north-west of England, 13 per cent below London and 15 Midland boroughs, and 10 per cent lower than in 23 boroughs in Yorkshire, Northumberland, Durham and Wales (table 25). Only when compared to 17 boroughs in the relatively rural, certainly less industrial, southern and eastern counties of England were Scottish real wages on a lowly par. Even compared to six Irish towns, Scottish purchasing power was 10 per cent weaker.

With English and Scottish wage-price differentials at their narrowest in 1912 the real wage disadvantage of Scots was also at a historical low.[92] Further refinements would be necessary to take account of greater irregularity of incomes in Scotland and a heavier dependence upon wage rather than salaried incomes, but the Board of Trade's statistical surveys demonstrated a mean Scottish real wage disadvantage of up to 10 per cent in 1912, and had the price disadvantage of the twentieth century been no greater, then prevailing mid century real wages in urban Scotland may have been at least 20–30 per cent below those in English and Welsh boroughs, and possibly even lower. Thus, in explaining why Scottish houses were 'mean, sordid and scantily furnished', the Presbytery Commission report of 1891 justifiably concluded that 'sheer poverty has much to answer for'.[93]

Tenement construction was also influenced by tenure. The management of urban estates required, in general, the balancing of short- and long-term considerations in an effort to maximize revenue and in this equation the controlled release of land was an established tactic. The Scottish feudal tenure system, however, attached a premium to this type of market strategy. In England the two principal methods of estate development were by the outright sale of land (freehold) or by a hire of the ground for a fixed term (leasehold). In Scotland land was sold outright by the vendor who relinquished all title to it, but an annual payment was also made – the feu duty.[94] The system was a mixture of the two English forms but possessed four unique features which tended to increase land prices. First, the vendor or superior was liquidating an irrecoverable asset in the same manner as the sale of freehold in England, and often withheld land in the expectation that the market would move upwards in the future, a reasonable assumption under the nineteenth-century conditions of rapid population growth and industrial development. In this respect the practice was no different from that in England. However, the second influence related to the superior's entitlement to an annual feu duty which was additional to the price of the ground. Thus, to take account of long-run inflation the superior was not encouraged 'to give his ground for a reasonable feu duty'[95] but compensated for the inevitable erosion of the real value in the long term by creating high-priced feus which were particularly onerous in the short term. Although this was superficially similar to the leasehold system, it was significantly different first because it was in addition to the maximized land value equivalent to the freehold sale, and second because with no reversionary rights and thus no participation in any betterment as under a leasehold tenure, the Scottish vendor had no interest in balancing the long-term appreciation of the land and buildings against the short-term, income-earning capacity. Or, as was described in contemporary terms, 'the superior, after feuing his land, is not interested in any increased value of the land over and above the amount of the feu duty, any increase in the value of the land being participated in by the vassal alone'.[96] The third feature of feuing was that it entitled the superior to a number of additional, though occasional, payments, equivalent to a second or even a third feu duty.[97] Where the successor to a feu was the heir of the previous vassal a payment of 'relief' equal to an annual feu duty was payable. The superior was bound to accept a successor who was not the heir if a 'composition' payment was made, a sum equivalent to the annual net rental on the property. No new 'casualty' payments of these types were admissible after the passage of the Conveyancing (Scotland) Act 1874, but by way of compensation 'duplicands' or double feu duties every nineteenth or so year became more frequent features of the feu contract. Further land burdens could also be levied in the form of ground annuals. Originally as an alternative to annual payments on land where sub-infeudation was prohibited, by mid Victorian times ground annuals were becoming additional to feu duties. The Scottish Land Enquiry Committee explained how the system worked and why it became increasingly attractive:

> [Ground annuals] are perpetual annual payments on the property and are not
> redeemable. As soon as they are created they can be sold. And this is precisely
> the explanation of their existence. The builder commonly disposes of them for
> cash as soon as they are created, and so finances his operations: he obtains
> his money at an earlier stage in building the premises and also secures this money
> at a lower rate of interest than a bond or mortgage.[98]

As a first mortgage on easy terms, never needing renewal, the attractions of extending the ground annual system of land burdens to the builder were obvious; to the resident, forgetting casualty payments, the combined effect of feu duties and ground annuals was generally to add 10–14 per cent to the gross rental of tenement property.[99]

The fourth inflationary influence on land values attributable to feudal tenure was the practice of 'sub-infeudation'.[100] The right to exact an annual feu duty passed successively with the transfer of land from landowner to developer, to builder to house factor, and then to house purchaser. A compound levy of feu duty was therefore effectively built into the transfer of land and landlords and house factors who found themselves the last lineal successors of the right to exact a feu duty accordingly passed on the accumulated charges so levied to their tenants. As each individual in the chain of sub-feuing was personally liable for payment to his immediate superior, there was a considerable incentive to ensure that this could be met and consequently successive tiers of the feuing pyramid tended to be substantially inflated. Furthermore, feu duties were also a first charge on an estate and thus a highly desirable security upon which capital could easily be raised. As such they were an attractive form of investment, competition for which may in itself have forced up the level of feu duties.[101] 'Feu-farming', the process of continuously building up the annual charge on land, became an accepted, if not acceptable, practice in Scotland as James Gowans, an Edinburgh builder, explained:

> A builder looks forward to the town increasing, and he takes up a lot of land
> from the superior at £50 an acre, and then by re-feuing or building himself he
> works it up to £200 an acre. That has been done within this city and large fortunes
> have been made out of it.[102]

From the point of view of the supply and price of building land the Scottish tenurial system worked to the disadvantage of all classes, though lower-income groups were particularly adversely affected. The English leasehold and freehold systems worked by different routes to maximize the landowner's receipts. Betterment and retention of title delicately balanced long- and short-term considerations. Under Scottish tenure arrangements there was no such trade-off but a reinforcing effect where both influences operated simultaneously to lever land prices upwards. In the power to sub-feu, a licence was granted to inflate the annual charge. Of course, such licences and price-inflating tactics were not unlimited, constrained as they were by what the market would bear, but they represented stronger reasons for a restriction in the supply of building land than existed in England and with such restrictions operating it was likely that the market would exact a higher price, with potentially serious implications for those who could least afford it – the Scottish working class. Feuing, therefore, tipped the balance of advantage towards land hoarding rather than estate development for building purposes, and landowners discovered that low-rating of vacant land gave a further stimulus to withholding land in the expectation of substantial future increases in land prices.

The proportion of rent attributable to the cost of land was undoubtedly higher in Scottish burghs than in English cities.[103] For example, properties of the London East End Dwellings Company and the London Common Trust, built in the last two Victorian decades, recorded 6–8 per cent of overall rent as due to ground rents; the proportion was in the 12–15 per cent range amongst comparable properties of the Glasgow Dwellings Company and the Improvement Trust during the same years, and 17 per cent in Clydebank.[104] Though strictly comparable sites are an impossibility due to the uniqueness of each plot, available building land in Liverpool in the 1890s cost between 22s.6d. and 24s., whereas it was in excess of 30s.per square yard in Glasgow at that time.[105]

The feuing system, construction of tenements and raising of builders' capital were intimately related, and it was these interconnections rather than simply the inflationary effect of feuing on land prices which reinforced the peculiarly Scottish pattern of high-rise construction. The Scottish Land Enquiry Committee stated:

> When the ground rent exceeds a certain figure (£20 to £25 an acre per annum) the erection of cottages at reasonable rents becomes impossible and it is necessary for the builder to erect tenements in order to spread the high cost of land over a large number of houses. . . . The high price of land and the erection of tenement housing react upon one another, that is to say, the high price of land requires the erection of tenements in order to make the maximum use of it and to spread the burden of the feu duty over as many payers as possible, and conversely the power to erect tenements and to impose upon the land a very considerable property maintains the high value of the land.[106]

It was indeed this degree of interconnectedness which had such an all-pervasive effect upon the built environment in Scottish towns where middle-class suburbanization and detached villa developments proceeded in much more limited ways than in English boroughs.

b. Structure of the Scottish building industry
If the power of the Scottish consumer was weakened by real wage and land price levels, in most burghs it was further eroded by a sizable component of interrupted employment. Under such conditions it was perfectly understandable that both quali-

tatively and quantitatively the standard of housing would be mean. To some extent, the structure of the Scottish building industry was a further force in this direction.

House-building in Victorian Scotland was skewed towards small operators (table 26).[107] Over half of the house-building in 102 burghs was undertaken as a 'one-off' project, that is 52.9 per cent of building proposals were for the construction of one house or tenement only. The number of projects for three or more properties represented only 17.2 per cent of all house-building projects, and in the smaller burghs the construction of several properties simultaneously by a builder was virtually non-existent (3.6 per cent) and in some completely unknown.

Table 26   The scale of building projects, Scottish burghs, 1873–1914

	no. of burghs	1 house	2 houses	3 or more houses
Cities	3	39.6	39.3	21.1
Major burghs*	30	53.9	25.8	20.4
Small burghs	69	74.8	21.6	3.6
Scottish burghs	102	52.9	30.7	17.2

* 'Major' status is accorded to any burgh which in the Census Reports 1841–1951 appeared as one of the twenty-five largest burghs in Scotland; any other burgh is designated as 'small'.
Source: Dean of Guild Court Registers of Plans and Sections in the individual burghs.

In the more populous urban communities of Scotland where the opportunities for a larger scale of operations might have presented themselves only 20.0 per cent of projects and 50.3 per cent of housing was built in projects of 3 or more units (table 27). Schemes for 3–5 houses represented 28.6 per cent of planned building, those for 6–10 formed 15.6 per cent of the total, and proposals for 11 or more houses in any one project accounted for only 6.1 per cent of applications to planning agencies in the 22 Scottish burghs: figures which would be considerably reduced if all 102 burghs were taken into consideration. Half the house-building work in Scottish burghs was left in the hands of builders whose activities were restricted to projects of one or two properties in a year.

Larger building operations were not systematically linked to those burghs experiencing most rapid population expansion. Between 1871 and 1911 the population of Kilmarnock increased by 64.7 per cent, and that of Falkirk by 251.7 per cent, and yet, as table 27 shows, the frequency of larger building projects was almost identical. In contrast, similar population growth rates, for example in Leith and Airdrie, of respectively 80.0 and 80.8 per cent over the same period 1871–1911, encouraged builders in these burghs to contemplate markedly divergent levels of larger scale residential construction, to the extent of 43.33 and 22.26 per cent of total house-building respectively. Much the same disparity applied to the smaller Scottish burghs, too, in that Lerwick, Fraserburgh, Buckie and Forres, the most rapidly developing burghs in northern Scotland, witnessed no more widespread a degree of large-scale construction than the more modestly expanding townships of nearby Elgin, Nairn or Peterhead.[108]

The existence and expected continuation of rapid rates of household formation in the Scottish urban population, it seems, was not a sufficient, or even a necessary, condition of large-scale building. Alternatively, there may have been a minimum

Table 27 Multiple house-building projects and urban growth in selected Scottish burghs, 1873–1914

	projects for 3 or more houses as a % of total projects	% contribution of projects of 3 or more houses to total house-building	population growth 1871–1911 (%)	average population of burgh 1871–1911
Rutherglen	2.5	11.3	163.1	14,648
Hawick	5.4	16.0	48.6	16,185
Airdrie	6.4	22.3	80.8	18,532
Kilmarnock	10.0	43.8	64.7	28,854
Falkirk	11.1	44.4	251.7	20,577
Irvine	11.5	40.1	47.8	8,857
Port Glasgow	12.0	23.7	64.0	14,682
Stirling	12.6	32.3	95.0	16,654
Dumbarton	12.9	34.6	92.5	16,822
Aberdeen	13.4	33.8	85.0	124,237
Hamilton	15.4	45.2	236.1	25,205
Galashiels	16.7	33.3	50.1	14,081
Dunfermline	17.7	44.3	70.8	22,375
Perth	18.0	36.7	60.8	29,585
Paisley	18.4	48.6	75.0	66,828
Musselburgh	22.5	70.3	112.0	10,387
Leith	22.5	43.3	80.0	66,168
Coatbridge	30.1	59.8	173.0	28,723
Edinburgh	30.1	66.7	62.6	264,716
Partick	34.3	61.8	277.5	40,560
Govan	39.0	80.4	366.7	58,497
Clydebank	48.8	83.6	275.0*	22,047*
Scottish burghs	(22) *[handwritten: (22) 20.0]*	20.0 *[handwritten: 50.3]*	50.3 *[handwritten: 80.1]*	— *[handwritten: 80.1]*

* Clydebank 1891–1911 only.
Sources: Dean of Guild Court Registers, Registers of Plans and Sections, and Town Council Minutes in the burghs; *Census of Scotland*, 1871–1911.

size of town below which the activities of larger builders were both impracticable and unprofitable, and which therefore acted as a powerful disincentive to build houses in projects of three or more units in certain burghs. Certainly, in the cases of the smallest Scottish burghs, the vast majority of residential building, 96.4 per cent in fact, was undertaken in projects for one and two houses only (table 26). Thus for urban focal points such as Huntly, Duns, Kirkcudbright, Stonehaven and St Andrews, the simultaneous construction of three houses by a single builder was a rare event, and in those communities such as Dunoon and Rothesay catering for the growing holiday resort traffic, or those burghs within the geographical orbit of the major urban centres, including for example, Bridge of Allan, Helensburgh and Inverurie,[109] the overwhelming form of residential construction was a single house. Although there is not an exact and progressive correlation between town size and the frequency of multiple house-building projects, it was predominantly in the major centres of population that a larger house-building scale emerged. Certainly, as table 27 shows, absolute town size rather than the rates of population growth was more closely linked with, and probably a more influential determinant of, urban house-building in Scotland in the Victorian period. Thus, below some critical average population level of approximately 20,000, with certain exceptions such as Musselburgh, Kilmarnock and Irvine, the demand for new houses, even where this was expanding rapidly, tended to be met by successively building single houses, rather than by the simultaneous construction of several houses.

As might be expected, heavy reliance on small-scale building operations constrained the extent of speculative construction. The nature of applications to the planning agency in most burghs, the Dean of Guild Court, reveals a variety of motives behind house-building. In Aberdeen 430 different individuals initiated 897 house-building projects in the years 1885 to 1894. Thus, almost every other house-building project, 47.9 per cent to be exact, came from a person who had not previously sought to build a house in that burgh, nor would they do so again, and in Edinburgh, too, much the same atomized structure existed in the building industry, where 41.9 per cent of planned house-building was on a once and for all basis. Of the 430 Aberdeen applicants, it was the initiative of shopowners (4.3%), manufacturers (4.2%), commercial interests (5.0%), professional groups (5.7%), artisans (2.0%) and occasionally unskilled labourers (0.7%) which accounted for the capital and the initiative to build. Widows and spinsters, returning Aberdonian exiles and other interests external to Aberdeen, together with company and institutional house-building, provided the stimulus for another 6.0 per cent, while an assortment of private individuals, some retired or without an acknowledged form of employment, and a small group of unclassified persons together instigated 18.2 per cent of planned house-building in Aberdeen. While the building trades of Aberdeen (41.1%) and quasi-building interests such as house-factors, architects, and solicitors (12.7%) brought a bare majority of house-building plans into being, a sizable element (46.2%) were formulated and financed by persons unconnected with the building industry. Over the same period, however, Edinburgh builders assumed a greater command of house-building, applying as they did for 72.6 per cent of houses approved by the Dean of Guild Court, with institutional and company building (7.1%), and private house-building plans (20.4%) rather less important than in Aberdeen. Nor were builders dominant in the finance of house-building in the smaller industrial centres. Their contribution was never more than 40 per cent, and on average only 28 per cent of the houses approved.[110]

The volume of financially guaranteed, unspeculative Scottish house-building was therefore substantial. Although initiating only 27.4 per cent of Edinburgh house-building, the stimulus for 46.2 per cent of residential building in Aberdeen, and 48.5 per cent in the major urban centres came from non-building industry sources; in the semi-rural towns never less than 60, and often closer to 70 per cent of planned house-building was backed by private, rather than builders' sources of capital. The occupational composition of these sources was extremely diverse, with retailers, manufacturers and professional groups most numerous. The majority planned only their own house, though a number combined with friends, relatives or business partners to cut the cost of legal, architects' and planning authority fees, as well as to reduce the unit costs by sharing party walls, splitting connection charges for gas, water and sewage and laying out of streets and pavements. Thus to a considerable degree the building of Scottish burghs was brought about non-speculatively; a sizable proportion of the finance for house-building was committed before the commencement of the project, and in many cases the sale of the property was assured upon completion.

If the speculative motive was muted, what there was combined with the small-scale building firms to produce variations in annual output of an order unprecedented in other Scottish industries. Nationally, building was 125 per cent more volatile

Table 28   Indices of housebuilding in Scottish burghs 1873–1914 (1900–09 av. = 100)

	Scottish burghs	Aberdeen	Dundee	Edinburgh	Glasgow	Gov
1873	168.2		232		152	
1874	194.6		281		157	163
1875	211.5		272		178	205
1876	247.2		316		218	190
1877	193.3		172		228	n.a.
1878	78.5		98		51	63
1879	52.3		69		35	16
1880	111.0	126	160	181	31	37
1881	71.7	100	58	129	27	37
1882	74.5	60	56	141	23	90
1883	57.7	64	54	109	20	79
1884	78.9	130	94	115	26	37
1885	76.7	129	56	106	39	11
1886	94.4	188	67	94	43	39
1887	105.5	155	125	150	44	32
1888	97.0	114	111	135	51	37
1889	96.0	126	111	125	49	47
1890	72.4	78	96	94	42	26
1891	76.8	85	91	74	75	21
1892	87.6	113	107	63	110	21
1893	107.3	134	138	65	119	37
1894	124.0	177	140	110	139	58
1895	125.7	177	129	105	133	63
1896	153.4	247	138	199	141	79
1897	156.5	249	160	210	168	126
1898	168.1	213	198	237	157	116
1899	138.4	204	178	205	108	79
1900	93.6	122	85	109	93	116
1901	121.4	123	120	97	141	190
1902	132.2	127	98	104	197	137
1903	125.7	154	107	110	148	111
1904	116.3	121	105	115	114	111
1905	113.0	118	131	123	106	84
1906	106.0	81	114	134	101	63
1907	69.6	54	71	88	71	68
1908	59.9	57	78	61	55	63
1909	62.9	44	91	58	58	58
1910	51.9	46	56	41	45	11
1911	35.1	23	47	30	28	16
1912	31.5	23	54	35	28	11
1913	25.9	23	36	17	27	
1914	25.3	17	42	17	23	

Source: R.G. Rodger, thesis, table 4.4, p. 97.

than industrial production as a whole. Compared to food, drink and tobacco, mining, chemicals or engineering, building instability was respectively 327, 108, 61 and 33 per cent greater than in these sectors. The Scottish building industry was more unstable than its English counterpart. Not unusually, building activity during depressed years ran to only 10–15 per cent of previous peak levels, and house-building variations of 20–30 index points were normal. Between 1880 and 1914 the annual changes in the house-building indices for Edinburgh, Dundee, Aberdeen,

nock	Kirkcaldy	Leith	Partick	Perth	Port Glasgow	
			75			1873
			82			1874
			109			1875
			136			1876
		231	95			1877
	50	269	14	52	109	1878
	82	58	14	89	22	1879
	88	180	20	104	65	1880
	44	96	34	47	22	1881
	82	115	34	52	44	1882
	26	19	41	42	109	1883
	44	77	27	68	22	1884
	24	83	61	37	44	1885
	35	154	34	57	22	1886
	68	128	109	57	22	1887
	56	83	88	57	44	1888
	50	109	n.a.	47	65	1889
	26	64	n.a.	68	109	1890
	47	90	n.a.	37	65	1891
	76	71	n.a.	73	22	1892
	123	122	n.a.	115	174	1893
	120	109	88	198	130	1894
	170	106	123	151	196	1895
	150	147	150	115	131	1896
	114	135	150	130	130	1897
	144	218	177	182	65	1898
	123	147	136	99	43	1899
	70	83	54	73	130	1900
	106	109	129	130	109	1901
	129	90	191	214	109	1902
	120	141	191	99	108	1903
	109	109	102	104	87	1904
	153	96	61	94	86	1905
	97	180	95	109	65	1906
	53	71	41	78	174	1907
	79	45	95	47	65	1908
	85	77	41	52	65	1909
	97	45	41	42	87	1910
	32	45	48	63	109	1911
	21	25	48	11	44	1912
	12	6		10	44	1913
	15	19		5	43	1914

Govan and Kircaldy were within this range though in Kilmarnock, Leith, Partick, Perth and Port Glasgow they varied annually by an average of 30–40 index points.[111] In some burghs, such as Coatbridge and Irvine, the house-building index moved 40–50 points on average each year. Such averages obscure actual year-to-year variations (table 28). In Clydebank, for example, the house-building index between 1894 and 1898 recorded successively 71; 129; 188; 106; 71. Even in Kirkcaldy during the depressed 1880s, the index ranged between 26 and 88 only, but the average change in the index of 26.4 points represented as much as 100 per cent variations in some years. It was not that there were just a few spectacular variations – 58 to 180 in Leith 1879–80, 174 to 65 in Port Glasgow 1907–8, or 204 to 122 in Aberdeen in 1899–1900 – but that there were many such examples and they were a recurrent experience for house-builders in urban Scotland. The framework of their operating conditions was, therefore, highly unstable, the margin of error very slight.

This extreme degree of instability in Scottish building emanated from various sources. Since lower real incomes restricted the duration of buoyant demand for housing, and higher land prices, and incidentally more exacting standards of structural strength, compressed the duration and extent of the cyclical phase when Scots could afford more and better housing, builders responded vigorously when the opportunity arose. Moreover, in many towns, the composition of Scottish demand was heavily dependent on the fortunes of a single industry. Few burghs enjoyed the diversity of an employment base such as that of Aberdeen and Edinburgh,[112] and consequently demand, already weakened because of the wage-price relations, was for structural reasons a source of uncertainty to Scottish builders.

In addition, the methods of financing house-building added to the instability. The sale of the right to exact feu duties, compounded at perhaps 25 to 30 years purchase of annual value, or the raising of a bond secured on this annual income, represented a source of working capital for builders.[113] Speculative builders, however, were confronted with greater difficulties in selling these sub-feus or in raising bonds using the feus as collateral. The absence of an assured sale for their intended dwellings meant that an investor might be left with the right to extract an annual charge on a non-existent or incomplete house without inhabitants from whom he could collect. The Scottish feuing system offered, therefore, an attractive source of capital for speculative builders in the expansion stage of the cycle, but at other times even the better class of villa housing or investment building could not always depend on raising capital on the basis of future feuing income. The system of house-building finance introduced instability from another direction too. Refinancing bonds on heritable property, another method of raising working capital, required skilful handling at maturity dates. These bonds, usually from one to five years in the first instance, though with annual maturities if they were renegotiated, put considerable strain on the builder's credit rating. Not surprisingly, the investment builder was better placed through his long-term operations in the industry, and his established network of informal financial contacts such as legal firms ensured a greater success rate in refinancing his bonds when a crisis came. For the speculative builder the dwindling availability of capital in such a situation spelled his impending ruin, and the bout of forced liquidations which resulted, coupled with the impact on confidence, delayed the point at which speculative builders resumed their activities. The abundance of capital in the upswing phase and the dearth of funds in the trough, allied to the particular susceptibility of the speculative builder to variations in the flow of capital, offers a partial explanation as to why severe instability was such a common characteristic of the Scottish building industry. Thus in Scotland the workings of the land tenure system of feuing in relation to the sources of capital for house-building conspired to restrict the volume of funds available to speculative builders. Perhaps predictably, therefore, their responses were dramatic when the valve was released; and equally violent when the flow of capital was turned off.

The combination of numerous small firms with limited capital, no barriers to firms entering the industry and easy credit for builders during limited phases of general economic prosperity produced substantial volatility in Dundee, Hawick, Clydebank and indeed in a great many burghs. Nowhere was the amalgam so potent as in Glasgow during the building boom of the 1870s and its legacies. The cessation of credit brought bankruptcy on a catastrophic scale; the number failing in the Glasgow building trades rose to 53 in 1877, over four times the average for 1870–6,[114] and the failure in the following year of the City of Glasgow Bank brought bankruptcy to two-thirds of the building businesses in the city.[115] In this case the basis and scale of credit advances was so unsound as to promote a level of speculation which outweighed the stabilizing influence of the guaranteed or contractual side of the house-building industry.[116] The speculative outburst of the mid 1870s left its legacy on the building history of the city not only in physically shoddy tenements, but also by sufficiently anticipating future housing requirements as to depress building for a decade,[117] and by promoting banking and building society reforms, notably the more rigorous examination of overdraft facilities and applications for loans, which prevented future excessive stage-by-stage advances being obtained by builders.[118] A constraint therefore existed in the 1890s which moderated the extent of the next cyclical boom by limiting the availability of capital and thus the contribution of speculative builders.

Some stability was introduced into the Scottish building industry by larger scale operators able to satisfy steadier middle-class and artisan demand for housing when working-class tenement demand faltered. James Steel, John White, William Ballantine, William Murray and James Slater – all Edinburgh builders – undertook 353 properties in the decade 1885–94, and together accounted for 18.7 per cent of all new residential building.[119] The Aberdeen firms of J. Green, and Cameron and Matthew constructed tenements to the value of approximately £150,000 in the same decade, while in Govan, A. Stewart and Co. were alone responsible for 152 tenements estimated to cost £176,550 during the years 1894–1904.[120] Prominent in Grangemouth, Kirkintilloch, Dunblane, Milngavie and Musselburgh were, respectively, the firms of George Primrose, W. Fletcher, C. Angus, John Wood and F. Cooper and Son, which by their longevity as much as by the size of their building interests provided some measure of stability in their respective burghs.[121]

Some signs of diminishing instability were evident from about 1880. The emergence of several larger scale firms with expectations of long-term commitment to the building industry was one such indicator. Another was the increasing percentage of small builders who appeared in bankruptcy proceedings after 1880.[122] In the 1850s, 1860s and 1870s the proportion of small builders – those with less than £100 for division to creditors – appearing in bankruptcy proceedings was declining. But the squeeze on credit from the late 1870s, the extended building depression of the 1880s, and admittedly a legislative change which made *cessio* decrees – effectively summary bankruptcy orders without a discharge – more attractive, saw a doubling in the percentage of small builders declared bankrupt after 1880 compared to the levels of the preceding 30 years.[123] The effect was to weed out many of those producers who responded to advantageous short-term market conditions but whose activities fouled the long-term prospects of other builders by saturating the housing market. By reducing their presence one element of instability was controlled.

Although at the aggregate level of analysis urban bankruptcies were apparently inversely correlated with the volume of building activity in the period 1870–1914

181

this relationship appeared strongest at the major turning points and was in any event weakening over time, something which would again suggest a developing degree of responsibility by builders, investors and credit agencies, as well as a much higher level of instability in the formative stages of early Victorian urban development.[124] More particularly, at the level of the individual burgh the inverse relationship was virtually non-existent after the trauma of plummeting building orders after 1877 and the impact on builders' liquidity. The case of Glasgow was typical of most Scottish burghs where the levels of building activity and bankruptcy appeared to be connected until 1880, but thereafter moved independently. Indeed, the independence of the series was more emphatic in Edinburgh, Dundee and Aberdeen than in Glasgow.

It was these forces which were translated into a declining dynamic to yearly building fluctuations in the last quarter of the nineteenth century and in the Edwardian period. The amplitude of the building cycle was subjected to less pronounced oscillations than in the first half of Victoria's reign. Feverish levels of peak building activity or dejected idleness in the troughs were never so extreme after the 1876–7 peak and 1878–9 trough. Annual changes in building activity levels in twelve burghs between 1900 and 1914 were 22 per cent below those of 1880 to 1900, while the amplitude of building fluctuations fell by appreciably more in Aberdeen (83%), Edinburgh (75%), Port Glasgow (47%), and Dundee (29%).[125] In Leith and Kirkcaldy building was respectively 17 and 10 per cent less unstable in the 1900s than in the 1880s and 1890s, though the Glasgow conurbation including Govan and Partick registered greater variations to building largely because of the highly depressed and thus almost static level of output in the 1880s. However, neither the generally lower amplitude of building fluctuations nor the increased presence of larger building firms in the period 1875–1914 should be construed as reversing the predominantly small-scale and highly unstable nature of the Scottish building industry; it merely represented the development of limited countervailing forces. Nor should it obscure the fact that for most of the nineteenth century such countervailing forces had been negligible, allowing the building industry consciously to produce the design and quality of housing previously described.

5. Housing problems and palliatives: corporate housing, public regulation and landlord/tenant tensions

Paradoxically, though the Scottish real wage disadvantage was diminishing, and despite the tendency towards a narrower dynamic range in house-building fluctuations, the Scottish building industry experienced a very real crisis from late Victorian times. Three crucial difficulties confronted urban builders in differing intensities according to local circumstances. From the 1860s the problems of institutional housing, rising costs of production, and a squeeze on landlords' profitability were clouds on the horizon; by the 1890s squeals of anguish confirmed the reality of a crisis in the Scottish building industry which the Edwardian period only intensified. Nor were these complaints simply associated with a depressed 'state of trade' and an 18–20 year periodicity in the building cycle. They were genuine fears amongst builders that the entire basis of production was undergoing redefinition.

Probably the least important of these fears perceived as a crisis was the role of institutional building. Cheap money, compulsory purchase, statutory clearance and rehousing were seen as municipal encroachments upon the domain of private enterprise builders.[126] From their pioneering inception – in Glasgow (1866), Edinburgh (1867), Dundee (1871), Greenock (1877), Leith (1877) and Aberdeen (1884) – City Improvement Trusts encountered scepticism and latterly outright opposition from builders who perceived municipal enterprise as a trespass upon their interests.[127] Opposition centred on these local authority clearance schemes, for although environmentally beneficial, in clearing congested housing they created overcrowding pressures in adjacent streets, usually failed to rehouse displaced residents, hoarded building land and participated in land speculation, and frequently paid excessive compensation to landlords. Builders argued that this inflated land prices, created uncertainty as to municipal intentions, and discouraged new building initiatives by attaching a premium to obsolescent properties which commanded unduly high rentals. Finally, the catalogue of complaints included the ability of municipal authorities to rent council property below market price through advantageous financial arrangements, thereby eroding the lowest segment of demand for private housing.

Clearance schemes of the 1860s to 1880s with limited housing possibilities caused some concern to builders; the initiation of municipal housing under private legislation and then by Part III of the Housing of the Working Classes Act, 1890, generated alarm.[128] In aggregate terms builders' fears were unfounded; in 1913 only 1.01 per cent of Scots were housed in local authority property, a level much in keeping with Liverpool and London where English municipal activities were most conspicuous.[129] The west central burghs were most active, but Edinburgh and, curiously, the relatively non-industrial burghs of Perth and Oban were also highly placed amongst vigorous housing authorities (table 29). Although in aggregate terms builders' fears were unfounded, as most of the local authority housing had been constructed between 1888 and 1913, as a proportion of new building it was less insignificant. In 25 years council building accounted for just over 1 per cent of the housing stock built by private enterprise during the preceding 100 years; over the quarter century, therefore, council building had housed 4–5 per cent of urban families. From 1890 the threat of municipal housing was therefore not unfounded,

Table 29 Families housed by local authorities, 1913

local authority	families housed	total families in L.A. area	% of families housed in L.A. houses
Aberdeen	131	36,804	0.36
Bo'ness	10	2,143	0.47
Clydebank	26	7,363	0.35
Edinburgh	601	74,645	0.81
Glasgow	2,199	167,896	1.31
Greenock	214	15,234	1.40
Hamilton	23	7,439	0.31
Kilmarnock	58	7,513	0.77
Leith	84	17,891	0.47
Oban	24	1,159	2.07
Perth	114	8,300	1.37
Totals	3,484	346,387	1.01

Source: City of Glasgow Housing Committee, *Housing Centenary: a Review of Municipal Housing in Glasgow from 1866 to 1966* (1966), 10.

and it was recognized as such by builders almost immediately. Houses constructed by hospitals, asylums, sanitoria, water and utility companies, and a number of other responsible authorities were further sources of infringement upon builders' territory. Accountable for housing their inmates, they also accommodated certain grades of supervisory staff, and collectively were sufficiently numerous to warrant separate classification in the censuses. Though quantitatively small this still removed some potential customers from private builders under normal market conditions.

Public housing before 1914 was primarily a response to deficiencies in the private housing provisions. Much the same rationale applied to philanthropic gestures and cooperative building projects. As concern for public health and morality lurched forward, so compassion and civic consciousness induced institutional agencies to build 'model' houses for the working class. The vicissitudes of Scottish house-building also impelled industrialists to intervene in the housing market after 1870. Workers' welfare was at stake here too, though employers were interested in it not from an altruistic viewpoint but from its impact on their primary interests – corporate profits. Insufficient or erratic housing provision potentially threatened industrial expansion, and as an insurance premium against an insufficient supply of labour, Clydeside shipowners and Lanarkshire and Lothian colliery-owners regarded company housing after 1870 as a central element in management strategy, just as time and travel allowances were for John Brown of Clydebank in securing a stable workforce.[130] As their shipyard manager commented:

> At present every available house in Clydebank is occupied and rents are from 10% to 20% dearer than in Govan. The building trade is at present stagnant and there is nothing for it but to arrange with a builder ourselves.[131]

That companies were motivated by labour supply considerations rather than by a commercial yield on their housing investment can be seen by the net returns of 1.8 per cent to the Summerlee Iron Works, 2.9 per cent to Beardmores, and on a dozen schemes for almost 1,000 houses in central Scotland between 1873 and 1912, the colliers' and ironworkers' firm of Wm Baird and Co. averaged a meagre 2.7 per cent net yield on their £128,593 housing investment, below the 3.0 per cent available on gilts during the period.[132]

Industrial firms might finance and erect housing themselves, offer builders capital and land to do so on their behalf, encourage a public utility society or other agency to build, or secure a loan through the Public Works Loan Board, and Alexander Stephen (Govan), Denny (Dumbarton), Yarrow (Scotstoun), John Brown, William Beardmore and George Thompson (all Clydebank) employed such methods in providing workers' housing principally after 1890. To a degree, company housing on Clydeside, in Lanarkshire and elsewhere, was a reflection of private builders' failures to meet the quantity, type and timing of demand. But company housing took the decision-making out of the hands of builders, and if it offered a degree of contractual assurance by way of compensation, local building autonomy was conceded. Subsequently, private enterprise building decisions were taken in the uncertain shadow of the housing policy of an industrial enterprise, and in the case of Clydebank, annual variations in house-building were in fact more pronounced after the involvement of Brown, Beardmore and Thompson in the provision of housing than before. Thus, like municipal housing, company housing though never an important contributor to the aggregate housing stock before 1914 could and did affect the nature of house-building operations in a manner disproportionate to its limited presence in a few burghs.

For a critical span of years, approximately 1820 to 1860, building had been unregulated in urban Scotland.[133] Medieval controls exercised under the jurisdiction of the Dean of Guild Court initially fell into disuse in the late eighteenth and early nineteenth centuries as burgesses sought to minimize the areas of aggravation which might fuel the argument for administrative reform. After municipal reorganization in 1833 few local authorities were inclined immediately to restore such a symbol of former feudal power as the Dean of Guild Court or its successor. Thus, in those crucial years when urban development was at its most formative building standards were virtually unsupervised. In Glasgow regulatory powers were defunct between 1844 and 1862.[134] Elsewhere, in Edinburgh and Dundee for example, they remained in force, but jurisdiction was limited to former medieval or early modern boundaries, beyond which the Victorian city was rapidly, often uncontrollably, developing.[135] The implications for the quality and amenity of Scottish housing were transparently obvious in the deficient accommodation repeatedly reported to official enquiries as late as 1917, even though half a century of public health and building control initiatives had gone some way to remove the worst excesses of unsupervised building during the early phase of industrialization in Scotland.

Almost as a reaction to this laxness, the Burgh Police (Scotland) Act 1862 made regulatory powers available and individual burghs used supplementary private legislation to provide what was later acknowledged to be an unduly severe building code.[136] Detailed guidance was given on the size of chimney flues, the quality of materials for mortar, wall thickness and even the quality of linen and binding for plans submitted to the resurrected Dean of Guild Courts. That Scottish building regulations were exacting can be illustrated by comparison with those in London, which proved a blueprint for control elsewhere in England. Under the London Act, the specification regarding the thickness of walls was much less demanding, and construction consequently cheaper. For a three-storey dwelling, wall thickness in London required two storeys to be of $13\frac{1}{2}$ ins and one of 9 ins while in Glasgow one storey was to be 18 ins and two $13\frac{1}{2}$ ins. This resulted in a 25 per cent increase in the quantity of materials; in addition, to support the heavier weight of the walls, and the stiffer code regarding roofing materials, depths of foundations had to be increased, adding 73 per cent to the equivalent London costs. In a one-storey building the requirements of the Glasgow bye-laws for walls and foundations imposed on average a 40 per cent excess on the London specifications. By 1903 compliance with Glasgow regulations imposed an additional 114 per cent to the cost of foundations for a two-storey house in comparison to London costs, and for 4-, 5- and 6-storey houses the foundation costs in Glasgow were respectively 116, 119 and 196 per cent greater then in London, and the cost of building walls, whether of stone or brick, was between 25–50 per cent above that of London.[137] These standards were very severe and imposed undue costs of construction upon the Glasgow building industry, with the result that some elements of demand remained unfulfilled, while across the entire range of working- and middle-class housing building regulations reduced the quantity and the quality of housing affordable. Coupled with this inordinate burden imposed by Scottish building bye-laws was a glaring inconsistency, for the regulation load-bearing capacity per square foot in tenements and warehouses was in the region of 2:1, yet the needs of industrial storage were unlikely to be approached in a domestic situation. The conclusion of architect T.L. Watson was that:

> As the requirements of the London Act are sufficient for all purposes of safety it is evident that the Glasgow Act involves an absolute waste of money and to that extent interferes with the erection of cheap dwellings.[138]

In Newcastle and Birmingham, in Lancashire and in Midland towns – indeed in most English boroughs – 'many economies were practised which would not be permitted by the authorities' in Scotland.[139] Wall thickness, depth of foundations, loading factors, quality of materials and various other aspects of Scottish construction were moulded into a tough, almost repressive, building code according to the sanitary and public health aspirations of the late nineteenth century.

By 1902 it was increasingly apparent that in the bid to improve the sanitary conditions of Scottish burghs, building regulations were having an adverse effect. Several witnesses to a Glasgow investigation of housing conditions were doubtful as to the continuing wisdom of this tough building code. Their views were cogently articulated by Watson, who noted that the local Glasgow Acts of 1892 and 1900 had 'raised the standard of building and improved the sanitation, particularly of the cheaper class of dwellings' but that this had also 'involved an increase of cost and consequently of rents'.[140] Subsequently, enquiries recommended a relaxation of regulations governing Scottish house-building. Building regulations therefore had two adverse effects on housing standards. The absence of structural standards before 1862 permitted very basic accommodation to be built; the introduction of a building code, however, added to construction costs, increased rents and reduced the space which tenants could afford. After their initial introduction in Glasgow in the 1860s building regulations spread rapidly to other burghs – Dundee, Partick (1873), Govan (1874), Irvine (1876), Leith (1877), Kirkcaldy, Perth, Port Glasgow (1878), Aberdeen, Edinburgh, Kilmarnock (1880).[141] By 1893 all large burghs compulsorily had to adopt minimum regulations of the Glasgow type, and by 1900 more than 200 burghs had done so.[142] The additions to cost had reduced builders' room for manoeuvre and increasingly in the last quarter of the nineteenth century the objective of improved housing standards was undermined by the abandonment of this section of the market by builders, notably after 1903. Public health and building laws had

> acted adversely on the supply of a sufficient quantity of new houses for a mere compliance with the letter of the sanitary law has added to the cost of erection and maintenance of new houses and has therefore lessened the profitable inducements to build.[143]

The substitution of sound but costly housing for cheap and inferior properties produced a paradox and the 'conflict between health considerations and economic considerations' had recorded a victory for the former. Scottish building bye-laws forced construction standards which were 'too substantial' and this had seriously affected the standard and distribution of working-class housing.[144]

Building regulations not only added to costs of construction, they presented a barrier to the introduction of new methods, materials and designs. Productivity gains associated with steel-framed buildings or the substitution of concrete for brick and stone were not extensive in late Victorian England, but neither were they so relevant given the prevailing cottage-style terraced dwellings. The opportunities for cost reduction from these sources were much greater in high-rise tenement blocks, yet they were unacceptable to Scottish building regulations which were so ultra-conservative to W.D. Weir, the Cathcart engineer, that he was determined to introduce pre-fabricated building.[145] Productivity gains to Scottish building were available from less spectacular sources, merely by substituting more brick for dressed stone, or removing Feu Charter requirements for stone boundary walls, or by reducing ceiling heights and wall thicknesses.[146] Neither did the small-scale unit of production allow for economies of scale, bulk purchasing discounts, or the widespread diffusion of labour-saving steam machinery for stone-dressing, planing, tongue and grooving, and other woodworking techniques. Perhaps it was not surprising therefore that building productivity was below the Scottish average and only 95.2 per cent of the UK levels in 1907, and in stone, glass and roofing was only 91.5 per cent of UK levels.[147]

Builders' costs of production were under pressure in the last quarter of the nineteenth century from increasingly demanding building and public health regulations. Water supplies, closets and general plumbing, particularly, but also guttering, fireclay, chimney copings and vents, ironmongery, drains and sewer pipes, dampcourses, roof joists and partitions, and other materials added 25 per cent to costs between 1861 and 1898, though this was mainly concentrated in the years 1885–98, once the cost levels of the 1870s had by the early 1880s returned to those of 1861.[148] A further 17% rise was recorded between 1904 and 1914.[149] Overall, therefore, materials cost 40–50 per cent more in the 30 years between 1885 and the start of the First World War. However, this was more than matched by increases in labour costs. Expert contemporary calculations assessed this as an 81 per cent increase between 1860 and 1902, with a further 2.3 per cent increase between 1904 and 1914.[150] Wage rates in the building trades increased by about 35 per cent in the 30 years before the war. Based on a 50:50 weighting,[151] wages and materials together added at least 63 per cent to builders' costs of production between 1860 and 1914, and from the 1880s, those years of mounting pressure from other directions – institutional building, regulations, company housing, and landlords' attitudes – builders' costs also posed a major headache, escalating by about 38 per cent.[152]

How far trade union activities were responsible for the squeeze on builders' margins after 1880 is difficult to assess. Certainly the tendency of unions and employers to negotiate annual wage rates and to conclude them at agreed dates introduced a lag before downward adjustment of wages took place. Greater harmony in industrial relations offered some degree of predictability to builders' production costs from the labour element, and if that meant a little over the market wage was paid during slack trade until the agreement could be renegotiated – and in any event laying-off labour was always an available alternative – then crucially it also meant that in buoyant building conditions, when turnover and profits were high, disruptive strikes for increased wages would not hold employers to ransom. Thus annual wage bargains, for example, between local builders and a branch of the Associated Carpenters and Joiners of Scotland, from 1865 may have provided a measure of predictability to builders' decisions, though at a price – long-term upward drift in wages despite an underlying current of generally falling prices.[153] This was the case in Aberdeen where representatives of the United Operative Masons and Granitecutters, and of the employers, jointly formed the Aberdeen

Granite Association.[154] This introduced orderly wage bargaining. Even the union recognized that anarchy had existed in 1868 and 1877 when proposed wage reductions were countered by damaging strikes, and from 1888 the Granite Association eradicated the worst of these disputes.[155]

Union activity may have also increased labour costs from another direction, a decline in labour productivity due to restrictive practices. The comments of one observer were typical of many union critics to restrictive practices. 'There is a tendency in the trade unions to lower the standard of competence to the least competent', and that as the 'first class workman ... shows the other men up. . . . The first class workman is told by his delegate not to do so much work.'[156] The case of an employer checking the progress of work illustrated the productivity implications:

> [The workmen] had been at it for half a day and they had done very little, so he dismissed them. They were taking far too long to do what others were doing in about two hours. The delegate came down and asked the reason of dismissal, which he was told. He then went into the other cottages and asked the men working there 'How long did you take to do this?' The men said 'Five hours'; the delegate then said 'Oh, well, in future you will take nine.'[157]

Union officials consciously adopted this approach to deter employers from the dismissal of incompetent workmen, but the effect was to impair labour productivity. Rather mischievously *The Builder* commented on restrictive practices in building by suggesting the amputation of the left arms of bricklayers, the lampoon being directed at unionists who had been recommended by the British Bricklayers' Association to lay bricks one-handed. *The Builder* argued that amputation 'would make it easy to distinguish at a glance . . . between a unionist and a non-unionist.'[158]

Constrained by structural and cyclical influences on housing demand, squeezed by rising production costs and advancing standards of construction, builders were exposed to further difficulties from the direction of Scottish landlords.[159] It was not simply the short-run phenomenon that from the Boer War money market rates drifted upwards, with capital for heritable property costing 4 per cent in 1912, at least 1 per cent more than in 1900.[160] These difficulties were intensified by the increasing attractiveness of consols to institutional investors and of investment trusts to private savers.[161] The progressive exhaustion of such supplies of capital for investment in housing after 1900, in conjunction with almost annual increases in landlords' rates, merely completed the profit equation which builders had already solved, namely that margins were so eroded that, with the possible exception of the highest paid artisans, working-class housing represented an unwise venture.

New house-building suffered accordingly. From 1905 it was virtually suspended.[162] But difficult circumstances in Edwardian Scotland could not disguise more fundamental problems for suppliers, and in this the role of the landlord and the unique nature of the rent bargain were central. The overwhelming majority of Scottish working-class tenancies, between 60–90 per cent of dwellings rented at £5–£10 p.a. and on average 80 per cent of all working-class properties, were contracted for a yearly term commencing on Whitsunday, 28 May.[163] Agreements were often signed as much as four months in advance of this 'term day' and desirable properties were let for the following year by 2 February. These fixed removal dates, statutorily stipulated in the late seventeenth century, were in stark contrast to the fluid weekly tenancies in England and Wales. Though 'term day' contained an element of farce, with cartloads of furniture and bundles of clothing and linen congesting the streets of urban Scotland, the reality was serious. The scramble for reliable tenants meant written testimonies from former landlords; the search for the best properties required an early agreement to take over the tenancy and avert the possibility of being out on the street. Often it was only at term dates that repairs and maintenance were undertaken, and the approach of Whitsun meant a brief spell of frenetic activity in the building trades. This springtime interlude brought a welcome injection of cash, a diminution in monthly bankruptcies and eventually an equally abrupt cessation to maintenance work once term day had passed.

The practice of yearly letting had serious disadvantages for the Scot. First, and most conspicuously, in the context of unusually variable employment prospects the standard of accommodation affordable over one year's lease had to take account of interrupted earnings. English short lets allowed a tenant, *in extremis*, to move to cheaper accommodation or to move easily to another location for employment purposes, though it has been argued that in fact this was more urgently required in Scottish towns.[164] In Scotland a very large segment of the working population – 25.5 per cent in the cities – was prone to interrupted income, yet committed to an expenditure pattern for twelve months from which escape was both difficult and incurred further financial penalties.[165] Understandably, tenants chose a level of accommodation which they felt reasonably confident they could sustain throughout the year, even in the face of irregular employment, and the quality of accommodation was therefore governed by the household income levels in the worst working weeks, rather than by an average weekly income. To reinforce this preference for a low-rented, and thus amenity-deficient housing, and contrary to the English experience where the balance of legal power moved in favour of the tenant in the nineteenth century, in Scotland the landlords' position became more secure. Easier summary eviction for the non-payment of rent inclined Scottish tenants to opt for a rental level commensurate with their ability to pay, whatever misfortunes befell them.[166]

Long lets introduced other disadvantages for Scots.[167] Firstly, as long as yearly lets remained so did annual rate collections and consequently opportunities for compounding, allowances for regular collections undertaken by landlords on the municipalities' behalf and deductions for unlet property, were reduced. Neither landlords nor tenants gained. Secondly, rates were based on gross rent in Scotland. not nett rent as in England where deductions for insurance, rates and repairs reduced the basis of assessments to local taxation. Thirdly, agreement to a short let in Scotland rendered the landlord himself liable for the payment of rates – a substantial incentive to resist letting reform. A fourth disadvantage was that yearly rates payments imposed considerable hardship on those Scottish tenants unable to budget for substantial lump sum amounts. One brutal penalty for non-payment of poor rates was disenfranchisement which in Glasgow in 1906 affected 14,500 or almost 9 per cent of householders. This divergence in revenue and expenditure patterns was a source of vitriolic condemnation by working mens' organizations, tenants' associations and private individuals, and their support for a short-letting system was heavily endorsed in parliamentary and municipal elections where 'the missive question' – the shorthand for the letting system, derived from the landlords' letters each January seeking the intent of tenants in the forthcoming letting period – became a contentious issue from the 1890s.[168] The rigidity of 'this absurd system'[169] caused burdens to be added to rents and rates payments which further dampened effective housing demand in urban Scotland, with consequential implications for the level of building activity, and the standard of housing affordable.

That the house-letting system imposed financial penalties and caused hardship was reflected not just in elections or in the flowering of tenants' associations after 1900 in Paisley, Clydebank, Glasgow and elsewhere, nor in the sympathetic stance of the town councils of Govan, Greenock, Glasgow, Ayr, Leith, Falkirk, Kilmarnock, and Clydebank, but also in the nine separate attempts between 1890 and 1905 to introduce amending legislation. Long before the first of these attempts in the 1890s the adverse implications of the letting system on tenants was thoroughly understood, and it was only the concerted and powerful opposition of landlords' and house factors' associations, for example, in Glasgow, Edinburgh, Leith, Dundee, Aberdeen, Partick, Rothesay and indeed a number of other urban locations, which repeatedly defeated the reformers' zeal.[170]

The mobilization of landlords' and house-factors' opposition delayed letting and rating reform and indicated a power disproportionate to that numerically represented in table 30 if the Glasgow example can be taken as typical. Glasgow landlords, Daunton has concluded, owned on average a large number of properties and thus were confronted with more tenants than their counterparts in English boroughs.[171] Management was more onerous, more costly, because of the number of tenancies and the nature of shared amenities. Though the average size of property

Table 30   (a) Ownership of rented accommodation in Glasgow, 1900–1

category of landlord	owners no.	%	properties no.	%	annual rental amount (£)	%
Private individuals	4,289	64.4	13,581	56.1	1,152,639	58.9
Trusts	1,698	25.5	6,178	25.5	502,658	25.7
House factors	115	1.7	1,202	5.0	107,292	5.5
Property companies	89	1.3	915	3.8	82,091	4.2
Other companies	197	3.0	1,316	5.4	57,772	3.0
Public bodies	273	4.1	1,029	4.2	53,667	2.7
Total	6,661	100.0	24,221	100.0	1,956,119	100.0

(b) Glasgow landlords, 1900–1

rental of	owners no.	%	properties no.	%	yearly rental £	%
Rent-free	177	2.7	210	0.9	nil	nil
Up to £100	1,887	28.3	2,657	11.0	98,890	5.1
£100 to £250	2,324	34.9	4,981	20.6	385,838	19.7
£250 to £500	1,389	20.9	5,534	22.8	483,006	24.7
£500 to £750	430	6.5	2,995	12.4	261,534	13.4
£750 to £1,000	161	2.4	1,482	6.1	140,391	7.2
£1,000 to £2,000	201	3.0	2,844	11.7	270,647	13.8
£2,000 to £3,000	52	0.8	1,207	5.0	123,660	6.3
Above £3,000	40	0.6	2,311	9.5	192,152	9.8
Total	6,661	100.0	24,221	100.0	1,956,119	100.0

Source: N.J. Morgan and M.J. Daunton, 'Landlords in Glasgow: a study of 1900', *Business History*, xxv (1983), 261, 274.

holding was above that in England, the concentration of ownership, as reflected by the largest five property owners, was weaker than in England. Under these considerations – higher average number of tenancies, lesser concentration of ownership – many Scottish property owners preferred professional managers, house factors, to superintend their interests, thus dividing ownership from control.[172]

The fragmentation of property ownership can be seen from table 30(a). In 1900, 12 per cent of the housing stock was owner-occupied, and of the rented accommodation, private owners accounted for 58.9 per cent of the annual rental. Tradesmen, shopkeepers, builders, small businessmen, almost entirely local interests, were the typical owners of property and to a large degree this corresponds with the diverse and small-scale nature of building projects previously noted (tables 26 and 27). Trust ownership, which accounted for 25.7 per cent of annual rental, was also very important.[173] Trusts were most commonly created by Disposition and Settlement, legal processes in association with a deceased person's will, to determine how legacies would be paid and income provided for a widow and her children. Though normally created at death, trusts could achieve the same purpose either by a marriage contract, or by arrangement during a person's lifetime, and it was this substantial volume of trust funds which sustained the Scottish solicitor, in a manner very different to that in England, as an important financial intermediary, not just in the provision of building finance but in other investment outlets too.[174] Indeed, as responsible agent for the trust, it was the solicitor who often passed rent collection and other daily matters to a property factor to ensure constant attention. House factors operated on their own account too, and 5.5 per cent of rentals were owned by them, and property companies with 4.2 per cent of annual rentals represented another category of professional property management. In Glasgow, the sizable presence of the Improvement Trust and other institutional house-ownership was greater than in the majority of Scottish burghs, and the 5.7 per cent of annual rented property owned by these agencies was unlikely to be matched elsewhere.[175]

Property management could be undertaken personally, by a rent collector, by a house factor with responsibilities beyond those simply of rent collection, or by a house 'farmer', paying a fixed rent to the owner and earning a living by the differential between this and the amount charged to tenants. In Scotland, the house factor and farmer were more conspicuous elements of owners' strategies.[176] What were the implications of the greater power of Scottish landlordism? Firstly, the greater reliance upon professional managers meant an acquaintance with the law and the active invocation of procedures for the redress of owners' grievances. Thus the pressure was more consistently kept up on tenants than under small personal supervision. For example, six cases for eviction could be included in an application to the Burgh Court, thus reducing the legal costs of the action.[177] Secondly, a greater degree of solidarity amongst landlords was achieved under the Scottish system and this, in conjunction with the annual reletting date, had a collusive effect upon rents. At the very least it avoided competitive underbidding by landlords in a tight market for tenants, when, for example, the percentage of empty houses reached 8 per cent and landlords might have been unilaterally inclined to reduce rents. Thirdly, the resistance to pressure for reform of the letting system and the method of rates collection was another manifestation of the concentration of landlords' power.[178] Even when confronted with a powerful reform lobby, landlords' agents and factors managed to exert considerable political pressure to delay disturbance to the status quo until 1911. And unlike England, the growth of tenant power was effectively resisted by means of further legal redress for the recovery of rent. The law of hypothec, a process of sequestrating a tenant's furniture, tools and possessions as a security for rent, was available to the landlord from the day the tenant leased a house. Hypothec was interpreted as the landlord's security for the credit implied by payment of rent in arrears, and the assault upon this process was effectively resisted by professional house factors.[179] Although delaying tactics were frequently employed, landlords could throughout the nineteenth century obtain eviction orders in the Small Debt Court and the Burgh Court, and these proved more effective and more frequently invoked than the equivalent English process under either the law of distress, or the Small Tenements Recovery Act 1838.[180] Warrants for eviction in London between 1886–90 were in a ratio of 1 to every 1,818 inhabitants; in Glasgow the ratio was 1 to 54. Swift and complete retribution in Scottish law was accentuated by an even speedier process of summary eviction in the Housing, Letting (Scotland) Act 1911.[181] Seven days' arrears of rent allowed the landlord to give 48 hours notice, and on expiry of this notice landlords could obtain a summary application for removal. The tenant then had a further 48 hours to vacate the house.

The implications of rapid summary eviction should not be overlooked. Apart from adding to the armoury of the professional manager concerned with large numbers of tenancies, the intensification of summary powers was given to landlords as a bribe for minor reforms in the collection of rates and amendments to long-letting conditions. Greater flexibility of leases was therefore instituted alongside firmer powers of summary eviction. One aspect assisted the wealthy tenant; the other deployed powerful additional weapons against poorer tenants. The consequence was the intensification of landlord-tenant hostilities, the culmination of which was a series of bitter rent strikes.

This is not to argue that Scottish landlords held the whip hand throughout; simply that the legal framework not only operated to their advantage but, against the national trend, moved in their favour. The market place still governed whether they could invoke legal processes. If there was a surfeit of housing, the possibility of vacant properties constrained their inclination to go to law to obtain rent arrears. Some rent, even delayed rent, was better than no rent. Landlords might, therefore, be forced either to accept increased levels of rent arrears, to reduce rents, or to endure a higher proportion of untenanted properties. Variations in the percentage of empty properties was pronounced in most burghs.[182] In some, such as Edinburgh, Perth and Aberdeen, with a broad occupational base, the percentage of empty houses varied only slightly, as was the case in more stagnant urban areas, such as Arbroath. But in a very great number of burghs the proportion of empty houses varied appreciably between 1881 and 1911. In these four census years the percentage of unlet houses in Partick was successively 17, 8, 6 and 10 per cent; in Clydebank, it was 4 per cent in 1891, 4.5 per cent in 1901 and 16 per cent in 1911. Between 1881 and 1891, eight burghs – Hamilton, Partick, Wishaw, Govan, Irvine, Glasgow, Rutherglen and Port Glasgow – recorded reductions such as 17 to 7 per cent or 11 to 4 per cent, and in the decade 1901–11, witnessed a reversal of the trend, the proportion of void houses typically increasing from about 4 to 10–11 per cent with similar abrupt upturns for other burghs, such as Kilmarnock, Leith and Coatbridge, albeit at lower absolute levels. Cairncross has explained that an excess housing stock, as measured by the percentage of empty houses, could take several years to reverse.[183] Annual changes to the stock of housing were normally no more than 1 per cent so that levels of 12 per cent might take fully 6–7 years to be taken up, assuming a 5–6 per cent level of vacancies was generally acceptable and that there was no new building, no new household formation or in-migration. In practice it generally took longer to work through an oversupply of housing. Empty levels of around 5 per cent were generally assumed to be normal; below this 'equilibrium' level the landlord held the whip hand, and rents rose. In the range 8–10 per cent of landlords might have to consider rent reductions, though beyond that further rent reductions only reduced gross revenue and so a higher level proportion of voids had to be tolerated.

Nor were landlords in the dominant position in respect of their obligations to local authorities. Municipal responsibilities introduced by central government, as well as those voluntarily undertaken by local councils, imposed a mounting strain on civic finance after 1870. The fiscal base, essentially property taxation, was under mounting pressure. General cleansing and house inspection in the worst Glasgow districts necessitated almost four times more expenditure than in the city as a whole.[184] Illegitimacy, infant mortality, nuisances and other areas of responsibility involved mushrooming expenditure levels in terms of staff time, not to mention capital facilities. In 1888, 9 per cent of city burials were at the expense of the rates and charities; in the worst districts 37 per cent were buried at public expense.[185] Vaccination, childbirth amd medical treatment in the poorer districts entailed twice the per capita levels of expenditure as in the city as a whole. Revenue presented an equally bleak picture. Of houses assessed at £10 or more, only 2.6 per cent of police rates and no poor or school rates were outstanding in 1888; for those houses between £4 and £10, 20.5 per cent of police rates and 28.5 per cent of school and poor rates remained unpaid.[186] The consequence, as table 31 shows, was that general, school, poor and police rates in all Scottish burghs rose appreciably between 1890 and 1914.

Table 31   Increase in rate of assessment per £, 1890-1914

	1890–1 s. d.	1913–14 s. d.	increase %
Glasgow	3 1.0	4 7.9	51.1
Edinburgh	2 5.5	4 0.5	64.4
Dundee	3 3.5	4 2.0	26.5
Aberdeen	3 4.0	4 3.8	29.5

Source: Scottish Land Enquiry Committee, *Scottish Land* (1914), 395.

Economic factors – costs of production, levels of effective demand, incidence of local taxation – conditioned the basis of landlords' operations. The distinctive characteristics of the Scottish legal framework determined landlords' responses to the economic realities, and only in the ascendant could landlords or their agents enforce the convincing legal advantages with which they were endowed. But when economic circumstances permitted, the house-letting and rating systems, largely intact from 1854, allowed punitive actions against tenants which were generally agreed by all, bar landlords, to transgress the boundaries of natural justice.[187] It was this deep-seated conviction which generated opposition from tenants in the second half of the nineteenth century, which ultimately politicized the rents issue, culminating in local tenants' associations and other working-mens' pressure groups from the 1880s, and which, in conjunction with other economic and legal circumstances, uniquely combined to differentiate Scottish housing from that in any other part of the kingdom.

6 Rents

Rents were in essence a summary of the economics of construction and house-letting. As a market price for accommodation, rents had to take into account the various costs of property management – maintenance and repairs, insurance, depreciation, collection and administration charges, allowances for untenanted property, rates and taxes – and cover the capital costs of building – site development costs, land and ground burdens, labour and materials elements of building work, interest on capital advances, legal and property transference fees – and finally provide a sufficient residue to persuade builders and landlords that the effort was worthwhile. In Scotland numerous additional charges were incurred – higher building costs, legal fees, land costs, increments to rates, annual adjustments to house duty – with a cumulative effect upon rentals charged.[188] All this was undertaken not only against a level of instability in the building industry unprecedented in other sectors of the economy or in the English building industry, but also against a level of effective demand substantially weaker than in comparable industrial districts elsewhere in the United Kingdom. It was not so surprising then that these circumstances should be translated into a mean standard of accommodation.

Rents reflected these additional burdens applicable in Scottish burghs. For two-roomed houses in 1911, the average rental in fifteen English boroughs ranged between 2s.11d. and 3s.10d. per week; in ten Scottish burghs the range was 3s.3d. to 4s.7d., an excess of between 11.4 and 19.6 per cent.[189] Indeed, in suitably subdued official language, a Board of Trade enquiry recognized that, 'the rent index numbers for the Scottish towns were somewhat high as compared with those for English and Welsh towns.'[190] Hence, working-class outgoings on rents, London excepted, were appreciably higher in Scotland, in fact 11 per cent higher than in the boroughs of nearby Northumberland and Durham, 11.5 per cent above urban areas in Wales and Monmouth, and 19–26 per cent in excess of 42 boroughs in Yorkshire, Lancashire, Cheshire and the Midlands.[191] This largely confirmed the observations of contemporary housing experts. For example, in 1911 average rentals per square foot of floor space in Glasgow compared to Liverpool, Govan compared to Sunderland, showed the Scottish rental levels respectively 10.3 and 9.7 per cent above the English boroughs.[192] Contemporary data confirmed how dominant Scottish burghs were in the national league table of rental levels (table 32). What was more, even relatively minor burghs which might by reason of distance from the cities have expected to enjoy appreciably lower rentals for working-class property were very much on a par with the major Scottish urban centres. As the Board of Trade concluded: 'The [rental] range is thus very much narrower than in England and Wales.'[193]

Over the longer term the course of Scottish rents also kept ahead of the upward movement in the English rent index. Between 1876 and 1910 English rents increased by 20.4 per cent compared to a 33.5 per cent increase in Scottish rents.[194] Working-class property rentals moved upwards even more emphatically. Table 33 (col. 1)

Table 32   Rent indices, 1905

town	rent index	town	rent index	town	rent index
London	100	Bradford	59	Wolverhampton	53
Edinburgh and Leith*	81	Sunderland	59	Rochdale	52
Croydon	81	Birmingham	59	Burton-on-Trent	52
Plymouth and Devonport	81	Swindon	59	Galashiels*	52
Glasgow*	76	Perth*	58	Derby	51
Newcastle-on-Tyne	76	Reading	58	Hanley	51
Dundee*	75	Darlington	58	Stockport	51
Greenock*	71	Carlisle	58	Blackburn	50
Birkenhead	70	Grimsby	58	Wigan	50
Paisley*	69	Portsmouth	57	Warrington	50
Falkirk*	69	Keighley	57	Methyr Tydfil	50
Aberdeen*	68	Normanton	57	Chester	50
Swansea	68	Dover	56	Chatham, Gillingham	49
Jarrow	68	Nottingham	56	Coventry	49
Kilmarnock*	66	Leeds	56	Bedford	49
Gateshead	66	Worcester	56	Northampton	49
Southampton	65	St Helens	56	Norwich	48
Liverpool and Bootle	65	Halifax	55	Hull	48
Huddersfield	64	Sheffield	55	Preston	48
Barrow-in-Furness	63	Stockton	54	Gloucester	48
Newport (Mon.)	63	Lincoln	54	Leicester	48
Manchester and Salford	62	Stoke-on-Trent	54	Crewe	48
South Shields	61	Bristol	53	Taunton	47
Luton	61	Burnley	53	Ipswich	44
Oldham	60	Castleford	53	Kidderminster	43
Middlesbrough	59	York	53	Walsall	43
Sheerness	59	Bolton	53	Macclesfield	32
Cardiff	59				

* Scottish burghs.
Source: PP 1908, CVIII, Report of an Enquiry by the Board of Trade into Working Class Rents,
    Housing and Retail Prices, xxxi, xxxviii.

records a rental increase of 44.7 per cent in properties under £20 p.a., a figure largely corroborated by the average floor space rent in Glasgow of 4.122d., 4.45d. and 5.225d. per square foot in respectively 1860, 1870 and 1902.[195] Against a background of generally falling prices by as much as 42 per cent[196] in the period 1873–96, Scottish working-class rents increased by 23.6 per cent in those years, though in the Edwardian period price and rent increases remained largely in step.[197] The introduction of building regulations, the costs associated with installing internal water closets, compliance with sanitary codes regarding lighting and ventilation, room size and number of occupants, increments to occupiers and landlords' rates due to burgeoning municipal activities (even replacing ashpits with ashbins added 1 per cent to rents), pressure on central land and the opportunities for increased feu duties and ground annuals, these and other developments of the period after 1870 directly contributed to an unequalled rise in real rents.[198] Whatever the preferences and opportunities created by rising real wages for improved housing, severe limitations on the standards of Scottish domestic comfort were imposed by substantial increases in the real value of rental payments in the 40 years before the First World War. The contemporary view that rents for two apartment houses in central Scotland would pay for a four-apartment English house, or that the rent of a Glasgow three-apartment flat would pay for a five-roomed house in Birmingham, Sheffield, Manchester, Leeds, Cardiff or any one of 60 boroughs throughout England and Wales was a measure of the disadvantage under which urban Scots were housed in the period 1850–1914.[199]

Building costs escalated by 63 per cent between 1860 and 1914.[200] Rents did not keep pace. Contemporary calculations and those based on table 33 suggest

Table 33   Scottish rent indices, 1875–1911 (1900 = 100)

	smaller houses (valued at less than £20 p.a.) (1)	larger houses (valued at more than £20 p.a.) (2)	total (3)
1875	78.1	103.6	79.8
1876	77.2	106.2	81.4
1877	81.4	106.5	84.5
1878	83.4	105.5	86.1
1879	84.9	106.9	88.5
1880	86.3	106.4	89.0
1881	86.6	106.5	89.2
1882	86.8	106.8	89.5
1883	86.6	107.2	89.3
1884	86.6	107.1	89.0
1885	86.6	107.3	89.1
1886	86.6	103.9	88.6
1887	87.9	106.2	89.2
1888	88.3	105.7	89.5
1889	88.7	105.4	89.6
1890	89.1	104.9	89.8
1891	92.2	105.0	90.7
1892*	92.0	104.2*	91.6
1893	91.9	103.7	92.5
1894	93.1	103.0	93.3
1895	93.7	102.7	94.0
1896	96.5	101.7	94.4
1897*	94.9	101.3	96.1
1898	97.1	100.8	97.9
1899	97.9	99.9	98.6
1900	100.0	100.0	100.0
1901	100.9	99.7	100.7
1902	102.2	99.0	101.5
1903	104.5	98.9	103.6
1904	106.6	98.3	104.9
1905	107.1	97.9	105.1
1906	109.0	97.8	106.4
1907	109.2	97.3	106.6
1908	110.7	96.6	107.7
1909	110.7	96.6	107.7
1910	111.7	97.2	108.7
1911	112.6	95.6	109.0

* Data missing; mean of adjacent years used.
Source: PRO, IR 16, 1–135.

that over a similar time span rents increased by no more than 35–45 per cent depending upon location. Hence builders' and landlords' margins were squeezed by an average 0.33 per cent each year and their mode of business operation was influenced by almost daily interference from officialdom as the century wore on. If the footsteps of sanitary, ticketing and building inspectors were not actually on their sites and premises the possibility of visits was an omnipresent one. In addition, municipal clearances and eventually rehousing and council building, though they did not reshape the business frontiers, added a pall of insecurity into an already uncertain business venture.

Paradoxically, the rising cost of labour – estimated at 81 per cent in the building trades between 1860 and 1902 though substantially less in other sectors (engineering, printing, textiles, iron and steel[201] – might reasonably have been expected to be translated into additional demand for housing space and quality. Two powerful factors prevented this. Firstly, many employees endured broken time. While wage rates improved over time and continued to add to producers' costs, take-home pay in certain casual trades, of which building was one, did not keep pace.[202] Secondly, for the poorest families, 75–80 per cent of the weekly budget was devoted to expenditure on food, with 20–25 per cent allocated to rent.[203] Increases in wages, however, went on additional food consumption for the simple reason that as dietary studies have shown, even though such a large proportion of income was devoted to food, it provided insufficient nourishment for the family.[204] On the eve of the First World War the point was emphatically made by two nutritional experts: 'while the labouring classes with a regular income of over 20s. a week generally manage to secure a diet approaching the proper standard for active life, those with a smaller income and those with an irregular income entirely fail to get a supply of food sufficient for the proper development and growth of the body or the maintenance of a capacity for active work.'[205] Increases in wages of the low paid therefore went on more food, not on more or better housing.

7 Conclusion: capitalism, construction and class

That such cramped, amenity-deficient living conditions were commonplace in Victorian Scotland did not mean that the market economy had failed. In a sense it was a testimony to its success. An efficient market for labour had obtained and sustained a niche for Scotland in the galaxy of industrial nations, and lower labour costs were an essential element which had ignited economic modernization in nineteenth-century Scotland. To this extent, the market and the price mechanism had worked effectively as far as labour inputs were concerned. It was only latterly, once forward industrial momentum had been achieved, that the distributional implications of the process were questioned, once the climate of morality shifted so as to query the disagreeable effects of industrialization on workers' lifestyles and daily behaviour. The impact of urbanization on immorality and irreligiousness came under closer scrutiny after 1850.[206] What had earlier been unnoticed, or was at least acceptable, was then subject to extended enquiry. Low labour costs had initially been central to industrial efficiency, but in the second half of the century below national average wage levels produced sufficiently deplorable living conditions and behavioural patterns that if the stability of the state was not itself a direct issue, then workforce discipline certainly was,[207] even though in the minds of the middle class the danger was exaggerated.

The market economy, as represented by the price mechanism and profit motive, had not then failed, at least as far as the building industry was concerned. Rents, builders' proxy for prices, largely determined how much housing was demanded and supplied; the gap between receipts of rents and expenditure on property maintenance, interest and capital repayments determined builders' and landlords' willingness to embark upon house-building. It was the erosion of profits and upwards movements in expectations regarding standards of accommodation which rendered working-class house-building increasingly unprofitable. Builders and landlords accordingly reduced their involvement in this lowest sector of the housing market.

This trend may have been operative after the collapse of the housing boom in 1877–8, with the peak of the later 1890s and 1902–4 more of an aberration than a recurrence of the cyclical pattern. Rational market decisions were, thus, the basis of a developing haemorrhage in the supply of adequate working-class housing in the 30 or so years before 1914. To conform to prevailing standards of morality and decency, to provide accommodation commensurate with these, substantial price increases and expanded profit margins were necessary. Scottish purchasing power could not respond sufficiently. It was low wages, substantially below the real purchasing power in England, which prevented a significant advance in housing standards for large sections of the Scottish working class, and in recognition of this, a powerful lobby for the dilution of building standards and sanitary requirements developed by the turn of the century.[208]

Weak consumption levels caused builders to quit the bottom rung of the market; they recognized unprofitability and acted accordingly. How else is the expansion of non-private enterprise residential building to be explained? Cooperative ventures such as Workmen's Dwellings Companies, municipal responses, for example council housing and, after 1890, town planning and garden suburb schemes, philanthropic initiatives in the guise of model dwellings, and company housing were each an acknowledgment that builders were unwilling to undertake house-building and land-lords were hesitant about managing property at the lower end of the market. It was not that the market mechanisms had failed; it was simply that those institutions and companies were dissatisfied with the outcome in terms of its impact on labour whether from a compassionate, Christian, or corporate viewpoint. In fact keen observation of the percentage of empty houses confirmed that builders noted the workings of the market place and reacted to changes in this percentage on a capital stock adjustment principle. Advances of 1d. per hour in building wages were known to add £10 to the cost of a house[209] and thus to strangle a portion of demand – a simple formulation of the elasticity of demand. The revenue equation of price times quantity was constantly monitored by landlords struggling to decide when to alter rents and thus influence the levels of voids in their efforts to maintain gross rental income. Many such instances of the workings of the market could be invoked. It was the unacceptable distributional implications of these workings which produced the search for alternatives.

Illustrations and explanations of housing conditions have drawn heavily on cases in the quarter century before 1914. Deliberately, such examples have been selected to convey Scottish working-class housing in its most favourable light, once reformist environmental measures had had some impact. Mortality rates, the frequency of one-roomed houses and other indicators reveal improvements over the previous half century which might justify cautious optimism that in general terms the Scottish urban population was better housed in 1914 than in 1850. Such as they were, improvements came from an extremely basic level, remained considerably adrift of English housing standards, affected a smaller proportion of Scots because of the irregular nature of much of their employment, were achieved not without greater additions to rents than in England, and added friction between landlord and tenant. Beneath statistics of aggregate environmental improvement the realities of daily life changed only slightly for many urban Scots. Raised, though unfulfilled, expectations of housing improvements and coveted visible advances for some elements of the skilled working class left poorer groups, and particularly women, with a deeper sense of discontent when the Edwardian era commenced. For the skilled worker, too, housing improvements during the period 1850 to 1914 were subject to similar additional costs of construction, land charges, fiscal levies and other premiums to rental, all of which limited participation in housing improvements, and did little to narrow the differential in the quality of skilled workers' housing on either side of the border. Throughout the entire spectrum of Scottish housing – labourers', artisans', petty bourgeois, and even middle class – the higher costs of building, land development and property management as reflected in the very high Scottish rentals shown in table 32, whittled away the amount of space and quality of amenity. In conjunction with the wage levels which were lower and prices significantly higher than in English boroughs, the volume of housing demand was weak throughout all phases of the building cycle and the living conditions earlier described were a logical, indeed inevitable, outcome. It was perhaps surprising that builders maintained an interest in this segment of the market for as long as they did, given the alternative attractions of assured contract work in public and industrial building, and indeed in the guaranteed consols' yield which in many years exceeded the return to building operations.

The combination of these forces produced not only a distinctive physical arrangement of domestic space and urban form in the tenement, but as a consequence a qualitative standard so basic as to redefine daily functions. Playing, washing, child-rearing, sleeping, even sex and death assumed different patterns where pressure on space was as acute as in Scottish housing. Housing space was used, therefore, 'as a necessary of life by the wage-earning class, but [was] used as a luxury by the wealthy.'[210] Cultural preference for tenements was weaker than supposed; consumer resistance to change was far from immutable as contacts with English workers, miners' housing and limited production of flatted cottages in pre-1914 Scotland showed.[211] It was, principally, the weakness of consumer demand, builders' often overreactive responses to it, and pre-determined tenure conditions which were mainly responsible for the creation and continuation of extreme density of occupancy in tenement blocks. Such factors ensured that the text of the Glasgow Presbytery in its enquiry into working-class housing would remain unfulfilled before 1914:

> My people shall dwell in a peaceable habitation,
> In sure dwellings and in quiet resting places.[212]

NOTES

1 F. Engels, *The Condition of the Working Class in England in 1844* (1936), 34.
2 *Ibid.*, 37.
3 *Ibid.*, 34, 37, 38.
4 PP, 1917–18, XIV, *Royal Commission on the Housing of the Industrial Population of Scotland, Rural and Urban, Report*, para. 2232 (subsequently RC, 1917).
5 *Ibid.*, 2232–3.
6 PP, 1912–13, CXI, *Census of England and Wales 1911*, vol. II, Tables XLVI, XLVII.
7 Scottish Land Enquiry Committee, *Scottish Land* (1914) (subsequently SLEC).
8 *Ibid.*
9 PP, 1912–13, CXIX, *Census of Scotland* (also parts 1–4).
10 *Ibid.*
11 RC, 1917, paras 46–50.
12 *Ibid.*, para. 2223.
13 J. Melling, *Rent Strikes: People's Struggle for Housing in West Scotland, 1890–1916* (1983), 18–26.

14 D. Englander, *Landlord and Tenant in Urban Britain, 1838–1918* (1983), 140–83.
15 B. Dicks, 'The Scottish medieval town: a search for origins', in *Scottish Urban History*, eds G. Gordon and B. Dicks (1983), 23–51.
16 RC, 1917, para. 396.
17 *Ibid*.
18 M.J. Daunton, *House and Home in the Victorian City: Working-Class Housing 1850–1914* (1983), 57.
19 RC, 1917, paras 337–8, 345.
20 *Ibid.*, para. 419.
21 *Ibid.*, para. 415.
22 J.B. Russell, 'Local vices of building as affecting the death-rate', *Sanitary J. Scotland* (1877), 407.
23 *Ibid.*, 408.
24 Glasgow Municipal Commission on the Housing of the Poor (subsequently GMC), *Report* (1904); Evidence, Eadie, 335, Chalmers, 17; Daunton, *op. cit.*, 22.
25 RC, 1917, paras 351–6.
26 F. Worsdall, *The Tenement: a Way of Life* (1979), 27.
27 RC, 1917, para. 340.
28 Daunton, *op. cit.*, 35.
29 Edinburgh District Record Office (subsequently EDCRO), Dean of Guild Court Plans, 1800–1914; Strathclyde Regional Archives, Dean of Guild Court Plans for Glasgow, Partick, Govan; Dundee City Record Office, Plans to 1914, and Aberdeen Town Planning Department, Plans 1880–1914. See also comments, by Worsdall, *op. cit.* and Daunton, *op. cit.*, and RC, 1917, paras 456–69.
30 RC, 1917, para. 481. See also para. 484.
31 Presbytery of Glasgow, *Report of Commission on the Housing of the Poor in Relation to their Social Condition* (1891), 11, and Evidence of Glasier, 170–1, 186–9.
32 PP, 1884–5, XXX, *Royal Commission on the Housing of the Working Classes*, Evidence of J.B. Russell, Q.19, 542; RC, 1917, para. 421, and A.K. Chalmers, Q.20, 219.
33 RC, 1917, para. 421.
34 M.W. Beresford, 'The back-to-back house in Leeds, 1787–1937', in *Working-Class Housing 1850–1914: A Symposium*, ed. S.D. Chapman (1971); Daunton, *op. cit.*, 21–31; I.C. Taylor, 'The insanitary housing question and tenement dwellings in nineteenth-century Liverpool', in *Multi-Storey Living: The British Working Class Experience*, ed. A. Sutcliffe (1974).
35 A.K. Chalmers, *Public Health Administration in Glasgow* (1905), 106, brackets added.
36 J.B. Russell, 'On the "Ticketed Houses" of Glasgow', *Proc. Royal Philosophical Soc. Glasgow* (1888), 19.
37 *Ibid.*, 18.
38 *Ibid*.
39 RC, 1917, paras 406, 412.
40 R.G. Rodger, 'Scottish urban housebuilding 1870–1914' (Ph.D. thesis, University of Edinburgh), 252–78 (subsequently 'thesis').
41 RC, 1917, para. 573.
42 *Ibid.*, paras 571–2.
43 *Ibid.*, paras 563, 575.
44 RC, 1917, Evidence of Dittmar, 340(10) and 347. See also Appendices CLXX, CLXXI.
45 *Ibid.*, and RC, 1917, Report, para. 560.
46 H.D. Littlejohn, *Report on the Sanitary Condition of the City of Edinburgh* (1865).
47 RC, 1917, Evidence of Kelso, 37,911(5).
48 *Ibid*.
49 RC, 1917, Report, para. 571.
50 *Ibid.*, Appendix xv.
51 J.B. Russell, '"Ticketed Houses" of Glasgow'; G. Best, 'The Scottish Victorian city',

Victorian Studies, XI (1968), 342; J. Mann, 'Better houses for the poor – will they pay?', *Proc. Royal Philosophical Soc. Glasgow*, XXX (1898–9), 83; GMC, Report, 2, and Evidence of Fyfe, and Appendix, 627;PP, 1884–85, XXX, *Royal Commission on the Housing of the Working Classes*, Evidence, W.J.R. Simpson, Q.19,996, Bailie Morrison Q.19,500, J. Gentle, Q.20,707. See also Glasgow Burgh Police (Scotland) Act 1903, *3 Edw. VII, C.33*, Para. 103, Sect. 66.

52 In 1913, 11.8 per cent of Edinburgh houses had sculleries, but only 3.5 per cent of one- and two-roomed houses possessed them.

53 For a general description of internal conditions see Chalmers, *op. cit.*, 96–113.

54 RC, 1917, para. 646.

55 *Ibid.*

56 J.B. Russell, 'On the sanitary results of the Glasgow Improvement Act', *Sanitary J. Scotland* (1876), 137–8

57 J.B. Russell, *Life in One Room, or Some Considerations for the Citizens of Glasgow* (1888), 17.

58 RC, 1917, Mary Laird, Q.23,066(7).

59 Medical Research Council, *Poverty, Nutrition and Growth: Studies of Child Life in Cities and Rural Districts of Scotland* (1926), 304; W.L. Mackenzie, *Scottish Mothers and Children* (1917), 22–8, 164–83.

60 RC, 1917, Report, para. 649.

61 *Ibid.*, para . 650.

62 Local Government Board for Scotland, *Report on the Administrative Control of Pulmonary Phthisis in Glasgow* (1911); City of Glasgow, *Report of the Medical Officer of Health for 1913* (1914).

63 RC, 1917, Appendices, CI, CXLIX; Evidence, Hay, Q.17,725–30; 17,734–48; 17,785–8; 17,937–42. The Report, para. 705, states that in Glasgow 14 per cent of one-room and 27 per cent of two-room houses had lodgers.

64 Russell, *Life in One Room*, 16.

65 J.B. Russell, 'The house in relation to public health', *Trans. Insurance and Actuarial Soc. Glasgow*, 2nd ser., no. 5 (1887), 5.

66 Russell, *Life in One Room*, 8.

67 *Ibid.*, 26.

68 Chalmers, *op. cit.*, 105.

69 See also Russell, *Life in One Room*, 23–4, 26–7.

70 M.A. Simpson, 'Middle-class housing and the growth of the suburban communities in the west-end of Glasgow, 1830–1914', unpublished Glasgow B.Litt. thesis (1970), 301–7; R.G. Rodger, 'The evolution of Scottish town planning' in Gordon and Dicks, *op. cit.*, 71–91.

71 RC, 1917, Report, para. 493.

72 *Ibid.*, para. 494.

73 *Ibid.*, para. 496.

74 Russell, *Life in One Room*, 15.

75 Russell, 'The house in relation to public health', 9–10 (brackets added).

76 RC, 1917, para. 493. See also Evidence of Hair, Q.38,424.

77 SLEC, *op. cit.*, 371.

78 J.B. Russell, *The children of the city: What can we do for them?* Edinburgh Health Society Lectures for the People (1886), 92–3.

79 *Ibid.*

80 Dundee Social Union, *Report of Investigation into Social Conditions in Dundee* (1905); City of Edinburgh Charity Organization Society, *Report on the Physical Condition of Fourteen Hundred Schoolchildren in the City together with some account of their homes and surroundings* (1906).

81 Scotch Education Department, *Report on the Physical Condition of Children Attending the Public Schools of the School Board for Glasgow* (1907).

82 RC, 1917, para. 479.
83 R.H. Campbell, *The Rise and Fall of Scottish Industry 1707–1939* (1980), 80. See also PP, 1887, LXXXIX and PP, 1893–4, LXXIII (ii).
84 R.G. Rodger, 'The invisible hand; market forces, housing and the urban form in Victorian cities', in *The Pursuit of Urban History*, ed. D.Fraser and A. Sutcliffe (1983), 194–6.
85 Calculated from R.H. Campbell, *op. cit.*, 190.
86 A.D. Campbell, 'Changes in Scottish incomes 1924–49', *Economic J.*, LXV (1955), 225–40.
87 R.H. Campbell, *op. cit.*; N.K. Buxton, 'Economic growth in Scotland between the wars: the role of production structure and rationalization', *EcHR*, XXXIII (1980), 538–55.
88 J.H. Treble, 'The market for unskilled male labour in Glasgow 1891–1914', in *Essays in Scottish Labour History: a Tribute to W.H. Marwick*, ed. I. MacDougall (1979), 115–42, and 'The seasonal demand for adult labour in Glasgow, 1890–1914'. *Social History*, III (1978), 43–60.
89 PP, 1912–13, CXIX; Treble, *op. cit.*; R.G. Rodger, 'Employment, wages and poverty in the Scottish cities, 1841–1914', in *Perspectives of the Scottish City*, ed. G. Gordon (forthcoming), table 9.
90 For an explanation of the letting system, see below.
91 PP, 1908, CVII, *Report of an Enquiry by the Board of Trade into Working Class Rents, Housing and Retail Prices*, Appendix III.
92 PP, 1913, LXVI *Report of an Enquiry into Working Class Rents, Housing and Retail Prices*, etc.
93 Presbytery of Glasgow, Report, *op. cit.*, 22.
94 SLEC, 307–12
95 *Ibid.* See also RC, 1917, paras 1523–44.
96 SLEC, 289.
97 R.G. Rodger, 'The law and urban change: some nineteenth-century Scottish evidence', *Urban History Yearbook* (1979), 79.
98 SLEC, 308 (brackets added).
99 RC, 1917, Appendix CXXI.
100 SLEC, *op. cit.*, 308, 325–31; Rodger, 'The invisible hand'. 201–2.
101 GMC, Binnie, Q.6527.
102 PP, 1884–5, XXX, *Royal Commission on the Housing of the Working Classes*, Gowans, Q.18,893.
103 RC, 1917, Appendix CLXVII.
104 *Ibid.*, Appendix CXXI; W. Thompson, *The Housing Handbook* (1903) and *Housing Up to Date* (1907).
105 RC, 1917, para, 592; Mann, *op. cit.*
106 SLEC, 293. Also quoted by Daunton, *op. cit.*, 70.
107 This section on the building industry is based on R.G. Rodger, 'Speculative builders and the structure of the Scottish building industry, 1860–1914', *Business History*, XXI (1979), 226–46. This in turn is based on a survey of building applications and approvals in the 34 principal industrial towns, and in a further 68 burghs.
108 Lerwick, Minute Book of the Commissioners of Police, 1/1/3 and 1/2/3; Fraserburgh, Town Council Minutes (TCM); Moray District Record Office (MDRO), Buckie, TCM, AB Bu A 2/3; MDRO Forres, Register of Plans and Sections (RPS); MDRO Elgin, ZB E1 D3; Nairn, Plans, 1893–1914; Peterhead TCM, 1/1/6–21; *Censuses of Scotland* 1871–1911. Unless otherwise stated, the location of documentary materials is the burgh to which reference is made.
109 Huntly, Commissioners of Police of Huntly, 1/1/2–3 and RPS 1/5/3; Duns RPS 3/1/1, Kirkcudbright, RPS 1/3/2; Stonehaven RPS 1/4/2; St Andrews, RPS 1894–1929; Dunoon, Register of Applications for Lining, 1/11/1–3; Rothesay, RPS DC 6/4/1 and

Petitions 1898–9 and 1902–4; Central Regional Archives (CRA) Bridge of Allan, Plans, 1893–1914; Helensburgh, Register of Plans 1/6/1–2; Inverurie RPS 1/4/1.
110 Aberdeen Town Council House Plans, A-C 1879–97; EDCRO, DGC, Registers 1885–94.
111 C.H. Feinstein, *Statistical Tables of National Income, Expenditure and Output of the UK, 1855–1965* (1972), Tables 111–12; Rodger, thesis, table 3.11, 118, and 3.13, 124.
112 C.H. Lee, 'Modern economic growth and structural change in Scotland: the service sector reconsidered', *Scottish Economic and Social History,* III (1983), 5–35.
113 PP, 1914–16, XXXV, *Departmental Committee on Increases in Rental of Small Dwelling Houses in Scotland,* Petrie, Q.1597–9; Collins, Q.245–50.
114 *Edinburgh Gazette,* 1856–1913; Scottish Record Office sequestration proceedings, CS 318.
115 GMC, Binnie, Q.7011.
116 W. Fraser, 'Fluctuations of the building trade and Glasgow; house accommodation', *Proc. Royal Philosophical Soc. Glasgow,* XXXIX (1907–8), 21–40.
117 A.K. Cairncross, *Home and Foreign Investment 1870–1913* (1953), 131.
118 PP, 1914–16, XXXV, *Departmental Committee on Increases in Rental,* Steel, Q.1117; R. Stewart, Q.1472; GMC, Binnie, Q.6631, 6962; McCallum, Q.8171, 8191, 8401, 8423, 8481.
119 EDCRO, DGC Registers, 1885–94.
120 Aberdeen Town Council House Plans A–C, 1879–97; Strathclyde Regional Archives, Govan DGC Registers H-Gov 36/2.
121 CRA, Grangemouth DGC Roll Book GR 1/3/2; Kirkintilloch RPS 9/1/2; Dunblane RPS 1/3/1–2; Milngavie DGC Minute Book 1/3/1; Musselburgh DGC Register 1898–1914.
122 SRO, CS 318; *Edinburgh Gazette,* 1856–1913.
123 R.G. Rodger, 'Business failure in Scotland 1839–1913', *Business History,* XXVII (1985).
124 *Ibid.,* figs. 2 and 3, pp. 81–2.
125 Rodger, thesis table 3.11, 119.
126 GMC, Binnie, Q.6555, McKellar, Q.10,936, Mann, Q.8488, Watson, Q.11,247, R. McCallum, Q.8260, Paterson, Q.7644.
127 C.M. Allan, 'The genesis of British urban redevelopment with regard to Glasgow', *EcHR,* XVIII (1965), 598–613; PP, 1884–85, XXX *Royal Commission on the Housing of the Working Classes,* J.K. Crawford, Q.18,701–66; Gentle, Q.20,594–703; Turnbull, Q.20,084–157; Laing, Q.20,270–300; Simpson, Q.19,945–20,000; D. Crawford, Q.18,479.
128 *55 and 56 Vict. C 22,* Housing of the Working Classes Act 1890 Amendment (Scotland) modified the 1890 legislation to conform to Scottish Law, and in 1893–4, 1895 was further amended to become applicable to Edinburgh and Glasgow respectively.
129 London County Council, *London Statistics,* XII (1901–2), 10.
130 J. Melling, 'Employers, industrial housing and the evolution of company welfare policies in Britain's heavy industry: West Scotland 1870–1920', *Int. Rev. Social History,* XXVI (1981), 235–301; RC, 1917, Report, paras 947–5, 982–9; Appendix CII, CVII demonstrate a rate of return of 1–3 per cent on company housing; Dean of Guild Court records in various burghs.
131 Melling, *op. cit.,* 280
132 RC, 1917, Appendix CIII; B.R. Mitchell and P. Deane, *Abstracts of British Historical Statistics* (1971), 455.
133 For a brief survey of building regulations in Scottish burghs see Rodger, 'Evolution of Scottish town planning'.
134 G.W. Barras, 'The Glasgow Building Regulations Act (1892)', *Proc. Royal Philosophical Soc. Glasgow,* XXV (1894), 155–69.
135 R. Miller, *The Edinburgh Dean of Guild Court: A Manual of History and Procedure*

(1896); J.C. Irons, *Manual of the Law and Practice of the Dean of Guild Court* (1895), 11–21.

136 A typical example of building regulations is reproduced in Rodger, thesis, Appendix III, 37–8.

137 GMC, Watson, Q.11,161, 11,199, 11,204; GMC Report, *op. cit.*, 156. See also K. Hudson, *Building Materials* (1972), Appendix 1; R.H. Harper, 'The evolution of the English building regulations' (Ph.D. thesis, University of Sheffield, 1978), and 'The conflict between English building regulations and architectural design 1890–1918', *J. Architectural Res.*, VI (1977), 24–33.

138 GMC, Watson, Q.11,080.

139 *Ibid.*, Burgess, Q.5880–7.

140 *Ibid.*, Watson, Q.11,080. See also Binnie, Q.7019, Eadie, Q.7282–5, Gilmour, Q.7226.

141 Rodger, thesis, Appendix I, 87.

142 PP, 1902, CXVIII, *Report on the Judicial Statistics of Scotland for 1900*.

143 Fraser, *op. cit.*, 32–3.

144 GMC, Binnie, Q,6482, 6475.

145 *Ibid.*, Watson, Q.11,080, 11,168, 11,212; Binnie, Q.6620, 6627; McDonald, Q.3606. Concrete was restricted to a few areas, such as lintels, steps and floors, see Mann, Q.8488, 8509; W.J. Reader, *The Weir Group* (1971), 100.

146 SLEC, 384.

147 PP, 1909, CII and 1912–13, CIX, *Census of Production 1907*. See also R.H. Campbell, *op. cit.*, 195–6.

148 PP, 1884–85, XXX, *Royal Commission on the Housing of the Working Classes*, Evidence, Colville, Q.19,133; GMC, Eadie, 336.

149 RC, 1917, J.W. Smith, Q.41,557 and Appendix CLIXX.

150 GMC, Binnie, Q.6415, Eadie, Q.7190, 7358, 7370; see also A.L. Bowley, 'The statistics of wages in the United Kingdom . . . Building', *J. Royal Statistical Soc.*, LXIII (1900), 485–97, and Rodger, thesis, tables 8.5, 8.8.

151 K. Maiwald, 'An index of building costs in the United Kingdom, 1845–1938', *EcHR*, VII (1954), 187–203, adopts this weighting, though Scottish evidence suggests a higher and more variable weight for labour might be more appropriate.

152 Calculated from the statistics cited.

153 Modern Records Centre, University of Warwick, MSS. 78/C JS/41/1 Evidence of Messrs Matson and Proudfoot before the Commissioners appointed to enquire into the organization and rules of Trades Unions and other Associations, 1868.

154 T. Donnelly, 'The granite industry – its problems and its records, 1750–1939', *Business Archives Council of Scotland Newsletter*, V (1970).

155 National Library of Scotland, MSS, United Operative Masons' and Granitecutters' Journal, May 1901, 1.

156 RC, 1917, Auld, Q.39,919–26.

157 *Ibid.*, Q.39,923.

158 *The Builder*, 20 Jan. 1877, 70.

159 See particularly, Daunton, *op. cit.*; Englander, *op. cit.*; N.J. Morgan and M.J. Daunton, 'Landlords in Glasgow: a study of 1900', *Business Hist.*, XXV (1983), 264–81; Rodger, 'The law and urban change'.

160 PP, 1914–16, XXXV, *Report of the Departmental Committee on Increase in the Rentals of Small Dwelling Houses in the Industrial Districts of Scotland*, Evidence of Binnie, Q.128, 193, Gillies, Q.238, 248; A.W. Flux, 'The yield of high class investments, 1896–1910', *Trans. Manchester Statistical Soc.* (1910–11), 109.

161 PP, 1914–16, XXXV, Gillies, Q.245, Petrie, Q.1597–8, Scrimgeour, Q.1698–1700.

162 See table 28.

163 PP, 1907, XXXVI, *Report of the Departmental Committee on House Letting in Scotland*, 3.

164 Englander, *op. cit.*, 169.

165 PP, 1907, XXXVI, *Report*, 3, 6, 13–14. Removal between terms might require a tenant to pay rent for the remainder of the lease. If a replacement was found by the outgoing tenant, a subletting charge of 5 per cent was commonly made on the yearly rental, or on the outstanding portion. An alternative to removal was to move in as a lodger if employment was obtained at a distance, leaving the family in the leased property until the term expired. Thus the letting system partly contributed to overcrowding.
166 Morgan and Daunton, *op. cit.*, 278.
167 Rodger, 'The law and urban change', 84–6; PP, 1907, XXXVI, *Report*, 12–16.
168 Englander, *op. cit.*; PP, 1907, XXXVI, *Report*, 11–12.
169 PP, 1908, XLVII, *Minutes of Evidence of the Departmental Committee on House-Letting in Scotland*, McBain, Q.5627.
170 PP, 1907, XXXVI, *Report*, 7–9; Englander, *op. cit.*, 170–83.
171 Daunton, *op. cit.*, 118.
172 GMC, Blackie, Q.7883–91; Mann, Q.8581, 8850, 9350.
173 PP, 1914–16, XXXVI, Gillies, Q.245, Steel, Q.1117.
174 J.D. Bailey, 'Australian borrowing in Scotland in the nineteenth century', *EcHR*, XII (1959), 268–79; J.H. Lockie, 'Executor and trustee business', *Scottish Banking Practice* (3rd edn, 1970), 5–11, quoted by Daunton, *op. cit.*, 121.
175 Allan, *op. cit.*; Thompson, *Handbook*, 61–2; GMC, Report, 12–13.
176 PP, 1914–16, XXXV, Appendix VII; GMC, Gilmour, 348; RC, 1917, paras 841–58.
177 Presbytery of Glasgow, *Report*, 96.
178 Englander, *op. cit.*, 59–60, 63–4; Presbytery of Glasgow, *op. cit.*, Evidence of Dansken, McBain, Dick.
179 PP, 1907, XXXI, *Report*, 15–16; PP, 1908, XLVII, Mann, Q.3830, 5083.
180 Daunton, *op. cit.*, 137.
181 *1 and 2 Geo. V, C.53.*
182 See Rodger, thesis, 338–62 for further details of empty property in Scottish burghs.
183 Cairncross, *op. cit.* See also B.F. Reece, 'The price adjustment mechanism in Glasgow's rental housing market 1871–1913: the claim of "sticky rents" reassessed', *Scottish J. Political Economy*, XXXI (1984) 286–93. I am grateful to Professor D.H. Aldcroft for drawing this to my attention.
184 J.B. Russell, 'Sanitation and social economics', *Proc. Royal Philosophical Soc. Glasgow* (1889), 1–21.
185 *Ibid.*, 9.
186 *Ibid.*, 12.
187 GMC, Report, 10; Evidence of Renwick, Q.2130, 2142, Gilmour, Q.7464, 7559, 7578, Mann, Q.8701, 8922, 8951, 9276, McKellar, Q.10,811, 10,829, 10,960, 11,001.
188 Rodger, 'The law and urban change', 78, 80, 82, 85–6.
189 PP, 1913, LXVI, *Board of Trade, Report*, 40–3.
190 PP, 1908, CVII, *Board of Trade, Report*, xxxviii.
191 See table 25.
192 RC, 1917, Appendix CLXVII; Thompson, *op. cit.*, 174–6.
193 PP, 1908, CVIII, xxi.
194 H.W. Singer, 'An index of urban land rents and house rents in England and Wales, 1845–1913', *Econometrica*, IX (1941).
195 GMC, Binnie, Q.6529.
196 B.R. Mitchell and P. Deane, *Abstract of British Historical Statistics* (1962), 472–5; GMC, Binnie, Q.6543 states that prices fell by 31 per cent, 1867/77 to 1902.
197 GMC, Binnie, Q.6529.
198 *Ibid.*, Gilmour, Q.7487.
199 *Ibid.*, Burgess, Q.5543, 5586–8; PP, 1908, CVII, 590–1.
200 See above, note 52.
201 A.L. Bowley, 'The statistics of wages in the United Kingdom in the last hundred years', *J. Royal Statistical Soc.*, LXII (1899), 708–15; LXIII (1900), 297–315; LXIV (1901), 102–12;

LXVIII (1905), 563–614; E.H. Hunt, *Regional Wage Variations in Britain, 1850–1914* (1973); PP, 1887, LXXXIX, *Returns of Wages Published between 1830 and 1886*; PP, 1893–4, LXXIII (i), *Wages of the Manual Labour Classes.*

202 J.H. Treble, 'Unemployment and unemployment policies in Glasgow, 1890–1905' in *The Origins of British Social Policy*, ed. P. Thane (1978), 147–72; 'The seasonal demand for adult labour in Glasgow 1890–1914', *Social History,* III (1978), 43–60.

203 SLEC, 379–80.

204 D.N. Paton, 'The family budgets and dietaries of forty labouring class families in Glasgow in war time', *Proc. Royal Soc. Edinburgh,* XXXVII–VIII (1916–18), 117–36; A.M.T. Tully, 'Nutrition and economic conditions of working class families in Glasgow in April 1921', *The Lancet,* 2 July 1921, 58, also concludes 'that food, the supply of energy, is the first charge upon income'.

205 D.E. Lindsay and D.N. Paton, *Report upon a Study of the Diet of the Labouring Classes in the City of Glasgow* (1913), 27.

206 See, for example, W. Logan, *The Moral Statistics of Glasgow* (1849), and A.K. Chalmers (ed.), *Public Health Administration in Glasgow* (1905).

207 GMC, Ross, Q.12,654, 12,669, Munro, Q.4387, Eadie, Q.7247, 7277, McGillivray, Q.13,269, 13,278, Binnie, Q.6568A, 6570.

208 SLEC, 535; GMC, Binnie, Q.6475, 6479, 6674, 6848, 7014–19, Fyfe, Q.834, 1199, Nisbet, Q.1302, 1311, McDonald, Q.3666, 3889, Bannatyne, Q.6204, Eadie, Q.7282, 7362, Watson, Q.11,134; *Presbytery of Glasgow*, Report, 17–18; RC, 1917, Report, paras 354–5, 2201(35).

209 RC, 1917, Fraser, Q.38,113.

210 Russell, 'The house in relation to public health', 16.

211 Daunton, *op. cit.*, 88, emphasizes 'the custom of living in tenements' and wishes to restate the importance of 'cultural variables'. For examples of Scottish flexibility regarding housing form see RC, 1917, Appendices CLXVIIA, LV, LIX; Report 859–88; Thompson, *op. cit.*

212 Isaiah, 32, v.18.

INDEX

Aberdeen, 153, 164, 171, 177, 178, 179, 180, 181, 182, 183, 186, 187–8, 190, 192
Aberdeen Granite Association, 187–8
Airdrie, 153, 161, 175
Akroyd, E., 96
Akroyden, 97
Almondbury, 28, 29
Anfield, 140
Angel Inn [building] Club, Paddock, 38
Anglesey, 109, 110, 114, 132, 139, 140
Arbroath, 161, 192
architects, 15, 39, 97, 131, 135–6, 186
Armitage, J. A., 48
Aspinall, P. J., 8, 11, 53
Aspley, 46
Assheton Smiths, 110
Associated Carpenters and Joiners of Scotland, 187
Ayr, 190
Ayrshire, 169

'back-to-back' houses, 9–10, 45, 48, 50, 60, 76, 79, 91, 96, 98, 116, 158; regulation of, 96
Bagillt, 114
Baird & Co., 184
Baker, R., 96
Bala, 111
Balfour, J. S., 70
Bangor, 114
Bar, W. B., 131
Barkerend Union Building Society, Bradford, 69
Barrhead, 153
Barrow in Furness, 162
Battye, F., 42
Beardmore, Wm & Co., 184
Beaumaris, 114
Berry Brow, 28
Bingley, 64, 68, 73, 75–7
Bingley Building and Investment Society, 75
Bingley, Morton and Shipley Permanent Building Society, 69, 73, 75, 77
Binns, J. A., 71
Birkbeck Building Society, London, 72
Birkby, 33, 43
Birmingham, 59, 60, 72, 79, 158, 186, 195
Board of Trade, 172, 194
Bootle, 108, 127, 134, 140
Bothwell, 164
Bower, J., 35–6
Bowkett, T. E., 84–6
Bradford, 10, 59, 61, 63, 64, 67, 80, 90–3, 96, 99, 137; building activity, 59
Bradford and Bingley Building Society, 59, 69
Bradford Commercial Building Society, 61, 67
Bradford Freehold Land Society, 87
Bradford Improved Commercial Building Society, 61, 63, 67

Bradford Moor Union Building Societies, 61
Bradford Second Equitable Building Society, 69, 87, 90–3
Bradford Third Equitable Building Society, 69, 71, 78, 79, 84, 87, 88, 90–3
Bradford Tradesman's Building Society, 61
Bradford Union Building Society, 64–5, 69
Bridge of Allan, 176
British Bricklayers' Association, 188
British Society, 112
Brook, J., 35–6, 38
Brook, R., 46, 48
Brown, John & Co., 184
Buckie, 175
Builder, The, 96, 188
builders, 3, 11–12, 133; Huddersfield, 34–5, 39, 46, 48, 50–2; Liverpool, 12, 113, 127–36; Scottish, 4, 173, 177, 180–1; Welsh, 3, 113, 127–36, 140, 143; *see also* builders' merchants; building firms; building industry; building, speculative; building trades; building undertakers
builders' merchants, 11, 131, 136–9; *see also* building materials
building activity, 2, 3, 5–8, 13–15, 58–9, 88, 117, 126, 128, 131, 139, 175–8; building societies', 88, 90–5; Huddersfield, 29–32, 38–40, 43, 46–52; Liverpool, 114–15, 117, 126, 127–36, 139; Scotland, 177–80, 181–2, 188, 198; *see also* building cycles; building projects, size of; house-building
building clubs, 3, 12, 38, 60, 80; *see also* building societies
building costs, 9, 13–15, 39, 46, 50, 198; Scottish, 157, 185–8, 194, 195–7, 199; *see also* building regulations; house prices
building cycles, 5–6, 8, 12, 13, 58, 88–9; Huddersfield, 31–2; Liverpool, 114–15, 130, 139; Scotland, 178–80, 181–2, 198; *see also* building activity
building, finance of, 3, 11–13, 46, 177, 180; building societies', 70–1, 88–9, 90–5, 99, 139–40
building firms: bankruptcies, 7, 180–2; Huddersfield, 39, 46, 50–2; Liverpool, 127–36; Scottish, 170, 174–88; sizes, 3, 7–8, 16, 46–7, 134, 175, 180–2; Welsh, 108, 127–36, 140; *see also* builders; builders' merchants; building industry; building, speculative; building trades
building industry: historical sources for, 4–6, 7, 13; output, 2–3, 5–8, 13–15, 59, 117, 126, 128, 131, 139, 175–8; Welsh in, 106–8, 113, 128–36; *see also* builders; building activity; building firms; building finance; building, speculative; building trades; building undertakers; house-building
building industry, structure of, 3, 6–8, 10, 16–17;

building industry (contd)
Huddersfield, 46; Liverpool, 127–36; Scottish, 170, 174–88
building land: costs, 9, 37, 48, 50, 174; Huddersfield, 25–7, 32–7, 42–5, 48; provision of, 9–10, 25–7; Scottish, 172–4, 183; *see also* land costs; land tenure
building materials, 3, 11, 136, 186–7; brick, 14, 129, 138; costs, 13, 14, 46, 187; firms, 137–8; imports, 14, 114, 136–7; production and transport, 14–15, 110, 154, 187; slate, 109–10, 138; stone, 138–9, 154; taxation, 15, 111, 138, 154; timber, 14, 114, 136–7; Welsh, 106, 108, 124, 129, 136, 138–9
building, non-residential, 2, 5, 8, 111, 130, 131, 132, 140
building plan registers: Huddersfield, 31–2, 47; Scottish; *see* Dean of Guild Courts
building projects, size of, 7–8, 12, 15; Huddersfield, 46–7, 50; Liverpool, 131–2, 135, 140; Scottish, 175–7, 181; *see also* building activity
building regulations, 3, 11, 26, 158; and building costs, 15, 121, 128, 185–8, 194, 195; evasion, 120–1; Liverpool, 115, 120–1, 131, 137; London, 185; Scottish, 155, 158, 163–4, 185–7, 194, 195, 198; *see also* bye-laws
building societies, 3, 11, 46, 181; advances, sizes of, 46, 72–3, 75–9, 90–5, 99; terms of, 46, 64–7, 70, 72, 86–7; early foundations, 60, 64, 79; finance of building, 11–13, 46, 70–1, 88–9, 90–5, 99, 139–40; financial practice, 60–1, 64–9, 70, 75–89, 91–5, 99; housing provision, 58–103; interest rates, 81, 83, 86–9; investments, 87–8; legal regulation, 69–70; Liverpool, 132, 135, 139–40; membership, 12, 61, 65–7, 71–4, 99, 140; mortgages, 75–9, 86–7, 91–5, 99; property, 89–90; rules and fines, 61, 64, 69–70, 71, 79, 86; shares and discounting, 61, 65–8, 69, 71, 79–87; and speculative builders, 11–12, 46, 70–1; standards of housing, 91, 96–8; subscription levels, 61, 64, 69, 71, 80–7; terminating, 12, 59–61, 64–9, 70, 72, 73, 79–82, 86, 87, 97, 99, 140; in West Yorkshire, 58–103; *see also* building clubs; Starr–Bowkett Building Societies
Building Societies Acts: (1836), 68, 69–70, 86; (1874), 68, 70, 89; (1894), 70, 78, 84
building, speculative, 6–8, 10, 25; finance of, 71, *and see* building societies; Huddersfield, 32, 34–5, 46, 48, 50–2; Liverpool, 126–36, 137; Scottish, 177, 180–2; *see also* builders; building activity; building firms; building projects; house-building
building trades, 6, 13–14, 71, 133–5, 177, 181
building undertakers, 36, 37, 39, 40, 42–3, 46, 50–2; Scottish, 177
Burgh Courts, Scotland, 191, 192
Burgh Police (Scotland) Act (1862), 185
Burnley Building Society, 69

bye-laws, 15, 32, 45, 115, 116, 120–1, 131, 137; *see also* building regulations; house design

Caernarvon, 109, 110, 114, 138, 139, 140
Cairncross, A. K., 192
Calderstones, 140
Camberwell, 71
Cambrian Permanent Building Society, 132, 135, 139
Campbell, A. D., 170
Cannadine, D., 10–11
capital formation, U.K., 5
Cardiff, 7, 195
Cathcart, 187
cellar dwellings, 40, 44, 45, 52, 60, 91; Liverpool, 120, 129, 154; *see also* house types
Census of Production (1907), 170
Chadwick, E., 96, 98
Chatham (Street) Building Society, 139
Cherry Tree [building] Club, 38
Cheshire, 194
Chief Registrar (of building societies), 70, 87, 90
Childwall, 140
cholera, 40, 117, 120
Cilgwyn Cefn du Slate Co., 138
City of Glasgow Bank, 181
City of Liverpool Permanent Building Society, 139
Clarence (Street) Building Society, 132, 135, 139, 140
Clydebank, 153, 161–2, 174, 179, 181, 184, 190, 192
Clydeside, 153, 184
Coatbridge, 153, 161, 179, 192
contracting in gross, 6
Conveyancing (Scotland) Act (1874), 173
Conway, A., 114
Cooney, E. W., 6–7
Co-operative Permanent Building Society, 98
Copley, 96–7
court dwellings, 115–16, 120–1, 126, 129, 130, 154, 158; *see also* house types
Cowdenbeath, 153
Crackenthorpe Gardens Building Club, 60, 96
Crosby, 127
Crosland Moor, 33, 43, 45
Crossley, J., 96, 97
Crown (Street) Building Society, 139
Cubitt, T., 6

Dalmuir, 162
Dalton, 29, 31, 34
Daunton, M. J., 155, 190
Davies, D. P., 140
Dean of Guild Courts, 155, 177, 185
Denbigh, 138
Denbighshire, 109, 139
Denny, Wm & Co., 184
Dennystown, 160
Dewsbury, 59, 69